The Guiltless Gourmet

*Over 300 Quick and Easy Recipes that Are
Both Delicious and Nutritious*

by Judy Gilliard

ADAMS MEDIA CORPORATION
Holbrook, Massachusetts

Published by
Adams Media Corporation
260 Center Street, Holbrook, MA 02343
www.adamsmedia.com

ISBN: 1-58062-447-2

Printed in Canada.

J I H G F E D C B A

Library of Congress Cataloging-in-Publication Data
Gilliard, Judy.
Guiltless gourmet / by Judy Gilliard.
p.   cm.
ISBN 1-58062-447-2
1. Low-fat diet--Recipes. 2. Reducing diets--Recipes. I. Title.
RM237.7 .G548   2001
641.5′63--dc21   00-065017

This publication is designed to provide accurate and authoritative information with regard to the subject matter covered. It is sold with the understanding that the publisher is not engaged in rendering legal, accounting, or other professional advice. If legal advice or other expert assistance is required, the services of a competent professional person should be sought.
—From a Declaration of Principles jointly adopted by a Committee of the American Bar Association and a Committee of Publishers and Associations

Cover illustration by Ken Jacobsen.

This book is available at quantity discounts for bulk purchases.
For information, call 1-800-872-5627.

Dedications

To Dan Bunker, who has weathered the years with me
as a true and dear friend.

Acknowledgments

When it comes time to write acknowledgments I could write a whole other book;
however, I will try to name but a few.

My editor: Cheryl Kimball, who is a delight to work with.

My assistant: Michele Tharp, who did the nutrient analyses and
formatting along with adding support.

My sister, Teri Gilliard, the artist.

My family: Aunt Rose and Uncle Walt Edgar, Aunt Ginny and Uncle John Hardacre,
my cousins Doug, Susan, Amanda and Bryson Edgar, Chuck and Jean Gilliard.

My former partner: Joy Kirkpatrick Richardson, R.D.
(more of her in the Introduction)

Jones Radio Network: for a wonderful opportunity
and a staff who are supportive and fun to work with!

My friends in California: Jan and Harvey Izen; Tom, Mona, Nicole, and Michele Virgilio;
Barbara Araluce; Nathan and Lillian Shuman; Diane Lubich; Helen Leika; Carol Supan;
Dr. Patricia McColm; Sandra and Milt Levinson; Debbie Westover; Nancy and Ken Hess;
Basil Slaymaker; Larry Johnson; Kirk Gregory; and Jim Wallace.

Mature Living Magazine in Palm Springs, California: for the opportunity
of being the Food Editor.

Table of Contents

Introduction

I don't remember a time when I did not love food. As in most families food was the center of our gatherings (as it should be). I always looked forward to the holidays with the traditional turkey with oyster stuffing and to barbecues with steak and chili beans or hamburgers and hot dogs when the budget did not permit steak. We were in the restaurant business so food was always first and foremost. So it is understandable that I went on to get my college degree in Hotel and Restaurant Management and my teaching credential in Restaurant and Food Technology. I loved everything about it, and I still do.

My early training was mainly in Classical French cuisine. I loved entertaining, and I don't think I ever cooked without using a cube of butter. I was young, had a quick metabolism, and never had to worry about weight. . . . Oh, how things change.

In the early 1980s I was diagnosed with Type 2 diabetes. It should not, have come as a surprise since diabetes runs on both sides of my family—but it did. However, luck was with me; I had the good fortune to go to an excellent doctor. The first thing he did was to send me to a registered dietitian, Joy Kirkpatrick Richardson. Joy taught me how to balance my food and my eating. She did not tell me what I could not have. Instead, she told me how I could incorporate what I wanted into my meal plans. Our encounter developed into a lifelong friendship, including writing five cookbooks together. This book is a revision of three of those books. So Joy is responsible for many of the recipes and ideas, and for me still being in total control of my diabetes through diet and exercise.

What Is a Guiltless Gourmet?

The dictionary defines **guilt·less** as free of guilt; innocent and **gour·met** as a connoisseur of fine food and drink.

In my definition, A Guiltless Gourmet is a person who loves the art of cooking, eating, and entertaining; a person who finds simple pleasure in the enjoyment of food and the creation and celebration of it, all within the guidelines of good health.

Today's Guiltless Gourmet also needs to factor time and the cost of ingredients into the equation. I consider this style of preparation real food for the real world, and you have my permission to alter the recipes a bit to fit your specific needs.

For instance, in this book I used real butter and sugar. If you wanted to modify the recipe to lower the fat, in almost all cases you can replace the butter with Butter Buds. If you are diabetic, you can replace the sugar with fructose or Equal. I used sugar because I found that some people had a difficult time finding fructose. Fructose is a sugar made from fruit—it is a little sweeter than sugar, so you use a bit less and it metabolizes easier. However, I was careful to balance the sugar in the recipes so they would fit into a diabetic meal plan.

I love hearing from readers and would love to have one of your family recipes in my collection. Who knows, it could end up in a book, with you recognized of course! However, I will admit I modify recipes to fit into healthier guidelines when I can. Please write to me with any questions c/o Adams Media Corporation, 260 Center Street, Holbrook, MA 02343, or you can e-mail me at *jagilliard@msn.com.*

I hope you enjoy cooking from this book and other books of mine to come. I wish you happy and healthful cooking.

Judy

Tips

Drying Lettuce

Use a salad spinner or lay the washed lettuce out on paper towels to dry.

Roasting Peppers

1. Cut the tops off the peppers, remove the seeds, and quarter them.
2. Place the peppers on a cookie sheet that has been sprayed with a nonstick cooking spray.
3. Place the cookie sheet under the broiler until the peppers are well browned, about 10 minutes.
4. Remove the skin and cut the peppers in strips.

Peeling Tomatoes

1. Remove the core of the tomato from the top. On the bottom of the tomato cut an "X."
2. Drop the tomato into a large pan of boiling water for 10 seconds. Remove it and place it in cold water. The skin will pull right off.

Buying and Peeling Garlic

Buy garlic in loose heads that are large, firm, and tight-skinned. Store them in a cool, dry place out of the sun. They will keep up to one month.

To peel garlic, press each clove with the flat side of a knife until it breaks and then peel the skin off.

If you're peeling several cloves, blanche them in boiling water for 1 minute. Then rinse them under cold water and peel. You can store the peeled cloves in olive oil.

Harnessing the Food Processor

One of my best tips is: Use a food processor. It cuts your preparation time in half.

CHOPPING

Garlic
With the steel blade running, drop the peeled clove of garlic down the feed tube. It will chop to a fine consistency and cling to the sides of the work bowl.

Onions
Peel the onions and cut them into fourths. Place them in the work bowl with the steel blade and use quick on/off

pulses with the processor. The onions will cut very quickly, so be careful you don't turn them into mush.

Parsley

Wash and dry the parsley. Then place it in the work bowl with the steel blade. Turn the processor on and run it until all of the parsley is chopped. You can keep chopped fresh parsley in your freezer to use as needed.

Zest

A mini–food chopper is great for making zest from lemons or oranges. Simple peel the skin from the fruit, cut it in pieces, and put it in the chopper. Chop until very fine.

SLICING

With the slicing blade, you can slice onions, mushrooms, carrots, celery, cabbage, zucchini, and whatever else you can think of to use in sauces, soups, or vegetable dishes.

Storing Fresh Lemon Juice and Broth

Squeeze the lemons and put the juice in ice-cube trays. When frozen, pop out the cubes and put them in a plastic bag. The lemon juice will be ready in convenient amounts when you need it.

The same process works for vegetable or chicken broth; first reduce the broth by boiling it. This intensifies the flavor and you don't have as much bulk to work with.

By storing broth this way, you won't waste any and it will always be handy.

Choosing Spices and Herbs

Spices and herbs are essential to many recipes. The fresher the spices, the better. If you're lucky enough to grow your own herbs and spices, you can dry them and store them, or freeze them, as I mentioned earlier with parsley.

Remember, fresh or dried, herbs and spices have a shelf life and will become stale. Heat and moisture from your kitchen will reduce their flavors, so avoid storing them near your range or oven.

Date each new spice or herb purchase with the month and year of purchase. This makes it much easier to keep track of the shelf life. You may consider buying them in smaller quantities, but this depends on how quickly you use a specific spice.

Notes about Ingredients

Here are some bits and pieces of information that may help make your life easier as you become a Guiltless Gourmet. Understanding ingredients and measuring correctly are two important steps in ensuring successful results.

Alcohol

In this book I have used various types of alcohol: vermouth, cognac, wine, tequila, and beer. The alcohol and its calories are generally burned off by heating or cooking, but the flavor and an insignificant amount of carbohydrates remain. I've used alcohol in these recipes to add to or enhance the flavor. It is optional, however, and if you choose to eliminate it, the results will not significantly change.

Beans

I encourage you to buy dried beans and peas of all varieties. Although they may seem bothersome to prepare, they really are not. Soak a pound of beans overnight in a large bowl with plenty of water to cover. Then, drain and rinse them well the next day and place them in a pot or slow cooker with fresh water. Add onion, celery, carrots, chilies, garlic, and herbs—whatever flavor you desire. Bring the beans to a boil, then reduce to a simmer until they are done. Some beans or peas take only about an hour to cook while others may take 4 hours or more. When the beans are done, cool them slightly, then package them in 1- or 2-cup portions. Label, date, and freeze. When a recipe calls for beans, you just pull a package from the freezer. Dried beans and peas are complex carbohydrates. They have good quality protein, vitamins, and minerals, and they are an excellent source of fiber.

Broth/Bouillon

Broth and bouillon generally have a very high sodium content, even though they are low in calories. I have found the paste varieties work very well, keep nicely in the refrigerator, and are always available to cook with. The calculations in this book for beef or chicken broth are based on homemade broth with virtually no salt added. If you choose to use canned broth or bouillon, look for brands that have a low sodium content.

Capers

Capers are actually the pickled buds of a low, prickly Mediterranean shrub. They are often used in delicate dishes like scampi and in omelets or as an ingredient in light sauces. Capers are very low in calories, yet high in sodium content—306 milligrams per tablespoon.

Cheese

I use a variety of cheeses, stressing the lower fat versions as much as possible. Although a good source of protein, cheese is quite high in fat and sodium. Using less cheese and buying low-fat types will allow for plenty of variety.

Chilies

There are numerous types of chilies, and many are available fresh through your produce department. Chilies range from sweet and mild to very hot. If fresh chilies are available, I encourage you to use them.

Ask your produce manager to help you pick out the appropriate variety for the dish you are going to prepare. Fresh chilies should be roasted, peeled, and seeded before using. They are very low in calories and usually high in vitamin C. Canned chilies are also low in calories, but may contain a higher sodium content depending on how they are packed.

Cilantro

This pungent herb is used a great deal in Mexican and Southwestern cooking. It resembles parsley in appearance but not flavor. Look for it in the fresh produce section of your grocery store or specialty market.

Cocoa

I prefer to use European-style or Dutch-processed cocoa powder. It imparts a much smoother, richer flavor to a recipe. If you and your family prefer a lighter cocoa flavor, use a regular American brand.

Cottage Cheese

I use low-fat cottage cheese in most recipes unless I am blending it with other foods that are high in fat, then I choose nonfat to keep the fat calories down. I also use the dry curd cottage cheese in some spreads that call for a high-fat cheese. By blending the two I get all real whole food, adding protein and calcium to the end results without adding fat. Many dairies have dry curd cottage cheese. It's just another way to keep the fat calories down.

Fructose

When I revised the recipes in this book, I used regular sugar to make it easier for the reader who may have a hard time finding fructose. However, I prefer to use fructose because I like the taste and texture it imparts. Fructose is not a sugar substitute—it is crystallized fruit sugar. It is several times sweeter than white sugar (sucrose) so much less is needed for a sweet taste. You should use about one-third less fructose than sugar in a recipe. Apparently, fructose does not require insulin in order to be used by the body, but it still should not be used by a diabetic who is not in control.

Check with your doctor or diabetes educator before using fructose in your diet. Fructose can be purchased in a regular grocery store or in a health food store. It is important to keep fructose in a dry place because it easily absorbs moisture.

Jicama

A root vegetable also called yam bean, jicama is a low-calorie cross between a turnip and a radish in texture and has a mild flavor and a crisp, crunchy texture. Jicama can be found in the fresh produce area of your grocery store. Peel off the heavy brown skin, and slice it into sticks or chunks to serve with other raw vegetables. Shred jicama into salads or slice it for a crudités tray.

Milk

I recommend nonfat evaporated milk, nonfat milk, or 1% milk in your cooking. Nonfat will work in all of these recipes, but I find 1% milk provides extra flavor and texture without adding significantly to fat calories.

Rice

When I cook, I like to use a variety of rice—both white and brown rice, and short and long grain. My favorite is the Italian arborio rice, a short-grain white rice used to make risotto. The U.S. alternative is Cal-Riso, grown in Northern California. It works very well. For more information, see the section "The Differences in Rice" on p. xiv.

Salt or Sodium

Although I have kept the sodium content in these recipes within the normal parameter for good health guidelines, if you or a family member have the need to further reduce the sodium intake, use low-salt or no-salt-added items when possible. If you don't need to restrict sodium intake, feel free to add salt to taste. Some of the ingredients I use—like capers, and certain types of canned tomatoes—have a higher sodium content. However, I leave the decision to add more salt to you. The sodium content per serving is listed for every recipe in this book.

Sour Cream

I find that the reduced-calorie sour cream products work well. Some brands are better than others, so experiment to find your favorites. Be sure to use them in order to keep the total fat calories down.

Tomatoes

I use tomatoes in many recipes. Sometimes, a particular cut or texture of tomato is important. Find the tomato products that you like. It is important to use good quality products since they will determine the flavor of the dish.

Tortillas

Tortillas come in two basic types—corn and flour. Corn tortillas, store-bought or homemade, are made without added fat. Flour tortillas are generally made with lard, vegetable shortening, or oil. Tortillas also come in different sizes. Flour tortillas often equal two corn tortillas in size and in calories. I use standard-size corn and flour tortillas for my recipes.

Yogurt

I use nonfat yogurt exclusively. Buy a good brand. Try to find one without added gelatin.

Yogurt Cheese

Yogurt cheese is a delightful product made from nonfat yogurt. When making yogurt cheese, it is important to use a yogurt without added gelatin.

The Differences in Rice

Over the past several years I have received a lot of questions about rice, the many varieties, and their uses. I found this information on the USA Rice Federation's Web site, *www.usarice.com.* Check it out! For example, did you know that in the United States rice is grown in Arkansas, California, Florida, Louisiana, Mississippi, Missouri, and Texas?

Arborio

Arborio rice is a traditional Italian rice used in making risottos. Arborio is also grown in the United States. In terms of its length/width ratio and starch characteristics, arborio is classified as a medium-grain rice. The traditional U.S. medium-grain rice also produces the creamy characteristics of risotto dishes.

Aromatic Rice

This rice has a natural aroma and flavor similar to roasted popcorn or nuts. It is also called fragrant rice. The United States grows different types of aromatic rices. Some varieties result in dry, separate grains when cooked; others cook up moist and tender.

Basmati

An aromatic rice native to Pakistan and India, basmati is also grown in the United States. It has a natural flavor and aroma similar to roasted popcorn or nuts. When cooked, the grains swell only lengthwise, resulting in long, thin grains, and they are dry and separate.

Boil-in-Bag Rice

This specially processed rice has been premeasured and packaged into perforated cooking bags for quick, easy rice preparation.

Brown Rice

Brown rice is the least processed form of rice. Only the outer hull is removed. It still retains the bran layers that give it that characteristic tan color and nutlike flavor.

Della Rice

Della, an aromatic rice, was developed in the United States. Similar to basmati, Della has the same flavor and aroma, and the grains cook up dry and separate. However, the cooked kernels are not as long and slender as basmati because the grains, when cooking, swell both lengthwise and widthwise, like regular long-grain rice.

Enriched Rice

Some of the nutrients lost during the milling process are replaced in enriched rice. Most rice is enriched with iron, niacin, and thiamin. The enrichment is applied as a topical coating. Therefore, do NOT rinse the rice before or after cooking, or cook it in large amounts of water. This would result in the loss of enrichment and other water-soluble vitamins and minerals.

Jambalaya

This traditional Louisiana rice dish is highly seasoned and flavored with sausage, ham, seafood, pork, chicken, or other meat.

Jasmine

An aromatic rice grown in the United States and Thailand, jasmine has a flavor and aroma similar to that of roasted popcorn or nuts, and a soft, moist texture that causes the grains to cling to one another.

Long-Grain Rice

Long-grain rice is four to five times as long as it is wide. The cooked grains are separate and fluffy.

Medium-Grain Rice

This rice is a little shorter and plumper than long-grain rice. After cooking, the grains are more moist and tender, and have a greater tendency to cling together than long-grain rice.

Milling

Milling removes the hulls and bran from the harvested, dried rough rice to produce a milled, polished or white rice.

Paella

This is a traditional Spanish dish of saffron-flavored rice, shellfish, chicken, chorizo, vegetables, and seasonings.

Parboiled Rice

Parboiled rice is produced by soaking rough rice in warm water under pressure, then steaming and drying it before milling. This process gelatinizes the starch in the grain, and ensures a separateness of grain. Parboiled rice also retains more nutrients than regular-milled white rice, but it takes a few minutes longer to cook.

Pearl Rice

See Short-Grain Rice.

Pilaf

For this light and fluffy rice dish originating in the Middle East, the rice is often sautéed in fat. Then it is cooked in a broth with onions, raisins, various spices, and sometimes meat.

Precooked Rice

Precooked rice is milled, completely cooked, and then dehydrated. Preparation takes only a few minutes, making precooked rice ideal for hurry-up meals and speedy desserts. Precooked rice is enriched and as nutritious as other rices. It is also called quick-cooking or instant rice.

Regular-Milled White Rice

This rice is also referred to as white or polished rice, and is the most common form of rice. The outer husk is removed and the layers of bran milled away until the grain is white. It takes 15 minutes to cook.

Reheating Rice

To reheat the rice, add 2 tablespoons liquid for each cup of cooked rice. Cover and heat on top of the range or in the oven for about 5 minutes until it is heated through. If you are using a microwave oven, cover and cook on high power about 1 minute per cup of rice. Frozen rice may be cooked 2 minutes on high for each cup.

Rice Products

RICE BRAN

Rice bran consists of the outer cuticle layers and germ directly beneath the hull. The bran is removed during the milling process to make regular-milled white rice. Rice bran has a sweet, nutty flavor and is rich in vitamins, minerals, and fiber. Research indicates rice bran is helpful in reducing blood cholesterol levels. Also, rice oil is extracted from rice bran.

RICE CEREALS

Rice cereals are made from the entire rice grain and can be puffed, flaked, or crisped like the ready-to-eat rice cereals found on the market. Rice cereals that require cooking are made with whole-grain or granulated rice.

Rice cereals can also be used to make very smooth rice pudding and other rice desserts.

RICE FLOUR

Rice that is ground into flour can be used instead of wheat flour for baking. Rice flour has no gluten, a protein found in wheat flour. Since rice is nonallergenic, the flour is particularly suited to individuals who are allergic to wheat-flour products.

Risotto

Risotto is a rich and creamy Italian rice dish in which the rice is sautéed in fat with onions and cooked in broth. It's often flavored with Parmesan cheese.

Short-Grain Rice

This rice is a little shorter than medium-grain rice. As a rule, the shorter the grain, the more tender it is after cooking, and the more the grains cling together.

Storing Cooked Rice

All forms of cooked rice can be refrigerated for 6 to 7 days, or frozen for 6 months. Be sure to store the cooked rice in a tightly covered container or sealable plastic bag so the grains won't dry out or absorb the flavors of other foods.

Wild Rice

Not a true rice, wild rice is the grain of an aquatic grass native to North America. It is dark brown and has a nutty flavor.

Making Life Easier in the Guiltless Gourmet Fashion

Getting to Know the Butcher

Life in the kitchen can become a lot easier when you find a good meat cutter. Most grocery stores offer a meat counter where you can get specialty items. It is very helpful to get to know the meat cutter so you feel comfortable asking him or her questions. Then when you shop at a meat counter, you can get just the amount you want, and the meat cutter can do much of your work for you.

You can choose the red meat you want and have it boned and well trimmed of fat. Here's an example of how the meat cutter can save you time and money: When you buy a leg of lamb, the meat cutter can bone it, cut up parts of the leg for making kebabs, and roll and tie another part to use instead of lamb loin.

There is nothing like fresh, grade A, grain-fed chicken. In Guiltless cooking I usually use boned, skinned chicken breasts. You can also have the meat cutter wrap the bones in a separate package to use for broth or soups, if you wish.

Find out what days the seafood comes in, and buy it that day. Unless you are going to cook it the same nights, it is better to buy seafood that has been flash frozen and keep it in the freezer until you're read to use it.

It's always a good idea to order ahead if you're planning a dinner party. If there is anything special you want, given enough time, the meat cutter can probably get it for you.

He or she will probably have special package deals so you can buy in quantity. Be sure to request lean, low-fat cuts. The meat cutter will often have ideas for you and your special needs, whether your are cooking for one or twenty-one. Always make sure to mention if you are freezing any of your purchases, so they can wrapped in freezer paper.

Traveling in Guiltless Gourmet Style

Exploring different cuisines also makes me think of traveling to delightful countries, so I thought I would give you some tips for watching those fat calories while traveling. My favorite way to travel is on a cruise.

CRUISE TO LOSE . . . WEIGHT, THAT IS!

Take a cruise? Who me? I'd be bored to tears, sitting around, playing bingo—not to mention the 10 pounds I'd gain! After all, what else is there to do on a cruise besides eat enormous amounts of outrageously fattening food?

Sound familiar? That's where I thought cruising would take me until my travel agent convinced me to sail. Considering that I'm the type of person who is very uncomfortable in small places and can gain five pounds just looking at food, it took some persuasion to get me on board. But at last, I surrendered and how that first cruise changed my opinion of travel forever!

The combination of my career and my passion, writing about and discovering new foods and wines, makes for a lifestyle of never-ending action. Cruising was a breakthrough! The total relaxation of the cruising environment and the many dynamic activities available dispelled all my cruising fears.

And the weight gain? Not me . . . now, I Cruise to Lose!

Yes, anyone can control his or her weight while cruising and perhaps drop a few pounds in the process. Typically, the American diet includes skipping many meals and consuming a lot of high-fat foods. The best way to maintain your weight is to eat moderate portions of low-fat foods on a regular basis—three to five times each day. Add exercise and you're on your way.

Although many Americans are taking an interest in eating a more health-conscious diet, having the proper foods available three to five times a day is difficult. The relaxed atmosphere of cruising allows you to concentrate on nutrition, and the food is readily accessible throughout the day! This makes cruising the perfect place to begin some healthful new eating habits.

Cruise lines are offering healthier food choices. Look for menus that are approved by the American Heart Association. Although the items on these menus are guaranteed low in fat and cholesterol, you don't necessarily have to select them to eat smart. Here, I'll share some tips with you that will send you ashore weighing less than when you boarded—and you won't miss one bit of onboard enjoyment.

1. Alert the cruise line. If you have certain dietary restrictions, have your travel agent notify the galley by writing in advance of your trip what specific requirements you would like to have met. Upon boarding, discuss these requirements with the headwaiter.

   Remember these waiters are trained in service, not nutrition. Tell the waiter just what you would like to eat and how you'd like it prepared. Once you discuss your needs, he or she will be anxious to serve you and happy to meet your demands. After all, throughout the centuries, our culture has based a lot of happiness on food consumption.

2. Plan your choices for the day. Cruise lines publish the menu for each day the evening before. By reviewing this menu you can consider your choices in advance. That will eliminate a lot of temptations when you sit down to order your meal. Ordering from an American Heart Association's approved menu will make it easy to make the correct choice.

3. Watch out for fats. The biggest culprits are foods laden with fat. Remember: Fat makes you fat. High-fat foods include butter and margarine, mayonnaise, cream, ice cream, cream soups and sauces, sweet rolls, cakes, pies, breakfast meats, red meat, and fried foods.

4. Make choices. You don't have to eliminate these foods completely. Limit your intake of high-fat foods to one portion each day (or even one each meal), and you can enjoy a bit of forbidden food, yet maintain your weight.

   For instance, if there is an excitingly rich dessert you absolutely must have, order a lighter item for your main course. If you are craving a juicy steak (or other red meat), have fresh fruit or sorbet for dessert. And if you plan ahead, knowing you're going to be eating a bit heavier, add a few extra minutes to your exercise routine.

5. Exercise is crucial. When you exercise you have increased energy and feel better. You will also digest your meals better and look better.

   There are many choices of exercise on board: walking or jogging the decks, swimming, taking exercise classes, and using the fitness equipment in the gym. So, swim an extra lap or take the stairs everywhere you go to help you burn calories and fat and to allow you to indulge in an occasional exciting dessert or entrée.

Here are some tried and true guidelines:

For breakfast, always have fresh fruit. Skip the sweet rolls. Instead, stick to whole-grain toast, or pancakes made with nonfat milk. Cereals, hot or cold, with nonfat milk are always a good choice. These foods will get you off to a good healthy start with lots of complex carbohydrates and little fat.

If choosing from the buffet for lunch or dinner, do a quick check of the entire buffet before you pick up your plate. Spend a moment thinking through a proper selection by balancing high-fat foods with low-fat choices.

When seated at your table in the dining room, read through the entire menu before making any choices. Balance the heavier choices with the lighter foods. Always order your salad dressing and sauces on the side.

The Guiltless Gourmet Way to Enjoy Entertaining

We all must eat to survive. Eating is meant to sustain life. But throughout history eating has also been a social event, a time for gathering with family and friends to share a meal. Good food, good friends, and good conversation make memorable times.

Entertaining at home is again on the upswing. People find it more personal, more intimate. Parties or gatherings may range from a cozy dinner for two to a brunch for twenty. Still, most of us juggle work and household tasks, which leaves little time to prepare for the much-loved entertaining at home.

Here are a few suggestions on how to make at-home entertaining easier.

If the budget allows, hire someone to help serve and do the cleanup. You'll be able to enjoy your guests, and when the last one leaves, you'll walk into a clean kitchen!

Form a dinner club. Gather a group of people who like to cook and try new things. Develop a menu and give each person a recipe to make and bring to the dinner. This takes all the work from one person and makes a fun evening.

For those who are excited about entertaining at home, but fearful of the cost, let me offer these ideas:

Invest in a basic set of plain white dishes. I prefer my serving plates to be 12-inch buffet plates. They are perfect for any type of dinner motif and will balance on a lap if needed in a more casual setting.

Now you can build around this set of white dishes with a many different accessories. Choose a few more formal-looking pieces for the center of the table. Select solid-color napkins and a tablecloth, and the setting becomes formal. A piece of crystal or Lucite in the center along with gray, red, or peach napkins is all it takes! Don't be limited by these colors. Use your imagination! Watch for sales to pick up different colored napkins, tablecloths, and placemats.

When you're traveling, pick up unusual serving pieces or centerpieces. Perhaps you will find a brightly colored vase or dried flower arrangement. Use bright, fresh-cut flowers laid around a small sombrero and patterned napkins with your basic set of white dishes and you've created a festival!

Have sets of individual vases for flower arrangements. Look for bargains. It doesn't take much to dress up a table and set a mood.

Another good, small investment for the casual party or afternoon brunch is the wicker paper-plate holder. These will make inexpensive paper plates look expensive, and they're great to have on hand for parties, lunches, or snacks.

It doesn't take a lot of money to entertain at home and you'll find the rewards more satisfying. Be creative! Have fun! And, most important, enjoy your company!

Cocktails

Here are recipes for a few basic people-pleasing cocktails.

BELLINI

 3 ounces champagne or
   sparkling wine
 $1/2$ ounce peach brandy
 1 ounce fresh peach purée

Pour the peach brandy and peach purée into a champagne flute. Fill the glass with the champagne or sparkling wine.

CHAMPAGNE COCKTAIL

 1 sugar cube
 1 splash cognac
 1 splash bitters
 $4^1/2$ ounces champagne or
   sparkling wine

Place the sugar cube in a tulip champagne glass. Add the cognac and bitters. Top with champagne or sparkling wine.

KIR ROYALE

 $1/4$ ounce creme de Cassis
 5 ounces champagne or
   sparkling wine
 1 twist lemon

Pour the liqueur into a champagne flute. Fill the glass with champagne or sparkling wine. Garnish with a lemon twist.

MIMOSA

 3 ounces freshly squeezed
   orange juice
 5 ounces champagne or
   sparkling wine

Pour the orange juice into a champagne flute. Fill the glass with the champagne or sparkling wine.

SEA BREEZE

  2 ounces vodka
  3 ounces grapefruit juice
  3 ounces cranberry juice
  1 scoop crushed ice

Mix all the ingredients, except the ice, in a shaker. Place the crushed ice in a highball glass. Fill glass with the vodka mixture.

A Good Cup of Coffee

Coffee is the symbol of hospitality the world over. Francis Bacon, 17th-century English philosopher and author, states, "They have in Turkey a drink called coffee. This drink comforteth the brain and heart and helpeth digestion." I agree: There is nothing quite like a "good" cup of coffee. Many coffee stores offer a wide variety of different coffees. A large selection of decaffeinated coffee, rich with flavor, is now available as well. Even supermarkets are carrying whole beans that can be ground at purchase or taken home if you have a coffee grinder.

To keep your coffee fresh, store in an airtight container in your refrigerator or freezer. If you keep different blends, be sure to label them. When you venture into a store that specializes in coffee, plan to spend some time talking to the clerk about the different blends. This will help you choose the right ones for your tastes and needs. Here are a few suggestions to help you get started:

BREAKFAST COFFEE

A good full-bodied morning coffee can be Mocha Java or Viennese. If you like a lighter tasting coffee, try Colombian. To get the most flavor with the least bitterness, use a drip method of preparation. Melita-style coffeemakers, using the cone-shaped filter, make a quick, wonderful cup or pot. I also like the coffee press or a Melior-type pot, which can be purchased in several sizes depending on your needs. Pour the boiling water on the beans, let steep, then plunge down again. I first had coffee served in this fashion in London. I think it makes a wonderful cup of coffee. For a change, add an inch of vanilla bean, or 1/2 teaspoon ground cinnamon to the beans before brewing.

AFTERNOON COFFEE

Iced coffee can be a real afternoon treat. With a bit of nonfat milk and some sweetener, it tastes like dessert! To make good iced coffee, brew the coffee double-strength and pour it over ice cubes in tall glasses (the extra strong coffee allows for the dilution caused by the ice). Or, you may brew extra breakfast coffee and freeze it into coffee ice cubes. Then make iced coffee anytime by pouring regular-strength coffee over the ice cubes.

AFTER DINNER COFFEE

Espresso, French, Viennese, Java, Mocha, or Mocha Java are good types of coffee to serve after dinner. These can all be found in decaffeinated beans as well. You may want to make your own special house blend. Don't boil it; that can give it a bitter flavor. The coffee press looks nice on your table, and is a good conversation piece. Few people are aware of presses, although they are widely used throughout Europe. Serve your after-dinner coffee in demitasse cups. Serve Espresso with lemon peel on the side or add the essence of anise to the coffee itself.

CAPPUCCINO

A good trick for making Cappuccino if you do not have a frother is to whip 1 cup evaporated skimmed milk with 2 teaspoons sweetener and 1/2 teaspoon vanilla. Fill a coffee cup halfway with whipped milk and pour the Espresso over it.

TURKISH COFFEE

Use very fine or pulverized coffee. Mocha or Mocha Java are good ones to use. If you have a coffee grinder, just grind the coffee twice as long. If you grind it at the store, the machines normally have a setting for Turkish Coffee. To make 4 demitasse cups, bring 1 1/2 cups water to boil in a saucepan or a pot designed for making Turkish Coffee. (These can be found at a coffee specialty store.) Add 3 tablespoons coffee and 1/8 teaspoon ground coriander. Allow the coffee to come to a boil and froth up twice. Take it off the heat each time to allow it to go back down. Stir in 1 tablespoon sweetener and allow it to froth up once more. Pour into the demitasse cups.

MOCHA COFFEE

Fill the coffee cup half with coffee and half with hot cocoa. (To make the hot cocoa, mix 2 teaspoons cocoa with 2 teaspoons sweetener and 1 tablespoon hot water. Stir in 2 cups hot, nonfat milk.)

The Basic Kitchen

When you love being in the kitchen, you will find that over time your basic needs grow and grow! The most important thing to remember is to buy quality merchandise, especially electric appliances. It is also fun to have a certain amount of variety. For instance, the colors of the linens can set the tone of the meal from fun and festive to soft and romantic.

Cookware

Take your time when choosing your cookware. Buy a good line and pieces that you will use.

colander
large Dutch oven
medium Dutch oven
pasta pot
sauté pan
small saucepan

small skillet
stockpot
vegetable steamer

Cutlery

Buy good knives and keep them sharp. They'll make kitchen work much quicker and easier.

boning knife
chef's knife
kitchen shears
knife sharpener
paring knife
serrated bread knife

Small Appliances

A good food processor will cut your time in half! Take the time to learn how to use it. A toaster oven can double as an extra oven for small items.

blender
coffee grinder
coffee maker
electric beater
food processor
toaster oven

Baking Needs

I like the French white Corningware because it bakes well and presents nicely at the table.

cake pans
cutting boards
glass mixing bowls
insulated cookie sheet
measuring cups
muffin pans
ovenproof baking dishes
rolling pin
rubber spatulas
sifter
soufflé dishes
soufflé ramekins
9-inch springform pan
wire whisk
wooden spoons

Miscellaneous

garlic press
pepper grinder
potato peeler
salad spinner
timer
wine opener

Accessories

I prefer to keep my accessories simple so they work well with my moods—casual or formal.

bread basket
oval serving platter
pasta bowl
pitcher
serving trays
serving utensils
tongs
wooden salad bowl

Stemware

Keep your basic stemware simple. Then pick up different pieces when they catch your eye. Martini glasses make interesting dessert dishes or centerpieces to hold floating flowers.

all-purpose wine glasses
champagne flutes
ice bucket and tongs
martini glasses
pitcher
red wine glasses
water goblets
white wine glasses

Linens

Your linens can change the whole look and mood of your meals—so keep an interesting variety.

apron
dishcloths
napkins
placemats
pot holders
tablecloths

The Basic Pantry
Salad Ingredients

Avocado
Carrots
Celery
Cucumber (English)
Fresh Herbs
  Basil
  Cilantro
  Marjoram
  Mint
  Oregano
  Parsley
  Rosemary
  Tarragon

Lettuce
Radishes
Red cabbage
Red onions
Scallions
Tomatoes

Leeks
Mushrooms
Peppers: Red, yellow, green
Potatoes: Yukon Gold, red, russet, white
Shallots
Squash

Fruits

Apples
Bananas
Berries
Grapes
Lemons
Oranges
Pears

Vegetables

Artichokes
Asparagus
Brussels sprouts
Carrots
Cauliflower
Corn
Eggplant
Green beans

Pasta

Pasta, various sizes and shapes

Rice

Arborio
Brown, long- and short-grain
White, long- and short-grain
Wild

Flour and Cereals

Bread
Reduced-fat Bisquick
Low-fat granola
Rolled oats
Self-rising flour
Whole-wheat flour

Spices, Seasonings, and Condiments

Almond extract
Arrowroot
Bouillon paste
Butter-flavored nonstick spray
Cinnamon
Cornstarch
Equal
Fructose
Garlic
Ginger
Italian blend seasoning
Ketchup
Mayonnaise, low-fat
Molasses
Mustard (powdered)
Mustard (prepared, Dijon)
Nutmeg, whole
Olive oil
Olive oil spray
Paprika
Peppers: Black, cayenne, white
Salsa
Sea Salt
Sugar: Brown, white granulated, confectioners'
Sunflower seeds
Vanilla extract
Vinegars: Balsamic, seasoned rice wine, variety of flavors
Walnuts

Frozen Foods

Corn
Egg substitute
Green beans
Low-fat or nonfat ice milk
Peaches
Stew vegetables
Strawberries
Waffles

Meat, Poultry, and Seafood

Beef tenderloin
Flank steak
Lean ground beef
Pork tenderloin
Chicken breast
Turkey breast
Shrimp
Halibut
Sole

Dairy

Cheddar cheese
Crumbled blue cheese
Farmer's cheese
Feta cheese
Light sour cream
Nonfat milk
Nonfat or low-fat cottage cheese
Nonfat or low-fat cream cheese
1% milk
Parmesan cheese (fresh)
Plain nonfat yogurt

Wine, Liquor, and Soft Drinks

Champagne or sparkling wine
Club soda
Dry vermouth
Mineral water
Port
Red wine
Sherry
White wine

American Cuisine

American Cuisine (continued)

Introduction

American cuisine contains influences from all over the world, reflecting our heritage as a melting pot for many cultures. And each part of our country has a different cuisine. However, when you think of typical American food, you probably think of Mom, apple pie, baseball, barbecues, and Thanksgiving dinner. Here's a sample menu for the all-American barbecue:

Iced tea with Fresh Lemon

Waldorf Salad

Pasta Salad

Barbecued Chicken

Oven Potato Chips

Green Beans

Peach Crisp

CAJUN CUISINE

Cajun and Creole cooking are interesting combinations of French and Spanish cuisine with the added influence of the Choctaw Indians. Cajun and Creole cooking are located primarily in Louisiana, but in recent years their popularity has grown throughout the United States. Cajun food preparation can be high in fat and sodium.

However, it is easy to modify by eliminating the high-fat meats and the heavy use of butter and oils. Cajun cuisine uses lots of fresh ingredients and spices that are full of flavor, so it's easy to create very tasty dishes that are low in fat and salt. Spices found in the Cajun kitchen include peppers—black, white, and red (cayenne)—powdered sassafras, parsley, bay leaf, Tabasco, garlic (fresh and powder), and onion powder.

Now here's the Cajun version of the all-American barbecue. Start your party in the late afternoon on your patio with Dixieland Jazz playing in the background. Serve:

Iced tea with Fresh Mint

Crudités and Green Onion Dip

Mugs of Corn Chowder

Then in the dining room, change your music to a light jazz, and serve:

Cajun Oven-Fried Chicken

Creole Corn

Guiltless Bananas Foster

Coffee

Raspberry Sauce

This recipe will work for almost all fruit sauces using frozen fruit. You may need to purée larger fruits in a food processor or blender.

SERVES 8

1 bag (12 ounces) frozen unsweetened raspberries
2 teaspoons cornstarch
1 tablespoon sugar
¼ cup apple juice concentrate

1. Combine all of the ingredients and cook over a medium heat until the sauce thickens (about 10 minutes).

2. Remove the sauce from the heat.

3. Serve it either hot or cold.

Nutritional analysis per serving:

CALORIES	PROTEIN, GM.	CARBOHYDRATE, GM.	FAT, GM.	SATURATED FAT, GM.
181	0.3	43.5	0.1	0.0

SODIUM, MG.	CHOLESTEROL, MG.	FIBER, GM.	CALCIUM, MG.	CALORIES FROM FAT
4.1	0.0	1.5	6	0%

Strawberry Apple Butter

This is a good, basic sauce to keep on hand. It can be used to spruce up many different foods, makes a lovely gift, and it freezes well.

SERVES 12

6 medium apples, cored and thinly sliced
(do not peel)
1 cup apple juice concentrate
1½ teaspoons cinnamon
½ teaspoon allspice
¼ teaspoon ground cloves
1 bag frozen unsweetened strawberries,
thawed
1 tablespoon sugar

1. Combine apples, apple juice, and spices in a large saucepan.

2. Bring to a boil, then simmer for 20 to 25 minutes until the apples are very soft.

3. Add the strawberries and simmer for 5 minutes.

4. Put into a food processor or blender, add sugar, and blend until very smooth.

Nutritional analysis per serving:

CALORIES	PROTEIN, GM.	CARBOHYDRATE, GM.	FAT, GM.	SATURATED FAT, GM.
69	0.3	17.7	0.3	0.05

SODIUM, MG.	CHOLESTEROL, MG.	FIBER, GM.	CALCIUM, MG.	CALORIES FROM FAT
1.6	0.0	2.4	16	4%

Apple Walnut Muffins

These muffins can also be baked in a 9-by-13-inch pan and cut into bars. The best apples to use are Fuji or Gala. These apples are usually a little smaller, so use two.

MAKES 12 MUFFINS

3/4 cup unbleached flour
3/4 cup whole-wheat flour
1/2 cup unprocessed bran
1/4 teaspoon nutmeg
1 teaspoon cinnamon
2 1/2 teaspoons baking powder
2 eggs
2/3 cup apple juice concentrate
1 large apple, cored and chopped
1/2 cup walnuts

1. Preheat the oven to 400°F. Line a muffin tin with paper cups or spray with a nonstick baking spray.

2. Mix all of the dry ingredients in a food processor or blender until well mixed.

3. Mix the eggs, apple juice, apple, and walnuts together in a separate bowl.

4. Pour the liquid ingredients into the dry ingredients and mix until well moistened.

5. Fill the muffin tin. Bake for 20 minutes.

Nutritional analysis per serving:

CALORIES	PROTEIN, GM.	CARBOHYDRATE, GM.	FAT, GM.	SATURATED FAT, GM.
118	4	17.4	4.4	0.6

SODIUM, MG.	CHOLESTEROL, MG.	FIBER, GM.	CALCIUM, MG.	CALORIES FROM FAT
129.8	35	2.6	71	34%

Banana Bran Muffins

A great way to use the bananas that are getting too ripe! These muffins are very high in fiber. You may also want to add a half cup of chopped nuts.

MAKES 12 MUFFINS

1 cup whole-wheat flour
3 teaspoons baking powder
1/2 cup rolled oats, uncooked
1 cup unprocessed bran
3 tablespoons dark molasses
2 very ripe bananas, mashed
1 whole egg
1 cup nonfat milk
2/3 cup raisins

1. Preheat the oven to 400°F. Line a muffin tin with paper cups or spray with a nonstick baking spray.

2. Combine all of the dry ingredients.

3. Add the rest of the ingredients, except the raisins, and mix well.

4. Fold in the raisins.

5. Spoon the batter into the muffin tin. Bake for 15 to 20 minutes.

Nutritional analysis per serving:

CALORIES	PROTEIN, GM.	CARBOHYDRATE, GM.	FAT, GM.	SATURATED FAT, GM.
126	4.3	28.1	1.1	0.3

SODIUM, MG.	CHOLESTEROL, MG.	FIBER, GM.	CALCIUM, MG.	CALORIES FROM FAT
183.9	17.9	4.2	115	8%

Bran Muffins

The standard bran muffin can be a great way to start the day. Just add some fresh fruit. The big difference in these muffins is far less fat. Try spreading a fruit-sweetened jam on them.

MAKES 12 MUFFINS

1 cup unprocessed bran
1 cup whole-wheat flour
1 tablespoon sugar
1½ teaspoons baking soda
1 egg
2 egg whites
1 cup buttermilk
¼ cup corn oil
2 tablespoons honey
¼ cup molasses

1. Preheat the oven to 350°F. Line a muffin tin with paper cups or spray with a nonstick baking spray.

2. Combine bran, flour, sugar, and baking soda in a bowl.

3. Mix together the egg, egg whites, buttermilk, corn oil, honey, and molasses.

4. Stir the liquid mixture into the flour mixture, enough to moisten.

5. Pour the batter into the muffin tin. Bake for 25 minutes and cool.

Nutritional analysis per serving:

CALORIES	PROTEIN, GM.	CARBOHYDRATE, GM.	FAT, GM.	SATURATED FAT, GM.
138	3.9	20.7	5.6	0.9

SODIUM, MG.	CHOLESTEROL, MG.	FIBER, GM.	CALCIUM, MG.	CALORIES FROM FAT
149.7	18.2	3.1	79	36%

Carrot-Prune Muffins

These muffins may sound strange, but they taste great. They have lots of texture and moisture from the carrots and prunes.

MAKES 12 MUFFINS

1/3 cup sugar
1/4 cup light molasses
2 eggs
1 cup grated carrots
1 cup pitted, chopped prunes
1/2 cup nonfat milk
2 teaspoons baking powder
1/2 teaspoon nutmeg
1 teaspoon ground cinnamon
1/4 teaspoon ground ginger
1 cup oatmeal, ground (grind it into flour in food processor or blender)
1/4 teaspoon cloves
1/4 teaspoon baking soda
1/2 cup unprocessed bran
1 cup whole-wheat flour
1/2 cup chopped walnuts

1. Preheat the oven to 350°F. spray a muffin tin with nonstick baking spray.

2. Mix the sugar, molasses, eggs, carrots, prunes, and milk together.

3. Mix all of the dry ingredients, except the nuts. Add 1/2 of the mixture to the wet ingredients and mix lightly. Add the rest of the dry ingredients, and mix. Add the nuts last.

4. Fill the muffin tin. Bake 25 minutes, then let stand 15 minutes before removing muffins from the pan.

Nutritional analysis per serving:

CALORIES	PROTEIN, GM.	CARBOHYDRATE, GM.	FAT, GM.	SATURATED FAT, GM.
165	4.6	28.6	4.7	0.7

SODIUM, MG.	CHOLESTEROL, MG.	FIBER, GM.	CALCIUM, MG.	CALORIES FROM FAT
165.3	35.2	3.9	92	25%

Oatmeal Breakfast Bars

These are delicious for a breakfast on the go, to carry for snacks, or even for dessert.

MAKES 16 BARS

1/3 cup butter
1/2 cup sugar
6 egg whites
1/2 cup nonfat milk
2 tablespoons molasses
2 1/2 teaspoons vanilla
1 cup whole-wheat flour
1 teaspoon baking powder
1 cup unprocessed bran
3 cups rolled oats, uncooked
2 teaspoons cinnamon
1 cup raisins

1. Preheat the oven to 350°F. Spray 9-by-13-inch pan with nonstick baking spray.

2. Cream together the butter and sugar.

3. Add the egg whites, milk, molasses, and vanilla. Mix well.

4. Stir in flour, baking powder, bran, oats, cinnamon, raisins. Mix.

5. Put mixture into baking pan.

6. Bake 15 minutes. Cool, cut into 16 bars.

Nutritional analysis per serving:

CALORIES	PROTEIN, GM.	CARBOHYDRATE, GM.	FAT, GM.	SATURATED FAT, GM.
191	5.8	34	4.6	2.4

SODIUM, MG.	CHOLESTEROL, MG.	FIBER, GM.	CALCIUM, MG.	CALORIES FROM FAT
132.7	9.5	4.8	53	22%

Raspberry Corn Muffins

These tasty muffins have a surprise inside. They freeze well and are good for breakfast or served with a salad.

MAKES 12 MUFFINS

1 cup cornmeal
1 cup whole unbleached flour
1 tablespoon baking powder
1 cup nonfat milk
2 egg whites
2 tablespoons corn oil
2 tablespoons sugar
36 raspberries (approximately ¾ cup)

1. Preheat the oven to 400°F. Line a muffin tin with paper cups or spray with a nonstick baking spray.

2. Combine the cornmeal, flour, and baking powder in a large mixing bowl.

3. Combine the milk, egg whites, corn oil, and sugar. Mix well.

4. Add the liquid ingredients to the dry ingredients, and mix well.

5. Fill each cup in the tin a quarter full. Place 3 raspberries in the center of each, then top with the rest of the batter.

6. Bake for 20 minutes or until golden brown.

Nutritional analysis per serving:

CALORIES	PROTEIN, GM.	CARBOHYDRATE, GM.	FAT, GM.	SATURATED FAT, GM.
120	3.3	20.4	2.7	0.4

SODIUM, MG.	CHOLESTEROL, MG.	FIBER, GM.	CALCIUM, MG.	CALORIES FROM FAT
127.3	0.4	1.2	92	20%

Cottage Cheese Pancakes

These pancakes have a soft, delicate texture and are delicious served with fresh fruit or apple butter.

SERVES 4

1 cup low-fat cottage cheese
1 whole egg
4 egg whites
¼ cup unbleached flour
1 tablespoon corn oil

1. Spray the griddle with a nonstick spray and heat it.

2. Process the cottage cheese in a blender or food processor until smooth.

3. Add the egg and egg whites, and blend.

4. Add the flour and oil; blend just until mixed.

5. Use ¼ cup measure for each pancake. Bake the pancakes on the hot griddle until they bubble. Turn them over and bake until firm and brown.

Nutritional analysis per serving:

CALORIES	PROTEIN, GM.	CARBOHYDRATE, GM.	FAT, GM.	SATURATED FAT, GM.
134	12.8	7.5	5.5	1.2

SODIUM, MG.	CHOLESTEROL, MG.	FIBER, GM.	CALCIUM, MG.	CALORIES FROM FAT
299.1	55	0.2	44	37%

Cornmeal Waffles

These waffles have a marvelous crunchy texture and are especially good with Strawberry Apple Butter (page 6). Freeze the leftovers to toast later.

MAKES 6 WAFFLES/SERVES 6

½ cup unbleached flour
1 cup cornmeal
2½ teaspoons baking powder
2 tablespoons sugar
¼ cup unprocessed bran
1 tablespoon butter, melted
2 cups nonfat milk
2 egg whites, beaten until stiff

1. Heat the waffle iron.

2. Sift the flour, cornmeal, baking powder, and sugar into a mixing bowl.

3. Add the bran and mix.

4. Add the melted butter and milk; mix well.

5. Fold in the beaten egg whites.

6. Bake according to the directions for your waffle iron. These waffles are best when they are very brown and crisp.

Nutritional analysis per serving:

CALORIES	PROTEIN, GM.	CARBOHYDRATE, GM.	FAT, GM.	SATURATED FAT, GM.
194	7.3	35.4	2.7	1.4

SODIUM, MG.	CHOLESTEROL, MG.	FIBER, GM.	CALCIUM, MG.	CALORIES FROM FAT
289	6.9	2.3	212	12%

Yeast Waffles

The beauty of these waffles is that you can make up the whole batch and freeze the leftovers. Just pop them into a toaster for a quick breakfast during the week or for a snack. They are good and crunchy all by themselves.

MAKES 8 WAFFLES/SERVES 8

1 package dry yeast
2 cups lukewarm nonfat milk (105° to 115°F)
2 egg yolks
1 teaspoon vanilla
1 cup sifted whole-wheat flour
1½ cups sifted unbleached flour
2 tablespoons sugar
2 tablespoons butter, melted
4 egg whites

1. Sprinkle the yeast over the warm milk and stir to dissolve.

2. Beat the egg yolks and vanilla, and add to the milk.

3. Sift the flour and sugar, and add to the milk mixture.

4. Stir in the melted butter, combining it thoroughly.

5. Beat the egg whites until stiff and fold into the batter.

6. Let the mixture stand in a warm place for 45 minutes or until it doubles in bulk.

7. Use ½ cup of batter per waffle and bake according to the directions for your waffle iron.

Nutritional analysis per serving:

CALORIES	PROTEIN, GM.	CARBOHYDRATE, GM.	FAT, GM.	SATURATED FAT, GM.
215	9	33.9	5	2.5

SODIUM, MG.	CHOLESTEROL, MG.	FIBER, GM.	CALCIUM, MG.	CALORIES FROM FAT
92.8	63.5	2.6	92	21%

French Toast

This is easy and fast to make for one person; just divide the recipe by four. Serve with Raspberry Sauce (page 5) or Strawberry Apple Butter (page 6).

SERVES 4

4 whole eggs
1 teaspoon cinnamon
¼ cup nonfat milk
1 teaspoon vanilla
¼ teaspoon nutmeg
8 slices whole-wheat bread

1. Mix all of the ingredients, except the bread, in a flat bowl that will hold one slice of bread.

2. Dip each piece of bread into the egg mixture, making sure all of it is soaked up.

3. Brown the bread in a large skillet sprayed with nonstick coating. (If your skillet will not hold 2 slices of bread, cut the slices in half to fit.)

Nutritional analysis per serving:

CALORIES	PROTEIN, GM.	CARBOHYDRATE, GM.	FAT, GM.	SATURATED FAT, GM.
195	13.1	25.2	6.1	1.8

SODIUM, MG.	CHOLESTEROL, MG.	FIBER, GM.	CALCIUM, MG.	CALORIES FROM FAT
329.8	210.5	6.5	102	28%

Salmon Omelet

This quick, tasty dish gives you the benefit of omega-3 fish oil.

SERVES 2

2 eggs
2 egg whites
1 can (7¾ ounces) salmon
¼ cup green onion, chopped
⅛ teaspoon dillweed
2 tablespoons tomato paste

1. Preheat the oven to 350°F. Spray a 9-inch baking pan with nonstick baking spray.

2. Beat the eggs and egg whites until frothy; fold in the rest of the ingredients.

3. Pour the mixture into the prepared baking dish. Bake for 20 minutes, or until done.

Nutritional analysis per serving:

CALORIES	PROTEIN, GM.	CARBOHYDRATE, GM.	FAT, GM.	SATURATED FAT, GM.
288	36.2	3.1	13.7	3.1

SODIUM, MG.	CHOLESTEROL, MG.	FIBER, GM.	CALCIUM, MG.	CALORIES FROM FAT
255.1	278	0.4	52	43%

Skillet Eggs

A great brunch dish—serve it with toasted Italian bread and fresh fruit. Reducing the chicken broth intensifies the flavor and richness, so the eggs taste as if they were cooked in butter.

SERVES 4

¾ cup chicken broth
2 cups mushrooms, sliced
1 medium onion, sliced
1 bell pepper, sliced
½ teaspoon Italian Blend seasoning
Crushed hot red pepper to taste
4 red potatoes, cooked and sliced in large pieces
3 whole eggs
3 egg whites

1. Reduce ½ cup broth to 1 tablespoon in a nonstick skillet.

2. Sauté mushrooms and set aside.

3. Reduce ¼ cup broth to 1 tablespoon and sauté the onion and bell pepper until tender.

4. Add the seasonings, sliced potatoes, and mushrooms; toss until warm.

5. Beat the eggs and egg whites together. Add to the vegetables, stirring until set.

Nutritional analysis per serving:

CALORIES	PROTEIN, GM.	CARBOHYDRATE, GM.	FAT, GM.	SATURATED FAT, GM.
205	11.2	31	4.5	1.4

SODIUM, MG.	CHOLESTEROL, MG.	FIBER, GM.	CALCIUM, MG.	CALORIES FROM FAT
242.9	157.7	3.7	45	20%

Basil Dressing

If you don't have fresh basil, use dried. Be sure to crush it in a mortar and pestle first. This dressing is very good on tomatoes and fresh mozzarella cheese.

SERVES 8

¼ cup olive oil
½ teaspoon ground black pepper
1 cup wine vinegar (red or white)
Juice from ½ lemon
1 cup water
2 tablespoons chopped fresh basil

Combine the ingredients and chill.

Nutritional analysis per serving:

CALORIES	PROTEIN, GM.	CARBOHYDRATE, GM.	FAT, GM.	SATURATED FAT, GM.
66	0.1	2.3	6.8	0.9

SODIUM, MG.	CHOLESTEROL, MG.	FIBER, GM.	CALCIUM, MG.	CALORIES FROM FAT
3	0.0	0.2	29	92%

Poppy Seed Dressing

Use it for Spinach Salad with Strawberries (page 29). It is also good on fruit salad.

SERVES 8

¼ cup egg substitute
1 tablespoon sugar
1½ teaspoons Dijon-style mustard
¼ cup raspberry vinegar, or apple cider
   vinegar
¼ cup water
½ cup corn oil
1 tablespoon poppy seeds

1. Combine the egg substitute, sugar, mustard, vinegar, and water in the blender.

2. While the blender is running, slowly drizzle in the corn oil, and blend until it is well mixed.

3. Pour into a storage container and add 1 tablespoon poppy seeds.

Nutritional analysis per serving:

CALORIES	PROTEIN, GM.	CARBOHYDRATE, GM.	FAT, GM.	SATURATED FAT, GM.
147	1.3	2.5	15	1.9

SODIUM, MG.	CHOLESTEROL, MG.	FIBER, GM.	CALCIUM, MG.	CALORIES FROM FAT
14.2	0.1	0.2	27	92%

Sherry Dressing

This dressing is very good served on baby spinach leaves, topped with grated hard-boiled eggs.

SERVES 4

1½ teaspoons olive oil
2 tablespoons water
½ teaspoon freshly ground pepper
3 tablespoons wine vinegar
3 tablespoons dry sherry

Combine all of the ingredients in a blender or covered container. Mix well and then chill.

Nutritional analysis per serving:

CALORIES	PROTEIN, GM.	CARBOHYDRATE, GM.	FAT, GM.	SATURATED FAT, GM.
23	0.1	1.7	0.5	0.1

SODIUM, MG.	CHOLESTEROL, MG.	FIBER, GM.	CALCIUM, MG.	CALORIES FROM FAT
10.8	0.0	0.0	45	21%

Vinaigrette Dressing

A good basic dressing, vinaigrette can also be used to marinate vegetables, meats, and poultry for grilling.

SERVES 8

¼ cup olive oil
Juice from ½ lemon
½ teaspoon garlic powder
2 teaspoons Worcestershire sauce
1 cup wine vinegar (red or white)
1 teaspoon dry mustard
½ teaspoon ground black pepper
Dash Tabasco sauce
1 cup water

Combine all of the ingredients in a blender or covered container and mix well. Chill in a covered container.

Nutritional analysis per serving:

CALORIES	PROTEIN, GM.	CARBOHYDRATE, GM.	FAT, GM.	SATURATED FAT, GM.
68	0.2	2.4	6.9	0.9

SODIUM, MG.	CHOLESTEROL, MG.	FIBER, GM.	CALCIUM, MG.	CALORIES FROM FAT
15.1	0.0	0.1	17	91%

Bibb Lettuce with Radishes

Bibb lettuce has big floppy leaves that cover smaller leaves that should be in a tight ball. The outer leaves are good to use for lining bowls and plates. This is a delicate, simple salad.

SERVES 4

2 heads Bibb lettuce
1/2 cup Vinaigrette Dressing (page 22)
1 bunch of radishes, thinly sliced

1. Wash the lettuce, drain it, and tear it into bite-sized pieces. Spin or pat it dry.

2. Toss the lettuce, radishes, and dressing together, and place on 4 salad plates.

Nutritional analysis per serving:

CALORIES	PROTEIN, GM.	CARBOHYDRATE, GM.	FAT, GM.	SATURATED FAT, GM.
113	0.8	5.9	10.7	1.41

SODIUM, MG.	CHOLESTEROL, MG.	FIBER, GM.	CALCIUM, MG.	CALORIES FROM FAT
34.6	0.0	0.6	46	85%

Chicken or Turkey Salad

Try a Raspberry Corn Muffin (page 12) or toasted English muffin with Strawberry Apple Butter (page 6) on the side for a festive luncheon.

SERVES 4

12 ounces turkey or chicken breast,
   skinned, steamed or baked, and diced
½ teaspoon celery seed
1 tablespoon sour cream
1 tablespoon low-calorie mayonnaise
3 stalks celery, diced
1 large apple, diced
¼ cup raisins
2 teaspoons sesame seeds
Lettuce leaves
Carrot sticks or curls

1. Combine all ingredients. Mix well and chill.

2. Serve on lettuce leaves garnished with carrot sticks or curls.

Nutritional analysis per serving:

CALORIES	PROTEIN, GM.	CARBOHYDRATE, GM.	FAT, GM.	SATURATED FAT, GM.
222	25.5	14.9	6.7	2.1

SODIUM, MG.	CHOLESTEROL, MG.	FIBER, GM.	CALCIUM, MG.	CALORIES FROM FAT
108.8	66.1	2	51	27%

Fresh Fruit Plate

You can use any variety of fruits in this and even mix in some canned fruit. The mixed fruit in the glass jars are excellent.

SERVES 4

Juice from 1/2 lemon
1 cup water
1/2 small banana, sliced
2 small apples, sliced
2 small oranges, peeled and sectioned
1 cup Fruit Salad Dressing (page 26)

1. Mix the lemon juice and water. Then dip the apple and banana slices in the lemon water. (It keeps them from turning brown.)

2. Arrange the sliced apples, orange sections, and banana slices alternately on 4 dessert plates.

3. Top each fruit arrangement with 1/4 cup Fruit Salad Dressing.

4. Then garnish with an orange slice or a sprig of fresh mint.

Continued on page 26

Continued from page 25

Fresh Fruit Plate

Fruit Salad Dressing

1½ cup low-fat cottage cheese
½ teaspoon freshly grated orange rind
¼ cup nonfat yogurt
¼ cup sour cream
¼ teaspoon vanilla
2 teaspoons fresh orange juice
1 teaspoon honey

1. Combine all of the ingredients in a blender or food processor and blend until smooth.

2. Chill and serve over fresh, canned, or frozen and thawed fruit.

Nutritional analysis per serving:

CALORIES	PROTEIN, GM.	CARBOHYDRATE, GM.	FAT, GM.	SATURATED FAT, GM.
193	12.8	27.6	4.3	2.5

SODIUM, MG.	CHOLESTEROL, MG.	FIBER, GM.	CALCIUM, MG.	CALORIES FROM FAT
363.7	10.4	3.3	132	20%

Pasta Salad

Pasta salad is always a hit at a picnic. You can easily double or triple this recipe for larger gatherings.

SERVES 4

3 cups cooked pasta shells
8 ounces cooked and cubed chicken,
   turkey, or water-packed tuna
2 stalks celery, sliced
2 green onions or scallions, sliced
1 cup Vinaigrette Dressing (page 22)
2 cups broccoli flowerets, steamed crisp-
   tender (3-5 minutes)
1/2 teaspoon crushed basil (optional)
Lettuce leaves

Combine all of the ingredients and chill for 2 to 3 hours. Serve on a bed of lettuce.

Nutritional analysis per serving:

CALORIES	PROTEIN, GM.	CARBOHYDRATE, GM.	FAT, GM.	SATURATED FAT, GM.
288	15.8	26	14.9	2

SODIUM, MG.	CHOLESTEROL, MG.	FIBER, GM.	CALCIUM, MG.	CALORIES FROM FAT
199.4	11.6	3.9	83	46%

Sherry Spinach Salad

Serve this salad as a first course with glasses of dry chilled sherry, the same sherry you use in the dressing.

SERVES 4

2 bunches fresh spinach
¼ red onion, very thinly sliced
½ cup Sherry Dressing (page 21)
1 hard-boiled egg, finely chopped

1. Wash the spinach carefully, because each leaf can hold dirt. Break the stems off the leaves. Drain, spin, or pat the leaves dry.

2. Put into a bowl with the onions and toss with the dressing.

3. Place on 4 salad plates and sprinkle each with a quarter of the chopped egg.

Nutritional analysis per serving:

CALORIES	PROTEIN, GM.	CARBOHYDRATE, GM.	FAT, GM.	SATURATED FAT, GM.
98	2.7	3.8	8.3	1.7

SODIUM, MG.	CHOLESTEROL, MG.	FIBER, GM.	CALCIUM, MG.	CALORIES FROM FAT
202.9	54	0.9	39	76%

Spinach Salad with Strawberries

You can find baby spinach prewashed in bags in the produce section of the grocery store. Check the dates on the bag to make sure it is fresh. It is a good idea to rinse it once more and spin it dry in a salad spinner.

SERVES 4

2 bunches fresh spinach
12 strawberries, cut in half
1/2 cup Poppy Seed Dressing (page 20)

1. Wash the spinach carefully (each leaf can hold dirt). Break the stems off of the leaves and spin or pat them dry.

2. Toss the spinach with the dressing.

3. Place on 4 serving plates and garnish each with 6 strawberry halves.

Nutritional analysis per serving:

CALORIES	PROTEIN, GM.	CARBOHYDRATE, GM.	FAT, GM.	SATURATED FAT, GM.
115	1.5	13.5	7.1	1.3

SODIUM, MG.	CHOLESTEROL, MG.	FIBER, GM.	CALCIUM, MG.	CALORIES FROM FAT
189.5	1.4	3.2	50	56%

Tomato-Cucumber Salad

This very simple, very tasty salad goes well with almost everything.

SERVES 4

1 cucumber, peeled and sliced
1 large tomato, sliced
1/2 cup Basil Dressing (page 19)
4 romaine leaves, washed and patted dry

1. Marinate the cucumber and tomato in the Basil Dressing for 2 hours.

2. On each of 4 salad plates, place 1 romaine leaf and one-quarter of the marinated cucumbers and tomatoes.

Nutritional analysis per serving:

CALORIES	PROTEIN, GM.	CARBOHYDRATE, GM.	FAT, GM.	SATURATED FAT, GM.
50	0.8	4.5	3.7	0.7

SODIUM, MG.	CHOLESTEROL, MG.	FIBER, GM.	CALCIUM, MG.	CALORIES FROM FAT
87	0.7	0.7	14	66%

Tuna Salad

This low-cal version of its traditional cousin is good on rolls, stuffed into pita pockets, or served on a bed of lettuce and garnished with crisp, raw vegetables.

SERVES 3

1 can (7½ ounces) tuna, water-packed
1 green onion, finely chopped
1 stalk celery, finely chopped
¼ cup low-calorie mayonnaise
pepper to taste

Combine all of the ingredients and chill.

Nutritional analysis per serving:

CALORIES	PROTEIN, GM.	CARBOHYDRATE, GM.	FAT, GM.	SATURATED FAT, GM.
125	13.7	7.1	4.6	0.8

SODIUM, MG.	CHOLESTEROL, MG.	FIBER, GM.	CALCIUM, MG.	CALORIES FROM FAT
292.2	20.5	0.8	18	33%

Waldorf Salad

This traditional American salad is served at most holiday celebrations. To keep the apples from turning brown, toss them in 2 cups cold water with the juice of ½ lemon, and pat them dry on paper towels.

SERVES 4

2 small apples, cored and chopped
2 stalks celery, chopped
¼ cup raisins
¼ cup chopped walnuts
¼ cup sour cream
2 tablespoons low-calorie mayonnaise
⅛ teaspoon nutmeg

1. Combine the apples, celery, raisins, and walnuts.

2. Mix the sour cream, mayonnaise, and nutmeg.

3. Add the sour cream mixture to the apple mixture.

4. Cover and chill.

Nutritional analysis per serving:

CALORIES	PROTEIN, GM.	CARBOHYDRATE, GM.	FAT, GM.	SATURATED FAT, GM.
171	2.2	21.8	9.7	2.6

SODIUM, MG.	CHOLESTEROL, MG.	FIBER, GM.	CALCIUM, MG.	CALORIES FROM FAT
66.7	8.3	2.7	41	51%

Brown Rice Pilaf

Pilaf goes well with just about anything. You can also add any leftover vegetables to this dish. Just chop them up, heat them, and fold them into the rice when it is ready to serve. That way you don't overcook the vegetables.

SERVES 4

1 onion, sliced
1/4 pound fresh mushrooms, sliced
2 1/4 cups vegetable broth or water
1 cup brown rice
1 tablespoon soy sauce
1 teaspoon oregano
1/4 cup sliced almonds, toasted

1. In a large nonstick skillet cook the onion and mushrooms in 1/4 cup broth until all the liquid is gone.

2. Add the rice, soy sauce, oregano, and the remaining broth. Bring it to a boil.

3. Turn down the heat, cover, and simmer for 45 minutes, or until all the liquid is absorbed.

4. Stir the toasted almonds into the rice when ready to serve.

Nutritional analysis per serving:

CALORIES	PROTEIN, GM.	CARBOHYDRATE, GM.	FAT, GM.	SATURATED FAT, GM.
138	5.8	18.9	4.8	0.6

SODIUM, MG.	CHOLESTEROL, MG.	FIBER, GM.	CALCIUM, MG.	CALORIES FROM FAT
403.8	0.0	2.2	47	32%

Bulgur Pilaf

Bulgur is cracked wheat. When cooked, it is similar in appearance and texture to brown rice. Bulgur has its own unique flavor and aroma with the nutritional bonus of whole-grain wheat.

SERVES 4

1¾ cup chicken broth
½ onion, chopped
1 tablespoon parsley, minced
¼ cup carrot, shredded or chopped
¼ cup zucchini, shredded or chopped
1 cup bulgur wheat
¼ teaspoon cumin
Dash of red chili pepper or cayenne

1. In a 1-quart saucepan reduce ¼ cup chicken broth in half.

2. Add the onion and brown.

3. Add the parsley, carrot, zucchini, and the remaining chicken broth, and bring to a boil.

4. Add the bulgur, cumin, and red pepper.

5. Cover, reduce heat, and simmer for 15 minutes, or until all the liquid is absorbed.

6. Fluff with a fork.

Nutritional analysis per serving:

CALORIES	PROTEIN, GM.	CARBOHYDRATE, GM.	FAT, GM.	SATURATED FAT, GM.
75	3.7	14.3	0.6	0.1

SODIUM, MG.	CHOLESTEROL, MG.	FIBER, GM.	CALCIUM, MG.	CALORIES FROM FAT
248.2	0.0	2.1	25	6%

Herbed Stuffed Potatoes

Get creative. Add cooked lean meat or chicken and any leftover vegetables to make a tasty one-dish meal.

SERVES 4

4 medium baking potatoes, washed
1 green onion, chopped
¼ cup nonfat milk
¼ teaspoon Italian Blend seasoning
1 tablespoon Parmesan cheese
2 tablespoons sour cream

1. Preheat the oven to 350°F.

2. Bake the potatoes 45 minutes or until soft.

3. Make a slit in each potato, press open carefully, and scoop out the inside.

4. Mix the potato with all of the other ingredients.

5. Put the filling into the 4 potato skins.

6. Bake for 10 minutes, or until hot.

Nutritional analysis per serving:

CALORIES	PROTEIN, GM.	CARBOHYDRATE, GM.	FAT, GM.	SATURATED FAT, GM.
141	3.7	27.8	2	1.2

SODIUM, MG.	CHOLESTEROL, MG.	FIBER, GM.	CALCIUM, MG.	CALORIES FROM FAT
41.9	4.4	2.9	61	13%

Oven Potato Chips

Bet you can't eat just one! For extra flavor, try sprinkling them with garlic powder or herbs before baking. You can also use different infused olive oils.

SERVES 4

4 small potatoes, very thinly sliced
Garlic powder or herbs (optional)

1. Preheat the oven to 450°F.

2. Spread the potatoes on a nonstick cookie sheet. Spray lightly with an olive-oil spray and sprinkle with garlic powder if desired.

3. Bake until the potatoes are lightly browned, 10 to 12 minutes.

Nutritional analysis per serving:

CALORIES	PROTEIN, GM.	CARBOHYDRATE, GM.	FAT, GM.	SATURATED FAT, GM.
104	2.1	24.3	0.1	0.03

SODIUM, MG.	CHOLESTEROL, MG.	FIBER, GM.	CALCIUM, MG.	CALORIES FROM FAT
6.1	0.0	2.4	10	1%

Oven-Roasted Potatoes

Roasted potatoes are always good. You can also roast carrots, celery, and onions along with them. Then you'll have all your vegetables ready to go to the table.

SERVES 4

4 small potatoes, cut into quarters
  lengthwise
Salt
Freshly ground black pepper

1. Preheat the oven to 450°F.

2. Place potato pieces on a nonstick baking sheet. Spray with olive oil and sprinkle with salt and pepper.

3. Bake for 30 minutes, or until tender when pricked with a fork, and brown.

Nutritional analysis per serving:

CALORIES	PROTEIN, GM.	CARBOHYDRATE, GM.	FAT, GM.	SATURATED FAT, GM.
109	2.2	25.3	0.1	0.03

SODIUM, MG.	CHOLESTEROL, MG.	FIBER, GM.	CALCIUM, MG.	CALORIES FROM FAT
6.3	0.0	2.5	10	1%

Parsley Potatoes

The flavor of potatoes alone is wonderful, but you can also lightly salt and pepper them.

SERVES 4

2 small red potatoes, sliced
Fresh parsley, minced

1. Steam the potatoes for 10 minutes.

2. Arrange the slices on serving plate, and sprinkle with fresh parsley.

Nutritional analysis per serving:

CALORIES	PROTEIN, GM.	CARBOHYDRATE, GM.	FAT, GM.	SATURATED FAT, GM.
109	2.2	25.3	0.1	0.03
SODIUM, MG.	CHOLESTEROL, MG.	FIBER, GM.	CALCIUM, MG.	CALORIES FROM FAT
6.3	0.0	2.5	10	1%

Potato Pie

This is a fun one to play with. You can use several different vegetables in the layering. Try shredded zucchini, red onions, green beans, broccoli, mushrooms.

SERVES 4

3 **medium** potatoes, thinly sliced
2 **medium** carrots, grated
3 **green** onions, chopped, including the green tops
1 **cup** chicken broth
1 **tablespoon** chopped parsley

1. Preheat the oven to 350°F. Spray a 9-inch pie or quiche pan with nonstick spray.

2. Arrange two layers of potatoes around the pan.

3. Spread the carrots and onions over the potatoes, layer the remaining potatoes on top, and pour the broth over.

4. Cover and bake for 45 minutes.

5. Uncover, sprinkle parsley over the top, and bake again, uncovered, for 10 to 15 minutes.

6. Let stand 10 minutes, and then cut into pie-shaped wedges.

Nutritional analysis per serving:

CALORIES	PROTEIN, GM.	CARBOHYDRATE, GM.	FAT, GM.	SATURATED FAT, GM.
130	3.6	29.1	0.4	0.1

SODIUM, MG.	CHOLESTEROL, MG.	FIBER, GM.	CALCIUM, MG.	CALORIES FROM FAT
116.4	0.0	4.3	41	3%

Wild Brown Rice

The water chestnuts really make this rice because they add great texture and crunch.

SERVES 6

2¼ cups chicken broth
1 medium onion, thinly sliced
¾ cup long-grain brown rice
¼ cup wild rice, washed
1 tablespoon soy sauce
1 teaspoon crushed dried thyme
1 can water chestnuts, sliced

1. Reduce ¼ cup chicken broth in half.

2. Sauté the onion in the broth until it is soft.

3. Add the rice and quickly stir until it is lightly browned.

4. Add the rest of the broth, soy sauce, thyme, and water chestnuts.

5. Bring to a boil and cover. Turn down the heat and simmer for 45 minutes.

6. Let rice stand 10 to 15 minutes until the liquid is fully absorbed.

Nutritional analysis per serving:

CALORIES	PROTEIN, GM.	CARBOHYDRATE, GM.	FAT, GM.	SATURATED FAT, GM.
94	3.7	18.8	0.6	0.2

SODIUM, MG.	CHOLESTEROL, MG.	FIBER, GM.	CALCIUM, MG.	CALORIES FROM FAT
303.6	0.0	2	21	6%

Artichokes

Growing up in California, I often had artichokes for dinner. I have always been surprised at how many people have never had them. When buying artichokes, look for large firm ones. The real treat is when you get to the heart. Be sure to remove the choke, the fuzzy stuff on top of the heart; it is not edible.

SERVES 4

4 medium artichokes
1 clove garlic
1 lemon
1 teaspoon dill

1. Cut the tops and stems off the artichokes, and trim off the thorns with kitchen shears. (This gives them a much prettier appearance.)

2. Fill a large pot one-fourth full with water, and bring to a boil.

3. Peel the garlic clove, and add it to the water.

4. Cut the lemon in half. Squeeze the juice into the water, then drop the lemon into the water. Add the dill.

5. Put the artichokes into the boiling water and reduce the heat. Cover and simmer for 45 minutes, or until you can insert a fork easily into the heart.

Nutritional analysis per serving:

CALORIES	PROTEIN, GM.	CARBOHYDRATE, GM.	FAT, GM.	SATURATED FAT, GM.
67	4.5	15.2	0.2	0.1

SODIUM, MG.	CHOLESTEROL, MG.	FIBER, GM.	CALCIUM, MG.	CALORIES FROM FAT
119.7	0.0	6.7	65	3%

Cabbage Confetti

The red cabbage adds great color to this dish. This is a good side for low-fat sausages cooked on the grill or broiled.

SERVES 4

3 cups fresh red cabbage, sliced
3 cups fresh green beans, thinly sliced
1 large carrot, coarsely grated
1 tablespoon onion, chopped
½ cup Vinaigrette Dressing (page 22)

1. Steam the cabbage and green beans until they are crisp-tender, about 2 to 3 minutes.

2. Sauté the onion lightly in a nonstick skillet sprayed with a nonstick spray.

3. Add the cabbage, green beans, carrot, and Vinaigrette Dressing.

4. Cook over a low heat 3 to 5 minutes, or until heated through.

Nutritional analysis per serving:

CALORIES	PROTEIN, GM.	CARBOHYDRATE, GM.	FAT, GM.	SATURATED FAT, GM.
117	2.4	12.9	7.2	1.3

SODIUM, MG.	CHOLESTEROL, MG.	FIBER, GM.	CALCIUM, MG.	CALORIES FROM FAT
183.1	1.4	3.3	67	55%

Cauliflower au Gratin

This recipe is excellent served in a buffet for family gatherings.

SERVES 4

1 large head fresh cauliflower (or 2 packages frozen, thawed)
1 cup nonfat milk
1 tablespoon cornstarch or arrowroot
½ teaspoon freshly ground black pepper
¼ teaspoon cayenne pepper
2 ounces cheddar cheese, grated
2 tablespoons dry bread crumbs
2 tablespoons freshly grated Parmesan cheese

1. Preheat the oven to 350°F. Prepare a baking or soufflé dish by spraying it with a nonstick cooking spray.

2. Cut the cauliflower into small flowerets. Wash them, then steam them until they are crisp-tender, about 3 to 5 minutes.

3. In a medium saucepan, mix the milk, cornstarch, and black and cayenne peppers. Cook over a medium heat until the mixture comes to a boil and thickens.

4. Remove the pan from the heat, and stir in the cheddar cheese until it is melted and is well blended. Add cauliflower and gently toss to coat all the pieces.

Continued on page 44

Continued from page 43

Cauliflower au Gratin

5. Place the cauliflower in the prepared dish. Sprinkle the bread crumbs and Parmesan cheese over the top.

6. Bake for 15 to 20 minutes, or until the mixture is hot and bubbly.

You could also add or substitute any of the following:
   asparagus
   broccoli
   brussel sprouts

Nutritional analysis per serving:

CALORIES	PROTEIN, GM.	CARBOHYDRATE, GM.	FAT, GM.	SATURATED FAT, GM.
125	8.4	10.7	5.8	3.5

SODIUM, MG.	CHOLESTEROL, MG.	FIBER, GM.	CALCIUM, MG.	CALORIES FROM FAT
193.9	17.8	1.9	237	41%

Corn Chowder

Although frozen corn works very well in this chowder, buy fresh when it's available and cut the kernels off the cob. You can also buy frozen corn on the cob and cut off the kernels after it thaws.

SERVES 6

1 cup celery (1 to 2 stalks), chopped
1 onion, chopped
¼ cup red pepper, chopped
2 small potatoes, peeled and diced
2 cups whole-kernel corn
1 cup 1% milk
¼ teaspoon cayenne pepper (or to taste)

1. Spray a large pot with nonstick spray. Sauté the celery, onion, red pepper, and potatoes until softened but not browned.

2. Add the corn, milk and cayenne pepper. Simmer—do not allow to boil—for 35 minutes or until the potatoes are cooked.

3. Remove about 2 cups of soup and put it into a blender. Blend until puréed. Then pour it back into the soup and stir.

4. Reheat gently. Remember: Do not allow this soup to boil.

Nutritional analysis per serving:

CALORIES	PROTEIN, GM.	CARBOHYDRATE, GM.	FAT, GM.	SATURATED FAT, GM.
157	6.9	30.4	2.1	0.9

SODIUM, MG.	CHOLESTEROL, MG.	FIBER, GM.	CALCIUM, MG.	CALORIES FROM FAT
85.5	4.9	3.5	165	12%

Creole Corn

The South comes into play with this side dish.

SERVES 4

1 cup whole-kernel corn, fresh or frozen
1 cup okra, fresh or frozen, chopped
1 cup canned diced tomatoes
Dash cayenne pepper

1. Place all of the ingredients in a small saucepan.

2. Heat slowly and simmer until done, about 10 minutes. Add water if needed.

3. Serve in a small bowl as a side dish.

Nutritional analysis per serving:

CALORIES	PROTEIN, GM.	CARBOHYDRATE, GM.	FAT, GM.	SATURATED FAT, GM.
72	2.8	15.8	0.8	0.1

SODIUM, MG.	CHOLESTEROL, MG.	FIBER, GM.	CALCIUM, MG.	CALORIES FROM FAT
16.6	0.0	4	53	10%

Glazed Carrots

Baby carrots can be used in this dish. Slice them in half on the diagonal.

SERVES 4

1/2 **pound** carrots, peeled and sliced
   diagonally
1 **tablespoon** apple juice concentrate
1 **teaspoon** cornstarch
1 **teaspoon** dry mustard
1/4 **cup** water

1. Steam carrots until crisp-tender, about 3 to 5 minutes.

2. In a nonstick skillet combine the apple juice concentrate, cornstarch, mustard, and water. Heat and stir continuously until the sauce thickens and is smooth.

3. Add the carrots. Toss until well coated and heated through.

Nutritional analysis per serving:

CALORIES	PROTEIN, GM.	CARBOHYDRATE, GM.	FAT, GM.	SATURATED FAT, GM.
36	0.8	7.8	0.4	0.03

SODIUM, MG.	CHOLESTEROL, MG.	FIBER, GM.	CALCIUM, MG.	CALORIES FROM FAT
21.5	0.0	1.9	27	10%

Green Beans

Green beans add great color to a plate, and everyone likes them.

SERVES 4

2 cups fresh green beans, stems removed
  (or 1 package frozen, thawed)
¼ cup chicken broth
2 teaspoons butter
½ teaspoon minced garlic

1. Steam the green beans until tender, about 5 minutes.

2. Heat the chicken broth and butter in a medium nonstick skillet.

3. Add the garlic and cook lightly.

4. Add the green beans and toss until well coated and hot.

Nutritional analysis per serving:

CALORIES	PROTEIN, GM.	CARBOHYDRATE, GM.	FAT, GM.	SATURATED FAT, GM.
43	1.5	5.4	2.3	1.3

SODIUM, MG.	CHOLESTEROL, MG.	FIBER, GM.	CALCIUM, MG.	CALORIES FROM FAT
31.6	5.5	0.8	33	47%

Julienne Carrots and Zucchini

The julienne cut truly makes this dish elegant looking. A mandoline (French vegetable slicer) comes in handy, making the slicing job a snap. If you have a good slicer, you don't need to steam the carrots first.

SERVES 4

2 medium carrots
2 medium zucchini
2 teaspoons butter
$\frac{1}{2}$ teaspoon dillweed

1. Steam the carrots until they are crisp-tender. (It makes them easier to cut.) Cut the carrots and zucchini into $\frac{1}{8}$-by-2-inch julienne pieces.

2. Melt the butter in a medium-size skillet. Add the dillweed, carrots, and zucchini, and gently toss.

3. Turn off the heat, cover, and let stand 2 to 3 minutes. Serve.

Nutritional analysis per serving:

CALORIES	PROTEIN, GM.	CARBOHYDRATE, GM.	FAT, GM.	SATURATED FAT, GM.
43	1.2	7.6	1.4	0.7

SODIUM, MG.	CHOLESTEROL, MG.	FIBER, GM.	CALCIUM, MG.	CALORIES FROM FAT
24.1	2.7	2.4	37	29%

Mushrooms and Chinese Peas

Chinese pea pods cook very quickly, so be careful not to overcook them. If you use frozen ones, defrost them under cold running water, and cook them long enough to heat them through.

SERVES 4

¼ cup chicken broth
3 cups sliced mushrooms
2 cups Chinese pea pods

1. Reduce the chicken broth in half in a medium nonstick skillet.

2. Add the mushrooms and sauté them until tender and all the liquid is absorbed.

3. Add the Chinese pea pods and stir for 30 seconds.

4. Turn off the heat, cover, and let stand for 3 minutes before serving.

Nutritional analysis per serving:

CALORIES	PROTEIN, GM.	CARBOHYDRATE, GM.	FAT, GM.	SATURATED FAT, GM.
81	5.5	14.9	0.4	0.1

SODIUM, MG.	CHOLESTEROL, MG.	FIBER, GM.	CALCIUM, MG.	CALORIES FROM FAT
120.5	0.0	3.4	25	5%

Savory Celery

This would be good added to a salad or to a crudités tray.

SERVES 4

1 bunch fresh celery, separated
1 cup chicken broth
¼ cup Sherry Dressing (page 21)

1. Wash the celery and cut it in even pieces on the diagonal

2. Place the celery and chicken broth into a large saucepan and bring to a boil.

3. Reduce the heat, cover, and simmer for 5 minutes.

4. Drain the celery and toss with Sherry Dressing. Serve warm or well chilled.

Nutritional analysis per serving:

CALORIES	PROTEIN, GM.	CARBOHYDRATE, GM.	FAT, GM.	SATURATED FAT, GM.
92	1.8	6.3	7.2	1.4

SODIUM, MG.	CHOLESTEROL, MG.	FIBER, GM.	CALCIUM, MG.	CALORIES FROM FAT
259.5	1.4	1.8	53	70%

Stuffed Tomatoes

When you want to add color, these tomatoes are perfect. For variation, add a dash of nutmeg or curry powder to the milk mixture and serve them cold.

SERVES 4

4 medium tomatoes
1 cup frozen petite peas
$1/2$ cup nonfat milk
3 teaspoons cornstarch
1 teaspoon butter
Dash cayenne pepper

1. Cut off the top of each tomato and carefully cut around the inside. About $1/2$ inch from the outside bottom, make a small slit in the bottom part of the core. Spoon out the pulp and seeds (reserve for use in tomato sauces).

2. Thaw the peas by running cold water over them in a strainer.

3. Preheat the oven to 350°F.

4. Mix the milk, cornstarch, butter, and pepper in a small saucepan, heat the mixture, stirring constantly until it thickens.

5. Combine the peas with the sauce and spoon it into the tomatoes.

6. Warm in the oven for 5 minutes at 350°F just before serving.

Nutritional analysis per serving:

CALORIES	PROTEIN, GM.	CARBOHYDRATE, GM.	FAT, GM.	SATURATED FAT, GM.
85	4.2	14.8	1.6	0.7

SODIUM, MG.	CHOLESTEROL, MG.	FIBER, GM.	CALCIUM, MG.	CALORIES FROM FAT
72.1	3.3	2.9	55	17%

Zucchini Boats

This dish can be made ahead of time. Just hold off adding the bread crumbs and Parmesan cheese until right before baking. Bake at 400°F until hot.

SERVES 4

4 medium zucchini
2 tablespoons tomato paste
1/2 teaspoon Italian Blend seasoning
1 clove fresh garlic, minced
1/4 cup dry bread crumbs
2 tablespoons Parmesan cheese,
  freshly grated

1. Wash the zucchini and cut them in half lengthwise.

2. Steam them until tender, about 3 minutes.

3. With a spoon, scoop out the zucchini pulp, leaving the "shell" intact. Place the pulp into a bowl and mash it with a fork.

4. Mix in the tomato paste, Italian Blend, and garlic.

5. Stuff the mixture into the "shells," and sprinkle with the bread crumbs and Parmesan cheese.

6. Place them under the broiler until the cheese and bread crumbs are brown.

Nutritional analysis per serving:

CALORIES	PROTEIN, GM.	CARBOHYDRATE, GM.	FAT, GM.	SATURATED FAT, GM.
74	3.6	13.2	1.6	0.6

SODIUM, MG.	CHOLESTEROL, MG.	FIBER, GM.	CALCIUM, MG.	CALORIES FROM FAT
90	2	3.1	95	19%

Red Beans and Rice

This comes straight from New Orleans. It is wonderful, full of flavor, inexpensive, easy to make—and people love it!

SERVES 4

1 medium onion, chopped
1 cup celery, finely chopped
1 cup green bell pepper, finely chopped
1 teaspoon Tabasco
1 teaspoon white pepper
1/4 teaspoon ground black pepper
1/2 teaspoon ground cayenne pepper
1 teaspoon ground thyme
1/2 teaspoon garlic powder
1/2 pound red beans, soaked in water
  overnight and rinsed
2 bay leaves
2 cups cooked brown rice
2 cups chopped tomatoes

1. In a Dutch oven sprayed with a nonstick spray, sauté the onion, celery, and bell pepper until soft. Add the Tabasco; white, black, and cayenne peppers; thyme; and garlic powder. Mix in well.

2. Add the red beans and cover with water. Add the bay leaves, cover, and simmer (about two hours) until done (stir occasionally, adding more water if necessary).

3. Remove the bay leaves. Take out 2 cups of beans including the liquid. Purée in a blender and return it to the pot.

4. Serve the beans over rice or mix them together. Garnish with the tomatoes.

Nutritional analysis per serving:

CALORIES	PROTEIN, GM.	CARBOHYDRATE, GM.	FAT, GM.	SATURATED FAT, GM.
484	20.7	97.6	2.3	0.5

SODIUM, MG.	CHOLESTEROL, MG.	FIBER, GM.	CALCIUM, MG.	CALORIES FROM FAT
239.6	0.0	16.2	159	4%

Baked Sole with Shrimp and Asparagus

This is an elegant dish. It is delicious served with Parsley Potatoes (page 38).

SERVES 4

4 large shrimp, uncooked
4 sole fillets, 3 ounces each
4 asparagus tips, steamed to crisp-tender
1 lemon
fresh dill sprigs (or dried dillweed)
Paprika

1. Preheat the oven to 350°F.

2. Shell, clean, and butterfly the shrimp.

3. Place a shrimp in the center of each sole fillet.

4. Put an asparagus tip on top of the shrimp and roll the fillets jelly roll–style. Secure it with a toothpick.

5. Place the fish rolls in a baking dish. Squeeze lemon juice over them and sprinkle with fresh dill and paprika.

6. Bake for 20 minutes, or until the fish flakes.

Nutritional analysis per serving:

CALORIES	PROTEIN, GM.	CARBOHYDRATE, GM.	FAT, GM.	SATURATED FAT, GM.
127	20.6	1.9	3.9	0.7

SODIUM, MG.	CHOLESTEROL, MG.	FIBER, GM.	CALCIUM, MG.	CALORIES FROM FAT
120.9	59.1	0.4	29	27%

Blackened Fish

Blackened fish has become one of the most popular items in Cajun cuisine. The traditional method of preparation is to cook the fish at a very high heat with lots of clarified butter. To transform it into a more healthful dish, broil, barbecue, or cook the fish in a skillet with a nonstick spray.

SERVES 6

1 teaspoon paprika
1 teaspoon onion powder
1 teaspoon cayenne pepper
¼ teaspoon ground white pepper
½ teaspoon ground thyme
2 pounds fish (red fish, halibut, swordfish, salmon, or shrimp)

1. Mix all of the seasonings together.

2. Rub the seasoning mix on both sides of the fish.

3. Cook the fish under a broiler, barbecue it, or sauté in nonstick skillet until done. (Each fish will have a different cooking time, but keep in mind that fish cooks quickly.)

Nutritional analysis per serving:

CALORIES	PROTEIN, GM.	CARBOHYDRATE, GM.	FAT, GM.	SATURATED FAT, GM.
203	33.1	1.3	6.6	1.3

SODIUM, MG.	CHOLESTEROL, MG.	FIBER, GM.	CALCIUM, MG.	CALORIES FROM FAT
194.6	83.7	0.2	37	29%

Barbecued Chicken

Barbecued chicken is the perfect standby when you don't know what to fix.

SERVES 4

Chicken or Beef Marinade
(enough to marinate 1 pound of chicken
  or beef)

Juice of 1 lemon
1/4 teaspoon ground ginger
2 tablespoons soy sauce
1/2 teaspoon paprika
2 tablespoons water
1/4 teaspoon garlic, minced

4 chicken breast halves, boned, split, and
  skinned

1. Marinate the chicken breast in the marinade overnight, or for at least 4 to 6 hours.

2. Barbecue or broil the chicken until done. They cook quickly, in about 20 minutes, so be careful not to overcook them.

Nutritional analysis per serving:

CALORIES	PROTEIN, GM.	CARBOHYDRATE, GM.	FAT, GM.	SATURATED FAT, GM.
150	27.2	1.9	3.1	0.8

SODIUM, MG.	CHOLESTEROL, MG.	FIBER, GM.	CALCIUM, MG.	CALORIES FROM FAT
587.9	72.7	0.3	61	19%

Cajun Oven-Fried Chicken

To give a little extra crunch, spray the chicken breast lightly with olive oil right before it goes into the oven.

SERVES 4

4 chicken breast halves, skinned
1/4 cup buttermilk
2 tablespoons flour
2 tablespoons cornmeal
1/4 teaspoon oregano
1/4 teaspoon marjoram
1/8 teaspoon paprika
1/8 teaspoon cayenne pepper

1. Preheat the oven to 350°F.

2. Place the chicken breasts into a dish and pour the buttermilk over them, turning to coat well.

3. Combine the flour, cornmeal, oregano, marjoram, paprika, and cayenne pepper. Put the mixture into a bag or large flat dish.

4. Coat each piece of chicken with the flour mixture. Then place the chicken onto a cookie sheet that has been sprayed with nonstick spray.

5. Bake, uncovered, for 35 to 45 minutes, or until done.

Nutritional analysis per serving:

CALORIES	PROTEIN, GM.	CARBOHYDRATE, GM.	FAT, GM.	SATURATED FAT, GM.
176	27.8	6.7	3.3	0.9

SODIUM, MG.	CHOLESTEROL, MG.	FIBER, GM.	CALCIUM, MG.	CALORIES FROM FAT
79.9	73.2	0.3	34	17%

Chicken Breast Supreme

Reducing the chicken broth intensifies the flavor, which will add a richness that you get from butter without the extra fat. You can also top the finished dish with sliced ripe black olives to add color and flavor.

SERVES 4

2 cups chicken broth
1/2 pound mushrooms, sliced
4 chicken breast halves, boned, skinned and split
1/4 cup unbleached flour
1/2 cup dry white wine or dry vermouth
2 teaspoons cornstarch
1/4 cup cold water
1/4 cup sour cream
1/4 cup chopped parsley

1. Reduce 1/4 cup chicken broth to half in a large nonstick skillet.

2. Sauté the mushrooms until tender, remove from the skillet, and set aside.

3. Add 1/4 cup chicken broth to the skillet and reduce to half.

4. Coat each chicken breast in flour. Brown each breast well on both sides. (You may need to add more chicken broth as you go.)

5. Add the wine and remaining broth, cover, and simmer until the chicken is done, about 20 minutes.

6. Remove the chicken breast and keep warm.

7. Dissolve the cornstarch in the cold water. Add it to the skillet, and cook to thicken the mixture.

Continued on page 60

Continued from page 59

Chicken Breast Supreme

8. Stir in the sour cream and cook just enough to heat it through.

9. To serve, spoon the sauce over the chicken, and top with the mushrooms and parsley.

Nutritional analysis per serving:

CALORIES	PROTEIN, GM.	CARBOHYDRATE, GM.	FAT, GM.	SATURATED FAT, GM.
265	30.6	12.1	6.7	2.9

SODIUM, MG.	CHOLESTEROL, MG.	FIBER, GM.	CALCIUM, MG.	CALORIES FROM FAT
273.4	79.1	1	63	23%

Chicken Creole

You can also make Shrimp Creole by substituting shrimp for the chicken. If you use precooked frozen shrimp, defrost it under cold water, remove the tails, and heat it through. Be careful because shrimp cooks very quickly, and overcooked shrimp can become tough.

SERVES 4

1 pound raw chicken breasts, boned and skinned
1 bay leaf
1 recipe Creole Sauce, heated (page 62)
2 cups cooked rice (brown rice preferred), heated

1. Place the chicken breasts in a skillet. Add enough water to barely cover them. Add the bay leaf and bring to a boil. Immediately reduce to a simmer and poach the chicken until tender. Do not boil.

2. Make the Creole Sauce. Heat the rice.

3. Place $1/2$ cup of rice on each plate. Place the chicken breast on top. Then cover with $1/4$ recipe Creole Sauce.

Continued on page 62

Continued from page 61

Chicken Creole

Creole Sauce
1 medium onion, chopped
1/2 green pepper, seeded and chopped
1 large stalk celery, chopped
1 can (16 ounces) tomatoes, no salt
  added
1/4 teaspoon black pepper
1/8 teaspoon cayenne pepper or a few
  drops hot pepper sauce
1 cup chicken broth

1. Spray a skillet with nonstick spray. Sauté onion, green pepper and celery until tender.

2. Add tomatoes, black pepper, cayenne pepper, and chicken broth. Simmer for a few minutes or until the sauce has reduced down and thickened slightly.

Nutritional analysis per serving:

CALORIES	PROTEIN, GM.	CARBOHYDRATE, GM.	FAT, GM.	SATURATED FAT, GM.
390	29.1	58.5	4	1.1

SODIUM, MG.	CHOLESTEROL, MG.	FIBER, GM.	CALCIUM, MG.	CALORIES FROM FAT
458.7	58.2	5.8	81	9%

Chicken Gizzard Jambalaya

A bit of the bayou is in this recipe—you will feel as though you're in Louisiana. If you are not fond of gizzards, just add more chicken thighs.

SERVES 4

1 pound chicken gizzards, trimmed of gristle and diced
8 ounces chicken thighs, boned and skinned, cubed
1 medium onion, chopped
1 cup celery, chopped
1 cup carrots, chopped
1 1/2 teaspoons ground white pepper
1/4 teaspoon ground cayenne pepper
1 teaspoon ground thyme
1/2 teaspoon ground sage
1 can (15 ounces) diced tomatoes in juice
2 cups brown rice, uncooked
1 1/2 cups low-salt chicken broth
2 bay leaves

1. In a Dutch oven sprayed with a nonstick spray, brown the gizzards and thighs. Remove from the Dutch oven and set aside.

2. Add the onion, celery, and carrots to the pan. Sauté until soft. Add the seasonings and sauté for 30 seconds.

3. Add the tomatoes and juice, rice, and chicken broth to the pan. Return the chicken to the pan and bring to a boil. Add the bay leaves.

4. Cover and cook 50 minutes or put in 350°F oven for 1 hour.

Nutritional analysis per serving:

CALORIES	PROTEIN, GM.	CARBOHYDRATE, GM.	FAT, GM.	SATURATED FAT, GM.
387	40.3	34.5	9.1	2.5

SODIUM, MG.	CHOLESTEROL, MG.	FIBER, GM.	CALCIUM, MG.	CALORIES FROM FAT
235	107.3	4.7	84	21%

Chicken Gumbo

Gumbo, a popular dish, is a perfect one-dish meal on a winter evening. You can substitute shrimp for the chicken—just add it at the last minute.

SERVES 6

2 large stalks celery, sliced
1 small green pepper, seeded and chopped
1 medium onion, chopped
2 cups frozen or fresh-cut okra
1 can (16 ounces) tomatoes, low-salt type preferred
2 tablespoons quick-cooking tapioca
1 teaspoon thyme
2 bay leaves
1/8 teaspoon cayenne pepper
12 ounces chicken, cooked and skinned
6 cups chicken broth
3 cups cooked brown rice

1. Spray a heavy soup pot with nonstick spray. Sauté the celery, green pepper, onion, and okra just until tender.

2. Add the tomatoes, tapioca, thyme, bay leaves, and cayenne pepper.

3. Add the chicken and chicken broth. Bring to a boil, then quickly reduce heat and simmer for about 30 minutes.

4. Serve in a soup bowl over brown rice.

Nutritional analysis per serving:

CALORIES	PROTEIN, GM.	CARBOHYDRATE, GM.	FAT, GM.	SATURATED FAT, GM.
291	23.3	36.2	5.6	1.6

SODIUM, MG.	CHOLESTEROL, MG.	FIBER, GM.	CALCIUM, MG.	CALORIES FROM FAT
355.8	49.6	5.1	107	17%

Cornish Game Hens

Even though Cornish Game Hens tend to be a bit messy to eat, they always seem special. They are very easy to make, and interestingly enough, they are all white meat.

SERVES 4

2 Cornish game hens
1¼ cup Orange Sauce (page 66)
1 orange, plus 4 slices

1. Preheat the oven to 350°F.

2. Cut each hen in half, then wash and pat dry.

3. Cut the orange into quarters, and squeeze the juice of each quarter over each half-hen.

4. In a roasting pan, place an orange quarter under each half-hen and bake for 1 hour.

5. After 30 minutes, baste the hens with ¼ cup of the Orange Sauce.

6. To serve, pour ¼ cup Orange Sauce over each hen and garnish with twisted orange slices.

Continued on page 66

Continued from page 65

Cornish Game Hens

Orange Sauce
1 can chicken broth
2 oranges
3 teaspoons cornstarch
1 teaspoon freshly grated orange rind
2 tablespoons Cointreau (or any orange-
flavored liqueur)

1. Reduce the chicken broth to 1 cup.

2. Juice the 2 oranges. Add the cornstarch to the juice and stir until dissolved.

3. Stir the mixture into the reduced broth. Stir over medium heat until slightly thickened.

4. Add the grated orange rind and Cointreau and stir.

Nutritional analysis per serving:

Calories	Protein, gm.	Carbohydrate, gm.	Fat, gm.	Saturated Fat, gm.
471	43.2	14.5	21	5.8

Sodium, mg.	Cholesterol, mg.	Fiber, gm.	Calcium, mg.	Calories from Fat
221.3	133.9	2.6	70	40%

Dirty Rice

This is a great one-dish meal. You can also take the basic concept and use your leftovers. This is a good dish to make in your rice cooker.

SERVES 4

1 teaspoon ground cayenne pepper
1 teaspoon ground black pepper
1¼ teaspoons sweet paprika
½ teaspoon dry mustard
½ teaspoon ground cumin
½ teaspoon ground thyme
1 medium onion, chopped
1 clove garlic, chopped
1 pound chicken breast, skinned, boned
   and cut into cubes
1 cup brown rice, uncooked
2½ cups low-salt chicken broth
2 bay leaves

1. Mix the spices together except for the bay leaves. Set aside.

2. In a Dutch oven sprayed with a nonstick spray, sauté the onion and garlic until soft. Add the spices and sauté for 30 seconds.

3. Add the chicken cubes and sauté 1 minute, stirring constantly.

4. Add the rice, chicken broth, and bay leaves. Bring to a boil. Reduce heat to simmer. Cover and cook 45 minutes or put in a 350°F oven for 45 minutes.

5. Before serving, remove the bay leaves.

Nutritional analysis per serving:

CALORIES	PROTEIN, GM.	CARBOHYDRATE, GM.	FAT, GM.	SATURATED FAT, GM.
262	26.8	29.2	3.7	1

SODIUM, MG.	CHOLESTEROL, MG.	FIBER, GM.	CALCIUM, MG.	CALORIES FROM FAT
243.9	58.2	2.6	51	13%

Pepper Pots

If you don't have Marinara Sauce in the freezer, use canned diced tomatoes with herbs, such as garlic and basil. There are many to choose from in the grocery store and they are a better alternative than canned sauce.

SERVES 4

4 large green peppers
1/2 pound ground turkey, raw
1/2 cup onion, chopped
1 cup brown rice, cooked
1/2 teaspoon freshly ground black pepper
1 teaspoon Italian Blend seasoning
2 cups Basic Marinara Sauce (page 247)

1. Preheat the oven to 350°F.

2. Cut circular openings in the tops of the peppers, wash them, and remove the seeds.

3. Poach the peppers in boiling water or steam them for 5 minutes.

4. Mix together the turkey, onion, rice, seasonings, and 1 cup of Marinara Sauce.

5. Stuff each pepper with one-quarter of the mixture.

6. Place the peppers in a covered backing dish and bake for 50 to 60 minutes.

7. Pour 1/4 cup hot Marinara Sauce on each pepper before serving.

Nutritional analysis per serving:

CALORIES	PROTEIN, GM.	CARBOHYDRATE, GM.	FAT, GM.	SATURATED FAT, GM.
300	14.1	44.5	8.4	1.7

SODIUM, MG.	CHOLESTEROL, MG.	FIBER, GM.	CALCIUM, MG.	CALORIES FROM FAT
684.7	24.8	5.7	65	25%

Spicy Apricot-Dijon Chicken

If you keep frozen chicken breasts, this recipe can be done at short notice; either defrost the chicken by running cold water over them or in the microwave on the defrost setting. The jam should be a pantry staple; fruit-sweetened jam tastes more like real fruit. If the chicken breasts you have are boneless, reduce the cooking time.

SERVES 4

4 chicken breasts, skinned
1/4 cup low-calorie or low-sugar apricot jam
2 tablespoons Dijon mustard
1/8 teaspoon cayenne pepper

1. Preheat the oven to 350°F.

2. Place the chicken breasts in a small baking dish.

3. Combine the apricot jam, mustard, and cayenne pepper

4. Pour or spoon the jam mixture over the chicken. Cover the dish loosely with foil and bake it about 35 to 45 minutes, or until done.

Nutritional analysis per serving:

CALORIES	PROTEIN, GM.	CARBOHYDRATE, GM.	FAT, GM.	SATURATED FAT, GM.
176	27	8	3.5	0.8

SODIUM, MG.	CHOLESTEROL, MG.	FIBER, GM.	CALCIUM, MG.	CALORIES FROM FAT
157.8	72.7	0.6	21	18%

Turkey Chili

It is really difficult to tell the difference between red meat and turkey in this chili.

SERVES 6

1 pound of dried beans: black, pinto, navy, or mixed.
2 teaspoons chicken, beef, or vegetable bouillon paste
1 tablespoon olive oil
2 medium onions, chopped
1 clove garlic, minced
2 bell peppers, chopped
1/2 teaspoon oregano
1/4 teaspoon cumin
3 teaspoons chili powder
1 teaspoon ground red pepper (or to taste)
1 pound ground turkey, raw
1 can (28 ounces) diced tomatoes
1 can (15 ounces) tomato sauce

1. Soak the beans overnight in cold water. Rinse them, then cook in water, 3 inches above the beans, with 2 teaspoons of chicken, beef, or vegetable paste until they are barely tender.

2. Heat a large Dutch oven, add olive oil. Sauté the onion and garlic until yellow.

3. Add the bell peppers and seasonings.

4. Add the ground turkey and cook constantly, stirring until done.

5. Add the tomatoes, tomato sauce, and drained beans.

6. Simmer for 1 hour.

Nutritional analysis per serving:

CALORIES	PROTEIN, GM.	CARBOHYDRATE, GM.	FAT, GM.	SATURATED FAT, GM.
424	31.6	60.3	7.8	1.7

SODIUM, MG.	CHOLESTEROL, MG.	FIBER, GM.	CALCIUM, MG.	CALORIES FROM FAT
64.3	33	15.86	149	16%

Flank Steak Roulade

Flank steak is very lean and full of flavor. You could ask the meat cutter to remove the extra fat and run the flank steak through the meat tenderizer.

SERVES 4

1 pound flank steak
1 recipe Beef Marinade (page 57)
1 box frozen spinach, thawed and
   steamed 1 minute
1 can (8 ounces) water chestnuts, sliced

1. Trim any fat from the flank steak and score it on both sides (shallow diagonal slices).

2. Marinate it in the Beef Marinade for several hours or overnight.

3. Drain the spinach thoroughly, squeezing to eliminate as much moisture as possible. Spread the spinach evenly over the steak.

4. Arrange the water chestnuts on top of the spinach and carefully roll it up, jelly roll-style. Secure with toothpicks and slice into 8 even pieces.

5. Brush with the marinade and broil or barbecue 5 to 7 minutes on each side or until cooked to desired "doneness."

Nutritional analysis per serving:

CALORIES	PROTEIN, GM.	CARBOHYDRATE, GM.	FAT, GM.	SATURATED FAT, GM.
246	35.1	4.2	9.2	3.4

SODIUM, MG.	CHOLESTEROL, MG.	FIBER, GM.	CALCIUM, MG.	CALORIES FROM FAT
106.4	90.8	1.4	75	34%

Pork Jambalaya

Jambalaya is like a Spanish paella, but with spicier seasonings.

SERVES 8

1 pound lean pork loin, cubed
2 medium onions, chopped
1½ cups celery, chopped
1 clove garlic, chopped
1 teaspoon ground white pepper
1 teaspoon dry mustard
1 teaspoon ground cayenne pepper
½ teaspoon cumin
½ teaspoon ground black pepper
½ teaspoon ground thyme
2 cups brown rice, uncooked
4 cups low-salt chicken broth
2 bay leaves

1. In a Dutch oven sprayed with a nonstick spray, brown the pork cubes. Take them out of the pan and set aside.

2. Put the onions, celery, and garlic in a pan and cook until soft, stirring constantly.

3. Add the seasonings to the mixture and sauté for 30 seconds.

4. Return the pork to the pan. Add the brown rice, chicken broth, and bay leaves. Bring to a boil.

5. Cover and reduce to a simmer. Cook for 50 minutes, or place in a 350°F oven for 1 hour.

Nutritional analysis per serving:

Calories	Protein, gm.	Carbohydrate, gm.	Fat, gm.	Saturated Fat, gm.
261	20.5	29.1	6.5	2.3

Sodium, mg.	Cholesterol, mg.	Fiber, gm.	Calcium, mg.	Calories from Fat
249.5	45	2.7	52	23%

Apricot Pudding

Apricot pudding is a light refreshing dessert, perfect for the end of a heavy meal.

SERVES 6

3 cans (16 ounces) water-packed apricot halves
2 envelopes unflavored gelatin
¼ cup orange juice
1 tablespoon sugar
¼ cup walnuts, chopped

1. Drain the apricots, reserving 1 cup liquid. Heat the liquid to boiling. Pour over the gelatin, and stir until it dissolves.

2. Mix orange juice and sugar together. Add the apricots and place the mixture in a food processor with a metal blade or in a blender and purée.

3. Add the gelatin mixture to the apricots and blend well.

4. Pour the mixture into a mold or bowl and chill until set (several hours).

5. To serve, unmold the pudding or spoon it into small bowls. Garnish with the chopped walnuts.

Nutritional analysis per serving:

CALORIES	PROTEIN, GM.	CARBOHYDRATE, GM.	FAT, GM.	SATURATED FAT, GM.
136	4.2	24.1	3.9	0.3

SODIUM, MG.	CHOLESTEROL, MG.	FIBER, GM.	CALCIUM, MG.	CALORIES FROM FAT
41.7	0.0	3.6	32	26%

Brown Rice Pudding

As well as being a good dessert, the leftovers make an excellent breakfast.

SERVES 8

2 cups short-grain brown rice
1/2 cup raisins, chopped
6 egg whites, slightly beaten
1/4 cup sugar
1 can evaporated skim milk
1 teaspoon vanilla
1 teaspoon cinnamon
Freshly grated nutmeg to garnish

1. Preheat the oven to 325°F. Spray a 10-inch baking dish with a nonstick spray.

2. Combine the rice and chopped raisins in the dish.

3. Mix the egg whites and sugar, and add the evaporated milk, vanilla, and cinnamon, and mix well.

4. Pour the mixture over the rice and raisins, and sprinkle liberally with nutmeg.

5. Place the baking dish into a large pan half-filled with water. Bake for 1 hour or until it sets in the center.

Nutritional analysis per serving:

CALORIES	PROTEIN, GM.	CARBOHYDRATE, GM.	FAT, GM.	SATURATED FAT, GM.
192	6.4	40.1	0.7	0.2

SODIUM, MG.	CHOLESTEROL, MG.	FIBER, GM.	CALCIUM, MG.	CALORIES FROM FAT
62.5	0.6	2.2	59	3%

Chocolate Prune Cake

Sounds strange, but tastes great! Prunes add moisture and sweetness. Here's a hint: Chop prunes so your guests won't know the secret. If they knew beforehand, they might have a preconceived notion about your delicious cake.

SERVES 10

1 cup whole pitted prunes
2 cups water
4 tablespoons butter
2/3 cup sugar
1/8 cup molasses
4 egg whites
1/2 cup European-style cocoa
2 cups self-rising flour
1/2 teaspoon ground cloves

1. Preheat the oven to 350°F. Prepare a loaf pan by spraying it with a nonstick cooking spray.

2. In a saucepan, simmer the prunes in 2 cups water for 10 minutes. Drain the water, reserving 1/2 cup.

3. Coarsely chop the prunes.

4. Cream the butter, sugar, and molasses. Add the egg whites and beat well.

5. Sift in the flour, cocoa, and ground cloves. Stir in the prunes and prune liquid.

6. Pour the batter into the loaf pan and bake for 50 minutes.

Nutritional analysis per serving:

CALORIES	PROTEIN, GM.	CARBOHYDRATE, GM.	FAT, GM.	SATURATED FAT, GM.
215	4.3	39.3	4.9	2.9

SODIUM, MG.	CHOLESTEROL, MG.	FIBER, GM.	CALCIUM, MG.	CALORIES FROM FAT
82.6	12.5	2.2	26	21%

Chocolate Soufflé

For the chocolate lover, this is a true delight. The European-style cocoa gives it a rich dark flavor. If you like lighter chocolate, use an American cocoa powder.

SERVES 4

¼ cup sugar
3 tablespoons cornstarch
3 tablespoons European-style cocoa powder
1 teaspoon instant coffee
¼ teaspoon cinnamon
1 can evaporated skim milk
1 teaspoon vanilla
2 egg whites

1. Combine the sugar, cornstarch, cocoa powder, instant coffee, and cinnamon in a 2-quart saucepan.

2. Add the milk and cook over a medium heat, stirring constantly until the mixture comes to a boil and thickens. Add the vanilla.

3. Pour the mixture into a 1-quart bowl and cover the surface with waxed paper to prevent "skin" formation. Chill for 1 hour.

4. Beat the egg whites until stiff, and then fold into the chocolate mixture until they are fully incorporated.

5. Spoon into individual 4-ounce dessert dishes.

Nutritional analysis per serving:

CALORIES	PROTEIN, GM.	CARBOHYDRATE, GM.	FAT, GM.	SATURATED FAT, GM.
164	9.5	30.5	0.3	0.2

SODIUM, MG.	CHOLESTEROL, MG.	FIBER, GM.	CALCIUM, MG.	CALORIES FROM FAT
155.8	3.6	0.2	318	2%

Guiltless Bananas Foster

This is a reduced-calorie version of the famous recipe served at Brennan's in New Orleans.

SERVES 4

1 tablespoon butter
2 tablespoons sugar
½ teaspoon banana extract
1 teaspoon rum extract
2 medium bananas, peeled, cut in half lengthwise, then quartered
1 pint low-calorie ice cream or nonfat frozen yogurt

1. Using a medium-size, heavy skillet, melt the butter (do not brown it).

2. Add the sugar and allow it to melt. Stir well; it makes a slightly thickened syrup. Add the extracts carefully because they will splatter.

3. Add the 8 banana quarters and brown them on each side.

4. Serve over ice cream or nonfat yogurt. Spoon a little sauce over each serving.

Nutritional analysis per serving:

CALORIES	PROTEIN, GM.	CARBOHYDRATE, GM.	FAT, GM.	SATURATED FAT, GM.
175	1.8	27.6	6.9	4.2

SODIUM, MG.	CHOLESTEROL, MG.	FIBER, GM.	CALCIUM, MG.	CALORIES FROM FAT
56.3	21.6	0.9	46	35%

Lemon Cheese Pie

Cheesecake, without the guilt! This is an excellent alternative to the traditional high-fat cheesecake. It is very good with raspberry sauce drizzled over the top.

SERVES 8

Crust
1 cup graham cracker crumbs
1/2 teaspoon allspice
1 teaspoon lemon peel
2 teaspoons butter

Filling
2 cups low-fat cottage cheese
1/4 cup sugar
2 teaspoons vanilla
1/2 teaspoon lemon extract

Topping
1 cup sour cream
1 1/2 teaspoons vanilla
3 tablespoons sugar

1. Preheat the oven to 350°F. Spray a 9-inch pie plate with nonstick cooking spray.

2. To make the crust, put the graham cracker crumbs, allspice, and lemon peel into a food processor or blender until well blended.

3. Melt the butter. Slowly pour it into the graham cracker crumbs while the blender is running.

4. Place the crumbs in the pie plate, and press down evenly with your fingertips all the way around.

5. Now, the filling. Put the cottage cheese, sugar, vanilla, and lemon extract into a food processor or blender and blend until smooth.

6. Pour the cottage cheese mixture into the graham cracker shell. Bake for 15 minutes.

Continued on page 79

Continued from page 78

Lemon Cheese Pie

7. While the pie is baking, combine the topping ingredients in a mixing bowl and mix thoroughly.

8. Remove the pie from the oven and spread the topping evenly over the top. Place the pie back into the oven and continue baking for 10 minutes.

9. Cool the pie to room temperature, then refrigerate it until chilled before serving.

Nutritional analysis per serving:

Calories	Protein, gm.	Carbohydrate, gm.	Fat, gm.	Saturated Fat, gm.
199	8.8	21.8	8.6	4.9

Sodium, mg.	Cholesterol, mg.	Fiber, gm.	Calcium, mg.	Calories from Fat
104.3	17.7	0.3	74	39%

Lemon Yogurt Cake

This cake is perfect for afternoon tea, a formal dinner party, or casual entertaining. Store the cake in the refrigerator wrapped in foil or plastic wrap.

SERVES 8

4 tablespoons butter
1/2 cup sugar
6 egg whites (or 3/4 cup egg substitute)
Peel of 1 lemon, finely grated
3/4 cup plain nonfat yogurt
2 cups presifted self-rising flour
1/2 cup dried apricots, diced

1. Preheat the oven to 325°F. Spray a loaf pan with a nonstick cooking spray.

2. Cream the butter and sugar until light and fluffy.

3. Add egg whites, 2 at a time, beating after each.

4. Fold in the lemon peel, yogurt, flour, and apricots.

5. Spoon the mixture into the prepared loaf pan. Bake for 1 hour.

Nutritional analysis per serving:

CALORIES	PROTEIN, GM.	CARBOHYDRATE, GM.	FAT, GM.	SATURATED FAT, GM.
231	7	36.2	6.4	3.8

SODIUM, MG.	CHOLESTEROL, MG.	FIBER, GM.	CALCIUM, MG.	CALORIES FROM FAT
120.8	16.8	0.8	54	25%

Peach Crisp

You can use frozen or canned peaches as well.

SERVES 4

2 cups sliced peaches, about 3 to 4
   medium peaches
2 tablespoons sugar
¼ cup flour
¼ cup graham cracker crumbs
½ teaspoon cinnamon
2 tablespoons butter

1. Preheat the oven to 375°F.

2. Place the sliced peaches into 9-by-9-by-2-inch pan or baking dish. Sprinkle with 1 tablespoon sugar.

3. Combine flour, graham cracker crumbs, cinnamon, and 1 tablespoon sugar. Cut in the butter until the mixture is crumbly.

4. Sprinkle the mixture evenly over the top of the peaches and bake for 30 minutes.

Nutritional analysis per serving:

CALORIES	PROTEIN, GM.	CARBOHYDRATE, GM.	FAT, GM.	SATURATED FAT, GM.
166	1.9	26.5	6.8	3.9

SODIUM, MG.	CHOLESTEROL, MG.	FIBER, GM.	CALCIUM, MG.	CALORIES FROM FAT
97.8	16.4	1.9	13	37%

Rum Custard

You can also use a good spiced rum, such as Captain Morgan's, in place of the extract. If you do, use 2 tablespoons.

SERVES 4

2 whole eggs
2 egg whites
1½ teaspoons rum flavoring
2 cups nonfat milk
2 tablespoons sugar

1. Preheat the oven to 350°F.

2. Put the whole eggs and egg whites into a bowl, and beat lightly. Add the rest of the ingredients and mix well.

3. Pour into 4 custard cups. Place the cups into a baking dish and fill it halfway with water.

4. Bake for 50 minutes, or until a knife inserted in the center of the custard comes out clean.

Nutritional analysis per serving:

CALORIES	PROTEIN, GM.	CARBOHYDRATE, GM.	FAT, GM.	SATURATED FAT, GM.
119	9.1	12.4	2.9	0.9

SODIUM, MG.	CHOLESTEROL, MG.	FIBER, GM.	CALCIUM, MG.	CALORIES FROM FAT
121.2	107.3	0.0	165	22%

Strawberries in a Cloud

This dessert is delicious and light and can be made with any fresh fruit.

SERVES 4

Meringue
2 egg whites
1¼ tablespoons sugar

Sauce
2 cups nonfat milk
4 teaspoons arrowroot
1 tablespoon sugar
2 tablespoons Cointreau or Triple Sec
1 pint fresh strawberries, hulled and
  halved

1. Beat the egg whites for the meringue until frothy. Gradually add the fructose or sugar and continue beating until the egg whites form stiff peaks.

2. Heat the milk in a 10-inch skillet until just before the boiling point.

3. Drop 4 large spoonfuls of the meringue into the milk. Poach for 2 minutes, then carefully turn, and poach for 2 minutes on the other side. Remove carefully with a slotted spoon to a flat dish.

4. Mix the arrowroot, fructose or sugar, and Cointreau in a small bowl. Gradually add the mixture to the steaming milk, stirring constantly until thickened.

Continued on page 84

Continued from page 83

Strawberries in a Cloud

5. Pour the sauce into a bowl and chill for about 30 minutes.

6. To serve, divide the sauce equally into 4 dessert bowls, then top with the poached meringue and strawberries.

Nutritional analysis per serving:

Calories	Protein, gm.	Carbohydrate, gm.	Fat, gm.	Saturated Fat, gm.
178	6.3	28.1	0.3	0.2

Sodium, mg.	Cholesterol, mg.	Fiber, gm.	Calcium, mg.	Calories from Fat
91.5	2.2	1.2	159	2%

Tapioca Pudding

This is Tapioca Pudding at its best. It can be topped with fruit, or dice the fruit and fold it into the tapioca.

SERVES 4

2 cups nonfat milk
4 tablespoons quick-cooking tapioca
¼ cup sugar
1 teaspoon vanilla
2 egg whites

1. Combine the milk, tapioca, and 2 tablespoons sugar in a 2-quart saucepan and let stand for 5 minutes.

2. Heat the milk mixture over a medium heat, stirring constantly until it comes to a boil.

3. Remove from the heat, add the vanilla, and allow it to cool for 30 minutes.

4. Beat the egg whites until foamy, slowly add the remaining sugar, and beat until it forms soft peaks.

5. Fold the cooled tapioca into the egg whites.

Nutritional analysis per serving:

CALORIES	PROTEIN, GM.	CARBOHYDRATE, GM.	FAT, GM.	SATURATED FAT, GM.
129	6	25.4	0.2	0.2

SODIUM, MG.	CHOLESTEROL, MG.	FIBER, GM.	CALCIUM, MG.	CALORIES FROM FAT
90.5	2.2	0.1	153	2%

Upside-Down Apple Gingerbread

A tube pan works very well here because the apples wrap around the cake and it presents nicely.

SERVES 8

2 cups unbleached all-purpose flour, sifted
1¾ teaspoons ground ginger
1¼ teaspoons ground cinnamon
¼ teaspoon ground cloves
2 teaspoons baking powder
¼ teaspoon baking soda
¼ cup corn oil margarine
⅓ cup sugar
2 egg whites
1 cup nonfat milk
⅓ cup molasses
1 apple, cored and thinly sliced

1. Preheat the oven to 350°F. Spray a tube pan with nonstick cooking spray.

2. Sift together the flour, ginger, cinnamon, cloves, baking powder, and baking soda.

3. Beat the margarine and sugar together. Add the egg whites and beat until light and fluffy.

4. Combine the milk and molasses.

5. Add the milk mixture and the flour mixture alternately to the margarine mixture until everything is well blended.

Continued on page 87

Continued from page 86

Upside-Down Apple Gingerbread

6. Put a layer of apples around the tube pan. Pour the batter over the apples.

7. Bake for 45 minutes, or until a toothpick inserted into the center comes out clean.

8. Let stand for 5 minutes, then turn onto a serving plate. Serve hot or cold.

Nutritional analysis per serving:

Calories	Protein, gm.	Carbohydrate, gm.	Fat, gm.	Saturated Fat, gm.
252	5	41.5	7.5	0.9

Sodium, mg.	Cholesterol, mg.	Fiber, gm.	Calcium, mg.	Calories from Fat
176.4	0.6	1.5	132	27%

English Cuisine

Introduction

London is my favorite city. Its history, art, and cab drivers are not to be matched anywhere. I have made several trips to this great city and the surrounding countryside.

Americans tend to think that English food is boring. I totally disagree, and I am sure this segment of English Cuisine from the Guiltless Gourmet will change your mind. The English accomplish their tasks with ceremony and tradition.

In London most people live in small flats with tiny kitchens that don't have much storage space, which means they shop daily for their evening meal and buy in small portions. Many people entertain at the local pub. On the contrary, if you travel to the countryside, you find large homes with magnificent kitchens!

One of my favorite English traditions is High Tea, usually served from 3:00 to 5:00 P.M. I thought it would be fun to include a segment on English tea. I hope you will enjoy putting on your own tea using the Guiltless methods to cut fat calories out of high-fat foods.

English cooking is also called white cooking because it uses very few spices, and the most frequently used sauce is the white sauce. I have modified the white sauce to make it very low in calories. Most meats are roasted, which is also easy to modify. So let's move on to the English kitchen and plan a High Tea.

ENGLISH TEA

Tea is one of the English traditions I truly enjoy. In the past few years, tea has become more popular in the United States. If you have not experienced a good cup of tea, it's time you did. You can find several good quality teas in bags, which work well if you're on the run or want to keep some in the office. However, for a truly good pot of tea, it's best to steep it with loose tea leaves. Start with a glass or china teapot and fill it with boiling water. Let it stand a couple of minutes, then pour out the water. Spoon 1 teaspoon of loose tea per cup into the pot, then pour boiling water over the tea. (Just bring the water to a boil; don't let it keep boiling because it will take the oxygen out of the water and make your tea flat.) Let the tea steep for 3 to 5 minutes (follow the directions on the tea tin). Pour the tea through a tea strainer into a cup. Serve with lemon wedges or milk (never cream) and the sweetener of your choice.

HIGH TEA

In England High Tea is served between 3:00 and 5:00 P.M. It's great fun. Plan a High Tea for your next get-together, whether it's a wedding or baby shower, or just for fun. Use your best dishes and play with the little touches like flowers and classical music to add to the atmosphere. Here's a sample menu:

Tea with Milk or Lemon

Variety of Tea Sandwiches

Crumpet Scones and Fruit Scones

Sugar-Free Jam and Yogurt Cream

Chocolate-Filled Sponge Cake

Sherry Trifle

If you find you enjoy tea, keep a lookout for special teapots and cups you might like to serve your friends with. To find the teas that you like best, go to a coffee shop that also specializes in tea and talk to the proprietors. They can help you select the tea best suited to your taste. Tea sandwiches are always very light and delicate. I've given you several choices here. Each recipe will make eight sandwiches. For tea you want to cut off the crust and slice the bread in thirds (strips) or cut it into 4 triangles. You can also make a heartier sandwich from these recipes by using more filling and leaving the crust on. Make the sandwiches as close to serving time as possible, and then cover with a damp cloth.

Basic Sandwich Spread

This very simple, easy spread can take the place of higher-fat alternatives.

SERVES 18

1 cup Yogurt Cheese (page 98)
2 tablespoons mustard

Mix together the Yogurt Cheese and mustard. Use 1 teaspoon of the mixture on each slice of bread for making sandwiches.

Nutritional analysis per serving:

CALORIES	PROTEIN, GM.	CARBOHYDRATE, GM.	FAT, GM.	SATURATED FAT, GM.
18	0.9	1.2	0.1	0.02

SODIUM, MG.	CHOLESTEROL, MG.	FIBER, GM.	CALCIUM, MG.	CALORIES FROM FAT
31.3	0.2	0.1	29	5%

Chicken Sandwiches

Cook the chicken enough ahead of time so it is cold. You can also poach the chicken in broth seasoned with herbs to add more flavor.

MAKES 8 SANDWICHES

16 teaspoons Basic Sandwich Spread
   (page 93)
16 slices extra-thin wheat bread
8 ounces skinless chicken breast, sliced
   and cooked

1. Spread 1 teaspoon of spread on each slice of bread.

2. Place 1 ounce of chicken in each sandwich.

3. Cut off the crusts, cut the sandwiches, and cover.

Nutritional analysis per serving:

CALORIES	PROTEIN, GM.	CARBOHYDRATE, GM.	FAT, GM.	SATURATED FAT, GM.
154	13.5	25.6	1.4	0.3

SODIUM, MG.	CHOLESTEROL, MG.	FIBER, GM.	CALCIUM, MG.	CALORIES FROM FAT
318.7	15.1	6.3	117	8%

Cucumber Sandwiches

I have always loved cucumber sandwiches. They are refreshing and add a nice variety when served with an array of different sandwiches on a big platter.

MAKES 8 SANDWICHES

16 teaspoons Basic Sandwich Spread
   (page 93)
16 slices extra-thin wheat bread
1 large English cucumber, thinly sliced
Salt and pepper to taste

1. Spread 1 teaspoon of spread on each slice of bread.

2. Place sliced cucumber on one slice, sprinkle it with salt and pepper, and top with another slice of bread.

3. Cut off the crusts, cut the sandwiches, and cover.

Nutritional analysis per serving:

CALORIES	PROTEIN, GM.	CARBOHYDRATE, GM.	FAT, GM.	SATURATED FAT, GM.
131	8.3	26.6	1	0.1

SODIUM, MG.	CHOLESTEROL, MG.	FIBER, GM.	CALCIUM, MG.	CALORIES FROM FAT
330.7	0.6	6.5	120	7%

Egg and Watercress Sandwiches

These are even better if you make the egg mixture a few hours ahead of time and keep it covered in the refrigerator for 2 hours before making the sandwiches.

MAKES 8 SANDWICHES

1 cup watercress, washed, patted dry, and chopped
5 hard-boiled eggs, shelled and chopped
5 tablespoons Yogurt Cheese (page 98)
2½ tablespoons Dijon mustard
White pepper to taste
16 slices extra-thin wheat bread

1. Mix all of the ingredients, except the bread.

2. Make the sandwiches; cut off the crust, cut the sandwiches, and cover.

Nutritional analysis per serving:

CALORIES	PROTEIN, GM.	CARBOHYDRATE, GM.	FAT, GM.	SATURATED FAT, GM.
164	11	24.7	4.2	1.1

SODIUM, MG.	CHOLESTEROL, MG.	FIBER, GM.	CALCIUM, MG.	CALORIES FROM FAT
366	131.5	6.5	94	23%

Tuna Sandwiches

It is best if the tuna is mixed a couple of hours ahead of time and chilled before making the sandwiches.

MAKES 8 SANDWICHES

1 can (7 ounces) water-packed tuna,
  drained and flaked
5 tablespoons low-calorie mayonnaise
1 tablespoon Dijon mustard
1 teaspoon sweet pickle relish
16 slices extra-thin wheat bread

1. Mix all of the ingredients, except the bread, and let stand for at least 2 hours in the refrigerator.

2. Make the sandwiches; cut off the crusts, cut the sandwiches, and cover.

Nutritional analysis per serving:

CALORIES	PROTEIN, GM.	CARBOHYDRATE, GM.	FAT, GM.	SATURATED FAT, GM.
155	11.3	25	2.8	0.5

SODIUM, MG.	CHOLESTEROL, MG.	FIBER, GM.	CALCIUM, MG.	CALORIES FROM FAT
402	8.2	6.3	55	17%

Yogurt Cheese

This is an excellent nonfat replacement for high-fat items like cream cheese, mayonnaise, or sour cream. You can make it into a sweet cream or a spicy dip!

MAKES 8 OUNCES

16 ounce plain nonfat yogurt, without any added gelatin

1. Place the yogurt in a colander lined with coffee filters. Place the colander in a bowl and cover the top. Refrigerate for 18 to 24 hours.

2. Throw out the liquid and store the Yogurt Cheese in a covered container until ready to use.

Nutritional analysis per serving:

CALORIES	PROTEIN, GM.	CARBOHYDRATE, GM.	FAT, GM.	SATURATED FAT, GM.
24	1.8	4.8	0.1	0.04

SODIUM, MG.	CHOLESTEROL, MG.	FIBER, GM.	CALCIUM, MG.	CALORIES FROM FAT
23.4	0.6	0.0	61	2%

Yogurt Cream

This no-fat topping is excellent on fruit desserts to give them just that little something extra!

MAKES 8 SERVINGS

1 cup Yogurt Cheese (page 98)
1 teaspoon vanilla
3 tablespoons sugar

Mix all of the ingredients, and store in the refrigerator in a covered container until ready to use.

Nutritional analysis per serving:

CALORIES	PROTEIN, GM.	CARBOHYDRATE, GM.	FAT, GM.	SATURATED FAT, GM.
60	1.8	13	0.1	0.04

SODIUM, MG.	CHOLESTEROL, MG.	FIBER, GM.	CALCIUM, MG.	CALORIES FROM FAT
23.4	0.6	0.0	61	0%

Yogurt Cream, Celery, and Walnut Sandwiches

Try adding some chopped dates. This spread also makes a great filling for quick breads or a tasty topping on scones.

MAKES 8 SANDWICHES

2 cups Yogurt Cream (page 99)
2 cups chopped celery
1/2 cup chopped walnuts
16 slices extra-thin wheat bread

1. Mix all of the ingredients, except the bread.

2. Make the sandwiches; cut off the crusts, cut the sandwiches, and cover.

Nutritional analysis per serving:

CALORIES	PROTEIN, GM.	CARBOHYDRATE, GM.	FAT, GM.	SATURATED FAT, GM.
300	7.6	44	7.1	0.9

SODIUM, MG.	CHOLESTEROL, MG.	FIBER, GM.	CALCIUM, MG.	CALORIES FROM FAT
325.3	0.6	3.6	126	21%

Asparagus and Spinach Soup

To make this soup a bit richer without adding fat calories, use evaporated skim milk. A side benefit is that you get extra calcium.

SERVES 6

1 pound fresh asparagus
6 cups low-salt chicken broth
2 large potatoes, diced
1 package (10 ounces) frozen chopped
   spinach, thawed
1 teaspoon white pepper
1 cup nonfat milk

1. Cut the tips off of the asparagus and set aside. Cut off the bottom 1/2 inch and discard. Cut the remaining stem into small pieces.

2. Bring the chicken broth to a boil. Add the asparagus stems and diced potatoes. Cover, reduce heat, and simmer for 30 minutes.

3. Add the thawed spinach, white pepper, and nonfat milk. Cover and simmer for another 30 minutes.

4. Pour soup into a food processor with a steel blade, or a blender, and purée.

5. Pour the soup back into the saucepan. Add the asparagus tips, cover, and simmer for 10 minutes.

Nutritional analysis per serving:

Calories	Protein, gm.	Carbohydrate, gm.	Fat, gm.	Saturated Fat, gm.
91	7.4	14.6	0.9	0.3

Sodium, mg.	Cholesterol, mg.	Fiber, gm.	Calcium, mg.	Calories from Fat
400	0.7	2.5	111	9%

Carrot, Leek, and Potato Soup

This favorite soup for a chilly winter evening can also be turned into a summer soup by serving it chilled. It is also very good served with a dollop of sour cream and sprinkled with chopped chives.

SERVES 6

5 cups low-salt chicken broth
2 leeks, washed and thinly sliced
2 sticks celery, sliced
3 large potatoes, diced with skin
2 carrots, grated
1/2 teaspoon ground white pepper
1/2 cup nonfat milk

1. Place 1/4 cup of the chicken broth in a Dutch oven and bring to a boil. Add the leeks and celery and stir fry, tossing the vegetables quickly for 2 minutes.

2. Add the remaining chicken broth, potatoes, carrots, and white pepper, and bring it to a boil. Reduce heat, cover, and simmer for 1 hour.

3. Pure the mixture either in a food processor or a blender.

4. Return the soup to the Dutch oven. Add milk, heat, and serve.

Nutritional analysis per serving:

CALORIES	PROTEIN, GM.	CARBOHYDRATE, GM.	FAT, GM.	SATURATED FAT, GM.
110	5	21.6	0.7	0.2

SODIUM, MG.	CHOLESTEROL, MG.	FIBER, GM.	CALCIUM, MG.	CALORIES FROM FAT
350	0.4	2.8	75	6%

Beetroot Salad

Be careful with beetroot; it stains easily. But I think you'll agree that using fresh beets make the extra care worthwhile.

SERVES 6

4 fresh beets, grated
2 green apples, grated
2 ounces walnuts, diced
2 cloves garlic, crushed
4 tablespoons low-calorie mayonnaise

Mix all of the ingredients. Cover and chill for 1 hour.

Nutritional analysis per serving:

CALORIES	PROTEIN, GM.	CARBOHYDRATE, GM.	FAT, GM.	SATURATED FAT, GM.
102	1.5	17.2	3.8	0.5

SODIUM, MG.	CHOLESTEROL, MG.	FIBER, GM.	CALCIUM, MG.	CALORIES FROM FAT
105.6	2.5	2.4	23	34%

Crab Salad

This makes a lovely first course or a salad to serve with finger sandwiches. Add a cup of soup or some freshly baked bread, and it can serve two as a main course.

SERVES 4

4 red potatoes, cooked and cubed
1 red apple, cored and cubed
½ English cucumber, diced
2 hard-boiled eggs, peeled and chopped
1 cup crabmeat (or use imitation)
4 tablespoons low-calorie mayonnaise
4 large red lettuce leaves

1. In a bowl, mix all of the ingredients except lettuce leaves. Cover and refrigerate for 1 hour.

2. Place one lettuce leaf on each of 4 salad plates. Divide the salad mixture into 4 parts, spoon onto the plates, and serve.

Nutritional analysis per serving:

CALORIES	PROTEIN, GM.	CARBOHYDRATE, GM.	FAT, GM.	SATURATED FAT, GM.
262	12.4	39.2	6.7	1.4

SODIUM, MG.	CHOLESTEROL, MG.	FIBER, GM.	CALCIUM, MG.	CALORIES FROM FAT
590.4	120.1	3.4	38	23%

Beef and Beer

It is much better to use a light beer or ale in this recipe. A heavy-flavored beer will overpower the beef.

SERVES 8

2½ pounds lean beef, cubed
½ teaspoon black pepper
2 large onions, thinly sliced
2 tablespoons flour
1 bottle light beer
½ cup low-salt beef broth

1. Preheat the oven to 275°F.

2. Toss the beef cubes and pepper together.

3. Spray a large skillet with nonstick spray and brown the beef cubes. Transfer the meat to an ovenproof casserole.

4. Put the onions into the hot skillet and cook until tender. Sprinkle the onions with flour and mix well. Add them to the casserole.

5. Pour the beer and the broth over the meat. Cover the casserole and bake for 2 hours.

Nutritional analysis per serving:

CALORIES	PROTEIN, GM.	CARBOHYDRATE, GM.	FAT, GM.	SATURATED FAT, GM.
253	30.3	4.4	10.8	4

SODIUM, MG.	CHOLESTEROL, MG.	FIBER, GM.	CALCIUM, MG.	CALORIES FROM FAT
60	96.3	0.5	19	38%

Creamed Chicken

If you don't have leftover chicken or turkey, you can used canned white chicken meat in broth.

SERVES 6

1 recipe Basic White Sauce (page 109)
1 leek, thinly sliced (cut off dark green top and discard)
1½ pounds cooked chicken breast, boned and skinned
2½ cups cooked brown rice

1. Make the White Sauce in a large saucepan.

2. In a skillet sprayed with a nonstick spray, sauté the leek until tender. Stir the leek into the White Sauce.

3. Fold in the chicken and heat thoroughly.

4. Serve over brown rice.

Nutritional analysis per serving:

CALORIES	PROTEIN, GM.	CARBOHYDRATE, GM.	FAT, GM.	SATURATED FAT, GM.
183	10.6	26.9	3.4	1.6

SODIUM, MG.	CHOLESTEROL, MG.	FIBER, GM.	CALCIUM, MG.	CALORIES FROM FAT
65.2	24.4	1.7	75	17%

Macaroni and Cheese

Use your favorite cheese in this. Reserve a bit of the grated cheese and sprinkle over the top and the last 5 minutes of baking.

SERVES 6

1 pound penne (or your favorite macaroni)
4 cups nonfat milk
1 tablespoon butter
6 tablespoons flour
$1/2$ teaspoon white pepper
$1/4$ teaspoon cayenne pepper
4 ounces sharp cheddar cheese, grated

1. Cook the macaroni in a large pot of boiling water until just tender. Pour it into a colander and rinse with cold water. Drain well and set aside.

2. Preheat the oven to 350°F.

3. In a large saucepan, mix the milk, butter, flour, and peppers, and bring to boil, stirring constantly. Reduce the heat. When the mixture thickens, add the grated cheese and continue stirring until it melts.

4. Mix the cheese sauce and macaroni together in an ovenproof casserole. Cover and bake 20 minutes. Uncover and bake another 5 minutes.

Nutritional analysis per serving:

CALORIES	PROTEIN, GM.	CARBOHYDRATE, GM.	FAT, GM.	SATURATED FAT, GM.
468	20.9	72.3	10	5.6

SODIUM, MG.	CHOLESTEROL, MG.	FIBER, GM.	CALCIUM, MG.	CALORIES FROM FAT
222.9	28	3.5	354	19%

Salmon Dill Pie

It's the perfect Friday night supper with a green salad and fresh bread.

SERVES 6

2 cups soft bread crumbs
½ cup nonfat milk
4 egg whites, slightly beaten (beat 2 together, reserve 2 for later)
¼ small onion, finely chopped
2 tablespoons fresh parsley, chopped
1 tablespoon melted butter
½ teaspoon white pepper
1 pound canned salmon, drained and flaked
4 medium potatoes, cubed, with skins on
1 recipe Basic White Sauce (page 109)
¾ teaspoon dried dillweed
½ cup low-fat sour cream

1. Preheat the oven to 350°F. Spray an 8-inch round baking dish with nonstick cooking spray.

2. Combine bread crumbs, milk, 2 egg whites, onion, parsley, butter, and white pepper. Mix in the salmon; blend well. Spoon the mixture into the prepared dish.

3. In a saucepan, boil the potatoes until done; drain and mash. Add the remaining 2 egg whites.

4. Spoon the potatoes around the salmon mixture. Bake for 30 minutes.

5. Make the White Sauce. Add dillweed and sour cream.

6. To serve, cut the pie in 6 wedges and put on serving plates. Pour the sauce over each wedge.

Nutritional analysis per serving:

CALORIES	PROTEIN, GM.	CARBOHYDRATE, GM.	FAT, GM.	SATURATED FAT, GM.
377	24.8	41.4	12.1	5.2

SODIUM, MG.	CHOLESTEROL, MG.	FIBER, GM.	CALCIUM, MG.	CALORIES FROM FAT
727.8	55.6	2.7	302	29%

Basic White Sauce

The most common of English sauces, the Basic White Sauce is very simple to make. You can add different flavorings to complement your dish.

SERVES 4

2 tablespoons flour
1 tablespoon melted butter
1 cup nonfat milk

Items you can add for flavor:

Celery salt
Chives, chopped
Lemon juice (mock hollandaise)
Onion juice
Parsley, chopped
Sherry
Tarragon
Worcestershire sauce

1. Mix all of the ingredients thoroughly and pour into a saucepan. Stir constantly.

2. Bring the sauce to a boil, reduce the heat, and keep stirring until the sauce reaches desired thickness.

Nutritional analysis per serving:

CALORIES	PROTEIN, GM.	CARBOHYDRATE, GM.	FAT, GM.	SATURATED FAT, GM.
61	2.5	5.6	3.2	1.9

SODIUM, MG.	CHOLESTEROL, MG.	FIBER, GM.	CALCIUM, MG.	CALORIES FROM FAT
62.6	9.3	0.1	77	47%

Creamed Spinach

This dish can be made ahead and reheated in the oven with toasted bread crumbs sprinkled on top.

SERVES 6

1 recipe Basic White Sauce (page 109)
2 packages (10 ounces) frozen chopped
  spinach, thawed

1. Make the White Sauce in a saucepan.

2. Squeeze the excess water from the spinach, then fold it into the White Sauce, and heat thoroughly.

Nutritional analysis per serving:

CALORIES	PROTEIN, GM.	CARBOHYDRATE, GM.	FAT, GM.	SATURATED FAT, GM.
50	2.8	5.2	2.2	1.3

SODIUM, MG.	CHOLESTEROL, MG.	FIBER, GM.	CALCIUM, MG.	CALORIES FROM FAT
69.4	6.2	0.9	105	40%

Onion-Potato Cake

You can also make this cake in a springform pan for easy removal. That way, you can serve it right from the baking dish, and it will stay warm longer.

SERVES 6

2 pounds potatoes, sliced, with skins on
1 large onion, thinly sliced
½ cup chicken broth
White pepper to taste
1 tablespoon melted butter

1. Preheat the oven to 375°F. Spray a 7-inch soufflé dish with nonstick spray.

2. In the dish, arrange a layer of potatoes, then a layer of onion. Drizzle with the chicken broth and sprinkle with white pepper. Continue layering, finishing with the potatoes and the melted butter.

3. Cover and bake for 1¼ hours.

4. Turn out on a round platter and serve.

Nutritional analysis per serving:

CALORIES	PROTEIN, GM.	CARBOHYDRATE, GM.	FAT, GM.	SATURATED FAT, GM.
146	3.6	28.8	2.3	1.3
SODIUM, MG.	CHOLESTEROL, MG.	FIBER, GM.	CALCIUM, MG.	CALORIES FROM FAT
50	5.5	2.7	16	14%

Peas in White Sauce

To make a very special vegetable dish, see the recipe for Stuffed Tomatoes on page 52. It adds lovely color to your plate.

SERVES 6

1 package (16 ounces) frozen petite peas, thawed
1 recipe Basic White Sauce (page 109)

1. Make the White Sauce in a saucepan.

2. Fold in the thawed peas and gently simmer until heated.

Nutritional analysis per serving:

CALORIES	PROTEIN, GM.	CARBOHYDRATE, GM.	FAT, GM.	SATURATED FAT, GM.
104	5.7	15.5	2.3	1.3

SODIUM, MG.	CHOLESTEROL, MG.	FIBER, GM.	CALCIUM, MG.	CALORIES FROM FAT
108.1	6.2	2.6	72	20%

Rice with Onions

This easy, foolproof rice dish holds well in a low oven until it's time to serve it.

SERVES 6

1 tablespoon butter
1 medium onion, chopped
1 cup long-grain white rice
2¼ cups hot water

1. Preheat the oven to 300°F.

2. Melt the butter in an ovenproof saucepan. Sauté the onion in butter. Add the rice and toss it in the butter and onions. Add the water and bring to a boil.

3. Cover and place in the oven for 30 minutes.

Nutritional analysis per serving:

CALORIES	PROTEIN, GM.	CARBOHYDRATE, GM.	FAT, GM.	SATURATED FAT, GM.
52	0.8	7.4	2.1	1.3

SODIUM, MG.	CHOLESTEROL, MG.	FIBER, GM.	CALCIUM, MG.	CALORIES FROM FAT
29.2	5.5	0.5	39	36%

Roasted Potatoes

Roasted Potatoes are a wonderful side dish with almost anything. You could also use beef broth to flavor the potatoes, or if you are making a vegetarian meal, use vegetable broth.

SERVES 6

1/2 cup low-salt chicken broth
3 medium russet potatoes, washed and
  cut into fourths
Paprika

1. Preheat the oven to 400°F. Spray a cookie sheet with a nonstick spray.

2. In a saucepan, bring the chicken broth to boil and continue boiling until the broth is reduced to 1/4 cup.

3. Place the potatoes on the cookie sheet. Brush each chunk with the chicken broth and sprinkle with the paprika.

4. Roast for 30 minutes, or until the potatoes are tender.

Nutritional analysis per serving:

CALORIES	PROTEIN, GM.	CARBOHYDRATE, GM.	FAT, GM.	SATURATED FAT, GM.
56	1.3	12.7	0.1	0.04

SODIUM, MG.	CHOLESTEROL, MG.	FIBER, GM.	CALCIUM, MG.	CALORIES FROM FAT
35	0.0	1.3	7	2%

Crumpet Scones

These scones are very easy to make. They come out like thick pancakes.

SERVES 8

1 cup all-purpose flour
¼ teaspoon baking soda
2 tablespoons sugar
⅔ cup low-fat buttermilk
2 egg whites, slightly beaten
2 teaspoons melted butter

1. Sift the flour and baking soda together.

2. Mix in the remaining ingredients.

3. Pour a large spoonful of batter onto a preheated griddle or large heavy skillet sprayed with a nonstick spray. When the batter is full of bubbles, flip the scone over, using a spatula.

4. Put the scones in a basket lined with cloth or paper towels. Serve then immediately. Scones can be reheated in your toaster if you have any leftovers.

Nutritional analysis per serving:

CALORIES	PROTEIN, GM.	CARBOHYDRATE, GM.	FAT, GM.	SATURATED FAT, GM.
84	3	14.9	1.3	0.7

SODIUM, MG.	CHOLESTEROL, MG.	FIBER, GM.	CALCIUM, MG.	CALORIES FROM FAT
78.5	3.4	0.4	24	14%

Fruit Scones

These heavier scones have a bit more flavor than plain oven scones. They can be served alone, or with jam or Yogurt Cream (page 99).

SERVES 8

2½ cups all-purpose flour
2 teaspoons baking powder
1 teaspoon baking soda
½ cup sugar
3 tablespoons melted butter
½ cup raisins
2 egg whites, slightly beaten
1½ cups nonfat plain yogurt
Grated peel of 1 lemon
Nonfat milk for brushing scones

1. Preheat the oven to 425°F. Spray a large cookie sheet with nonstick baking spray.

2. Sift the flour, baking powder, and baking soda together.

3. With a fork, stir in the sugar, butter, raisins, egg whites, yogurt, and lemon peel until the dough barely holds together.

4. Turn it onto a floured surface and roll it out with a floured rolling pin or pat it out to ½ inch thick. With a cookie cutter (it's fun to use different shapes), cut out the scones and place them 1 inch apart on the cookie sheet. Brush the tops with nonfat milk.

5. Bake 10 to 12 minutes or until the scones have risen and are golden.

Nutritional analysis per serving:

Calories	Protein, gm.	Carbohydrate, gm.	Fat, gm.	Saturated Fat, gm.
276	7.6	50.5	5.1	2.9

Sodium, mg.	Cholesterol, mg.	Fiber, gm.	Calcium, mg.	Calories from Fat
344.7	13.1	1.5	167	16%

Orange Tea Loaf

To make this cake a bit more festive, poke some holes into it with a toothpick after the cake has cooled, and drizzle ¼ cup of orange-flavored liqueur over the top before wrapping and refrigerating it.

SERVES 8

2 cups self-rising flour
1½ teaspoons baking powder
¾ cup plain nonfat yogurt
⅔ cup sugar
2 egg whites, room temperature
2 tablespoons orange juice
Grated peel of ½ orange
½ teaspoon orange extract
½ teaspoon vanilla extract
½ cup nonfat milk

1. Preheat the oven to 375°F. Spray an 8-by-4-inch loaf pan with a nonstick baking spray.

2. Sift the flour and baking powder into a bowl and set aside.

3. Mix the yogurt and sugar in a separate bowl and set aside.

4. Beat the egg whites to soft peaks. Fold the orange juice, orange peel, orange and vanilla extract, the yogurt mixture, and the milk into the egg whites.

5. Fold the flour into the egg-white mixture.

6. Pour the batter into the loaf pan and bake 40 to 50 minutes.

7. Cool for 10 minutes, remove from pan and cool for 15 minutes. Wrap the loaf with plastic wrap and refrigerate it for 24 hours.

Nutritional analysis per serving:

CALORIES	PROTEIN, GM.	CARBOHYDRATE, GM.	FAT, GM.	SATURATED FAT, GM.
188	5.7	40.1	0.4	0.1

SODIUM, MG.	CHOLESTEROL, MG.	FIBER, GM.	CALCIUM, MG.	CALORIES FROM FAT
120.2	0.7	0.8	118	2%

Sherry Trifle

Trifle is one of the most often served English desserts. It is popular at High Tea and at Christmas.

SERVES 12

1 Sponge Cake (page 119)
1/2 cup sugar-free raspberry jam
1/2 cup sweet sherry
4 peaches, thinly sliced
4 tablespoons cornstarch
2 cups 1% milk
1 teaspoon vanilla
2 tablespoons sugar
1/2 cup toasted almonds, chopped
2 cups low-calorie whipped topping
1 cup raspberries

1. Spread the cake with jam, cut it into pieces, and place them in a large pretty bowl.

2. Pour the sherry over the cake and cover with the peaches.

3. In a saucepan, mix the milk and cornstarch. Bring to a boil, stirring constantly. Add the vanilla and sugar, stirring until thickened (like pudding). Remove from the heat, and let cool.

4. Pour the cooled pudding over the cake. Sprinkle the top with almonds.

5. Spread on the whipped topping, then pour the berries over the top.

Nutritional analysis per serving:

CALORIES	PROTEIN, GM.	CARBOHYDRATE, GM.	FAT, GM.	SATURATED FAT, GM.
232	7.1	49	5.3	1.7

SODIUM, MG.	CHOLESTEROL, MG.	FIBER, GM.	CALCIUM, MG.	CALORIES FROM FAT
102.2	9.1	2.2	130	21%

Sponge Cake

This is a basic cake that you can fill with sugar-free jam, custard, Yogurt Cream (page 99), or chocolate mousse.

SERVES 8

1½ cups self-rising flour
Grated peel from ½ lemon
¾ cup plain nonfat yogurt
1 cup nonfat milk
½ cup sugar
4 egg whites, room temperature

1. Preheat the oven to 350°F. Spray two 8-inch round cake pans with a nonstick baking spray.

2. Sift the flour into a bowl. Stir in the lemon rind.

3. Mix the yogurt, milk, and sugar.

4. Whip the egg whites to soft peaks and fold the yogurt mixture into them.

5. Fold the flour into the mixture.

6. Divide the batter into the pans and bake 25 minutes, or until the cake springs back when touched. Cool on racks.

Nutritional analysis per serving:

CALORIES	PROTEIN, GM.	CARBOHYDRATE, GM.	FAT, GM.	SATURATED FAT, GM.
157	6.3	31.9	0.3	0.1

SODIUM, MG.	CHOLESTEROL, MG.	FIBER, GM.	CALCIUM, MG.	CALORIES FROM FAT
61	1	0.5	88	2%

French Cuisine

Introduction

French cuisine is known for perfection in both appearance and taste, with soft, delicate flavors. Traditionally, French food has been heavy in fat, using butter, heavy cream, and lard unsparingly. However, with a few modifications, we can eliminate most of the fats and a lot of the preparation time.

France is also known for wine and champagne. Always remember to cook with the wine you are serving. If you are not serving wine, but your recipe calls for it, select a dry vermouth.

When planning your French lunch, brunch, or dinner party, you can determine the formality of the affair by your choice of table settings, linens, and other accompaniments. Here are a few suggestions.

FORMAL DINNER PARTY

For a formal dinner, use table settings of white, black, and silver linens, and don't forget the napkin rings. Add black candles and small individual vases with single red roses. Serve the appetizers with cocktails in the living room. Here's a sample menu.

> *Appetizers*
>> Pâté
>> Crudités
>
> *Cocktail*
>> Kir Royal
>
> *Soup*
>> French Onion
>
> *Salad*
>> Caesar
>
> *Main Course*
>> Coq au Vin
>> French-Cut Green Beans
>> Red Wine
>
> *Dessert*
>> Floating Island
>> Port
>> Coffee

Serve the Port and coffee in the living room.

INFORMAL FRENCH LUNCHEON

For an informal luncheon, use table settings with a
red and white checkered tablecloth and/or napkins.
Put bread sticks in glasses on the table. This will
give your luncheon a French country atmosphere.

Soup
    Tomato-Carrot
    Bread Sticks
Main Dish
    Beef Provençal
Dessert
    Pears à la Cream
    Coffee

French Onion Soup

This soup is a meal in itself and makes a perfect lunch or light dinner when served with a green salad and fruit.

SERVES 6

1½ pounds yellow onions, peeled, halved, and thinly sliced
½ teaspoon black pepper
2 tablespoons all-purpose flour
9 cups low-salt beef broth
1 tablespoon cognac (optional)
6½-inch slices French bread, toasted
6 ounces grated mozzarella cheese

1. Spray a large saucepan with a nonstick cooking spray; cover and cook the onions and black pepper on low for 15 minutes. Stir occasionally.

2. Uncover, raise the heat to medium, and continue stirring until the onions are light brown.

3. Sprinkle the flour over the onions and stir for about 3 minutes.

4. Add the beef broth and simmer, partially covered, for 45 minutes.

5. Add cognac and stir well.

6. Place French bread slices on a cookie sheet. Put 1 ounce grated cheese on each. Put under the broiler for 30 seconds.

7. Place the bread slices in 6 serving bowls. Ladle the soup on top.

Nutritional analysis per serving:

CALORIES	PROTEIN, GM.	CARBOHYDRATE, GM.	FAT, GM.	SATURATED FAT, GM.
253	15.8	27.7	8.3	4.7

SODIUM, MG.	CHOLESTEROL, MG.	FIBER, GM.	CALCIUM, MG.	CALORIES FROM FAT
1482	19.6	2.6	275	29%

French Potato Salad

French Potato Salad is prepared while the potatoes are warm so they will absorb the dressing. You can serve it either warm or cold.

SERVES 8

2 pounds small red potatoes, washed
1 teaspoon Dijon mustard
1 cup Vinaigrette Dressing (page 22)
1 tablespoon parsley

1. Boil the potatoes until they are just tender when pierced with a knife. Drain. As soon as you can handle them, cut into fourths or slice them.

2. Mix the mustard into the dressing.

3. Place the potatoes in a mixing bowl, pour the dressing over, and toss gently.

4. Sprinkle with fresh parsley before serving.

Nutritional analysis per serving:

CALORIES	PROTEIN, GM.	CARBOHYDRATE, GM.	FAT, GM.	SATURATED FAT, GM.
159	2.5	22	7.2	1

SODIUM, MG.	CHOLESTEROL, MG.	FIBER, GM.	CALCIUM, MG.	CALORIES FROM FAT
130.8	0.0	1.8	12	41%

Pâté

If you love liver pâté, this will be a delightful hit. It has a very smooth texture and the Neufchâtel mellows the flavor slightly.

SERVES 12

2 tablespoons butter
4 green onions, including tops, finely chopped
1½ pounds chicken livers
½ teaspoon salt
2 teaspoons dry mustard
½ teaspoon ground nutmeg
¼ teaspoon ground cloves
8 ounces Neufchâtel cheese
¼ cup cognac

1. In a large skillet, melt the butter. Add the green onions and sauté until tender.

2. Add chicken livers, salt, mustard, nutmeg, and cloves. Cover and cook on low for 10 to 15 minutes, until the livers are cooked.

3. Place the mixture into a food processor with a steel blade or into a blender. Use high speed. While running, process in the Neufchâtel, then the cognac.

4. Pour the mixture into a soufflé dish or a pâté tureen. Chill for at least 12 hours before serving.

Nutritional analysis per serving:

CALORIES	PROTEIN, GM.	CARBOHYDRATE, GM.	FAT, GM.	SATURATED FAT, GM.
171	11.4	8.6	8.8	4.3

SODIUM, MG.	CHOLESTEROL, MG.	FIBER, GM.	CALCIUM, MG.	CALORIES FROM FAT
330.5	221.5	0.7	42	46%

Quiche

This can be a very versatile dish. You can use any leftover vegetables. Be creative and have fun! Adding the nonfat dry milk makes the Quiche richer without adding any extra fat. Instead it adds extra calcium.

SERVES 4

¼ cup chicken broth
½ teaspoon garlic, minced
2 medium zucchini, shredded and well drained
2 tablespoons Parmesan cheese, grated
½ pound broccoli, chopped and steamed
3 ounces cheese, shredded
1¼ cup nonfat milk
3 tablespoons nonfat dry milk powder
2 eggs, separated
2 tablespoons tomato paste
1 tablespoon dried basil leaves
Dash crushed red pepper
1 egg white

1. Preheat the oven to 350°F. Prepare an 8-inch quiche pan by spraying the bottom with a nonstick cooking spray.

2. Reduce the chicken broth in a nonstick skillet to 1 tablespoon. Add the minced garlic and sauté for 1 minute. Add the shredded zucchini and cook for about 3 minutes. Add 1 tablespoon Parmesan cheese and cook for 1 more minute.

3. Spread the vegetable mixture thinly on the bottom of the quiche pan to form a crust.

4. Arrange the broccoli on top, and sprinkle with shredded cheese.

5. Mix the nonfat milk, nonfat milk powder, and egg yolks.

6. Add the tomato paste, basil, and red pepper.

7. Beat the egg whites until stiff and fold them into the milk mixture.

Continued on page 129

Continued from page 128

Quiche

8. Pour the mixture into the quiche pan and sprinkle with 1 tablespoon of Parmesan cheese.

9. Bake for 30 minutes or until it sets in the center.

Nutritional analysis per serving:

CALORIES	PROTEIN, GM.	CARBOHYDRATE, GM.	FAT, GM.	SATURATED FAT, GM.
217	17.5	15.1	10.5	5.5

SODIUM, MG.	CHOLESTEROL, MG.	FIBER, GM.	CALCIUM, MG.	CALORIES FROM FAT
352.6	128.9	3.3	426	43%

Salad Niçoise

This is a perfect main-course summer salad. You can have all the ingredients ready in advance, so all you have to do is arrange it any way you wish. I like to place separate arrangements of the green beans, tomatoes, potato salad, tuna, and eggs on a large plate lined with Boston lettuce. Sprinkle with capers, parsley, and dressing.

SERVES 6

1 head Boston lettuce, separated, washed, and dried

3 cups green beans, cooked and chilled

3 tomatoes, quartered

3 cups chilled French Potato Salad (page 126)

12 ounces water-packed solid tuna, drained

3 hard-boiled eggs, quartered

3 teaspoons capers

2 tablespoons chopped fresh parsley

½ cup Vinaigrette Dressing (page 22)

1. Either arrange the salad on 6 salad plates or in 1 large salad bowl.

2. Pour the dressing over the top of the salad.

Nutritional analysis per serving:

CALORIES	PROTEIN, GM.	CARBOHYDRATE, GM.	FAT, GM.	SATURATED FAT, GM.
300	23.2	42.4	10	5.1

SODIUM, MG.	CHOLESTEROL, MG.	FIBER, GM.	CALCIUM, MG.	CALORIES FROM FAT
773.3	122.1	4.3	80	30%

Soufflé

This out-of-the-ordinary soufflé doesn't have to be served immediately. It is unmolded so it makes a nice appearance, and it can be kept warm or reheated. It makes a nice first course for eight or a main course for four.

SERVES 4

1 ounce grated Parmesan cheese
2½ tablespoons butter
3 tablespoons flour
¾ cup nonfat milk, hot
¼ teaspoon white pepper
2 egg yolks
6 egg whites
¼ teaspoon cream of tartar
3 ounces cheddar cheese
8 ounces fresh mushrooms, sliced and cooked
10 ounces frozen chopped spinach, thawed (squeeze out extra water)

1. Preheat the oven to 350°F. Spray a 2-quart straight-sided baking dish with a nonstick cooking spray and cover the bottom and sides with the Parmesan cheese. (You'll also need a larger baking dish to hold the soufflé dish.)

2. Melt the butter in a saucepan. Add the flour and stir slowly over a low heat for 2 minutes. Do not let it brown.

3. Slowly stir in the hot milk. Bring to a boil, stirring vigorously with a wire whisk. The mixture will be very thick.

4. Remove it from the heat, and add the white pepper.

5. Beat the egg yolks in a bowl. Add a little of the milk mixture, beating as you do so you don't scramble the yolk. Do this a little at a time, then add to the milk mixture and beat in well.

6. Place the egg whites in a clean bowl and whip at a moderate speed until they begin to froth. Add the cream of tartar and beat at a high speed until the egg whites form stiff peaks.

7. Stir a quarter of the egg whites into the hot mixture to lighten it.

Continued on page 132

Continued from page 131

Soufflé

8. Stir in the cheddar cheese, mushrooms, and spinach.

9. Fold in the rest of the egg whites quickly with a rubber spatula, taking about 30 seconds.

10. Put the mixture into the prepared soufflé dish. Place that dish into a larger baking dish; add hot water to come halfway up the sides of the soufflé dish. Bake slowly for 1¼ hours. The soufflé will be brown on top with slight shrinkage from the dish.

11. Unmold by turning it onto a serving platter. Garnish with fresh parsley and diced tomatoes, if desired.

Nutritional analysis per serving:

CALORIES	PROTEIN, GM.	CARBOHYDRATE, GM.	FAT, GM.	SATURATED FAT, GM.
299	20.1	12.7	19.3	11.1

SODIUM, MG.	CHOLESTEROL, MG.	FIBER, GM.	CALCIUM, MG.	CALORIES FROM FAT
491.4	155.9	2.3	418	58%

Tomato-Carrot Soup

The sweet potato adds a hint of sweetness to the soup.

SERVES 8

1 large sweet potato
1 tablespoon butter
1 medium onion, chopped
3 cans (15 ounces) diced tomatoes in
  purée
1 clove garlic, minced
½ cup fresh chervil (1 tablespoon dried)
¼ cup chopped parsley
3 medium carrots, sliced
1 teaspoon sugar
½ teaspoon ground white pepper
4 cups chicken broth
Fresh parsley to garnish

1. Bake the sweet potato for 45 minutes at 375°F. Peel and cut into cubes.

2. In a large Dutch oven, melt the butter over a medium heat. Add the onion and sauté until soft.

3. Add the tomatoes and garlic. Simmer for 15 minutes.

4. Add the chervil, parsley, carrots, sugar, and white pepper. Cover and cook on low until the carrots are tender, about 15 to 20 minutes.

5. Transfer the vegetables and sweet potato to a food processor or blender and blend until smooth.

6. Return the soup to the Dutch oven. Add the chicken broth and heat on medium heat until warm.

7. Garnish with fresh parsley.

Nutritional analysis per serving:

CALORIES	PROTEIN, GM.	CARBOHYDRATE, GM.	FAT, GM.	SATURATED FAT, GM.
91	3.8	15.6	2.3	1.1

SODIUM, MG.	CHOLESTEROL, MG.	FIBER, GM.	CALCIUM, MG.	CALORIES FROM FAT
242	4.1	4.5	78	23%

Tomato Salad

This recipe is very low in calories, but it does have a high percentage of calories from fat—even though very little fat is used. You can omit the olive oil if you wish.

SERVES 6

3 large tomatoes
3 scallions, washed, trimmed, and
  chopped
2 tablespoons chopped fresh parsley
3 tablespoons fresh lemon juice
1 teaspoon oregano
1/2 teaspoon ground black pepper
2 tablespoons white wine vinegar
1 tablespoon olive oil

1. Cut the tomatoes in eighths.

2. Mix all of the other ingredients, and gently toss in the tomatoes.

Nutritional analysis per serving:

CALORIES	PROTEIN, GM.	CARBOHYDRATE, GM.	FAT, GM.	SATURATED FAT, GM.
38	0.7	4	2.6	0.3

SODIUM, MG.	CHOLESTEROL, MG.	FIBER, GM.	CALCIUM, MG.	CALORIES FROM FAT
7.4	0.0	0.9	12	62%

French Brussels Sprouts

The classic way to cook these Brussels sprouts would be to sauté them in butter. The Guiltless way is to use chicken broth and just a little butter. It gives you the flavor without the extra fat calories.

SERVES 4

1 pound fresh Brussels sprouts, washed, and trimmed (or 2 packages frozen and thawed)
1/2 cup chicken broth
1 teaspoon butter

1. Steam the Brussels sprouts until they are crisp-tender.

2. In a nonstick skillet, reduce the chicken broth in half.

3. Add butter to the skillet and melt.

4. Cut the Brussels sprouts in half. Add them to pan, and sauté until all are well coated and hot.

Nutritional analysis per serving:

CALORIES	PROTEIN, GM.	CARBOHYDRATE, GM.	FAT, GM.	SATURATED FAT, GM.
55	3.2	9.8	1.7	0.7

SODIUM, MG.	CHOLESTEROL, MG.	FIBER, GM.	CALCIUM, MG.	CALORIES FROM FAT
92	2.7	4.8	43	27%

Molded Brown Rice

The molded rice makes a lovely presentation on a buffet or on the dinner table.

SERVES 8

2 cups short-grain brown rice, uncooked
1 red bell pepper, diced
5 cups chicken broth
Fresh parsley to garnish

1. Put all of the ingredients in a rice cooker and cook until done. If you use a saucepan, bring the chicken broth to a boil. Add the rice and bell pepper. Cover and simmer until done, about 45 minutes.

2. Place the cooked rice in a 5-cup mold that has been sprayed with a vegetable spray. Press down firmly. (This can be made ahead and reheated.)

3. Place the mold in the oven, preheated to 350°F, for 10 minutes. Unmold onto a serving platter and garnish with fresh parsley.

Nutritional analysis per serving:

CALORIES	PROTEIN, GM.	CARBOHYDRATE, GM.	FAT, GM.	SATURATED FAT, GM.
131	4.3	25.9	1	0.3

SODIUM, MG.	CHOLESTEROL, MG.	FIBER, GM.	CALCIUM, MG.	CALORIES FROM FAT
194.2	0.0	1.8	22	7%

Crêpes Coquille St. Jacques

The classical Coquille St. Jacques has an extremely high fat content. Here is a modified, lighter version that still keeps the familiar flavor. As a first course serve one crêpe, or serve it in a shell with piped mashed potatoes; brown under the broiler right before serving

MAKES 12 CRÊPES

Court Bouillon

1 small onion, sliced
1 stalk celery, cut up
1 bay leaf
3 slices lemon
1 cup water
1/2 cup dry white wine
1 pound sea scallops, washed and drained

1. In a medium saucepan, combine all of the ingredients except the wine and scallops, and bring to a boil. Simmer for 10 minutes.

2. Add the wine and scallops. Cover and simmer for 6 minutes or until tender. Drain, reserve the liquid.

Continued on page 138

Continued from page 137

Crêpes Coquille St. Jacques

Sauce

½ cup Court Bouillon + 2 tablespoons
¼ cup chopped onion
½ pound mushrooms, sliced
¼ cup flour
¼ teaspoon white pepper
1 cup 1% milk
6 ounces Gruyère cheese
2 tablespoons dry white wine
12 crêpes
Parsley to garnish

1. Put 2 tablespoons Court Bouillon in a skillet. Bring to a boil. Add the onions. Sauté 1 minute, stirring constantly. Add the mushrooms. Reduce the heat. Cover until the mushrooms are soft. Remove the cover. Sauté until all liquid is absorbed.

2. Mix the flour, pepper, and milk. Pour into the onions and mushrooms. Stir until thick.

3. Add the Gruyère cheese. Stir until melted. Turn off the heat. Add the wine, ½ cup Court Bouillon, and the scallops. Mix well.

4. Divide the scallops into 12 portions. Wrap them in the crêpes with a small amount of sauce. Place them on a serving platter or on 6 plates, 2 crêpes per serving.

5. Spoon the sauce across the middle of the crêpes. Garnish with fresh sprigs of parsley.

Nutritional analysis per serving:

Calories	Protein, gm.	Carbohydrate, gm.	Fat, gm.	Saturated Fat, gm.
471	34.3	46.1	14.3	6.7

Sodium, mg.	Cholesterol, mg.	Fiber, gm.	Calcium, mg.	Calories from Fat
421.3	126.5	2.3	483	27%

Sole with Shrimp Sauce

*This is a delicate dish that is perfect served with **Molded Brown Rice** (page 136).*

SERVES 6

6 fillets of sole (2½ pounds)
2 tablespoons lemon juice
1 clove garlic, crushed
½ teaspoon dried tarragon leaves
½ teaspoon dried basil leaves
1 cup dry white wine
Shrimp Sauce (page 140)

1. Brush both sides of the fillets with lemon juice. Cut lengthwise. Roll them up with the dark side to the inside. Arrange the rolls standing up in a single layer in a large skillet.

2. Mix the garlic, tarragon, and basil in the wine. Pour over the fish. Bring to a boil. Reduce to a simmer and cover. Cook for 10 to 12 minutes.

3. With a slotted spoon, remove the fillets from the skillet to a warm serving platter. Cover and keep warm.

4. Strain the cooking liquid and measure 1¼ cups (if there is not enough, add water to make up the difference). Now make the Shrimp Sauce.

Continued on page 140

Continued from page 139

Sole with Shrimp Sauce

Shrimp Sauce

1¼ cup liquid from cooking fish
1 shallot, chopped
1 tablespoon chopped parsley
1 tablespoon flour
3 tablespoons tomato paste
⅛ teaspoon cayenne pepper
⅔ cup nonfat milk
¼ cup dry white wine
½ pound shrimp, cooked and cleaned

1. Place 3 tablespoons of the cooking liquid from the fish in the skillet. Bring to a boil. Add the shallot and parsley. Reduce heat and sauté for 1 minute.

2. Mix the flour, tomato paste, cayenne pepper, and milk into the remaining cooking liquid. Bring to a boil, cooking until thick and smooth.

3. Add the wine and shrimp, and heat.

4. Pour the sauce over the fillets and serve.

Nutritional analysis per serving:

CALORIES	PROTEIN, GM.	CARBOHYDRATE, GM.	FAT, GM.	SATURATED FAT, GM.
203	35.8	1.2	2.3	0.5

SODIUM, MG.	CHOLESTEROL, MG.	FIBER, GM.	CALCIUM, MG.	CALORIES FROM FAT
156.7	90.8	0.1	42	10%

Chicken Stroganoff

The popular stroganoff recipe uses chicken as an alternative to beef. Serve with rice or noodles.

SERVES 6

1 pound boneless, skinless chicken breast
  cut in strips
1 cup low-salt chicken broth
1/2 medium onion, thinly sliced
1 pound sliced mushrooms
1/4 cup dry white vermouth
3 teaspoons cornstarch
1/4 teaspoon ground black pepper
1 cup low-fat sour cream

1. In a skillet sprayed with a nonstick cooking spray, brown the chicken on all sides on high heat. Remove from the skillet. Set aside.

2. Heat 1/4 cup chicken broth in the skillet. Add the onions and cook until soft on medium heat. Add the mushrooms. Cover and simmer for 5 minutes. Remove the cover and continue cooking until all the liquid is absorbed, stirring constantly.

3. Add the vermouth. Bring it quickly to a boil, then reduce the heat to simmer.

4. Mix the cornstarch in the remaining chicken broth and add to the skillet. Stir until thickened.

5. Add the chicken and black pepper. Gently stir in the sour cream.

Nutritional analysis per serving:

CALORIES	PROTEIN, GM.	CARBOHYDRATE, GM.	FAT, GM.	SATURATED FAT, GM.
160	17.4	7	6	3

SODIUM, MG.	CHOLESTEROL, MG.	FIBER, GM.	CALCIUM, MG.	CALORIES FROM FAT
176.9	47.3	1.1	38	34%

Chicken with Lemon and Capers

Capers always give a lovely zip to a dish. Coating the chicken with flour will keep it moist.

SERVES 6

1 tablespoon butter
1 medium onion, sliced
3 cloves garlic, chopped
6 chicken breasts halves, boned and skinned
2 tablespoons flour, seasoned with salt and pepper
2 cups dry white wine (or dry vermouth)
2 lemons, very thinly sliced, with skins
2 tablespoons small capers
¼ cup chopped fresh parsley
3 cups cooked brown rice

1. In a large skillet or a Dutch oven, heat the butter. Add the onion and garlic. Sauté until tender.

2. Coat the chicken breasts with the flour and brown on both sides.

3. Add the wine. Bring to a quick boil and reduce heat to simmer.

4. Add the lemons and capers. Cover and simmer until the chicken is done, about 8 to 10 minutes. Add the parsley.

5. Serve over brown rice.

Nutritional analysis per serving:

CALORIES	PROTEIN, GM.	CARBOHYDRATE, GM.	FAT, GM.	SATURATED FAT, GM.
399	30	35.2	5.8	2.3

SODIUM, MG.	CHOLESTEROL, MG.	FIBER, GM.	CALCIUM, MG.	CALORIES FROM FAT
217.1	78.2	2.5	52	13%

Coq au Vin

This is a hearty chicken stew. You can use any part of the chicken or a mixture of different parts, just be sure to remove all of the skin. To cut preparation time, you can use frozen or canned pearl onions and baby carrots.

SERVES 6

2 tablespoons olive oil
12 small pearl onions, peeled
3 ounces Canadian bacon, cut in thin strips
1/4 cup flour
6 chicken legs with thighs, skin removed
1 teaspoon garlic powder
1 teaspoon rosemary
1 teaspoon thyme
1/2 teaspoon ground black pepper
1/2 cup cognac
12 small new potatoes
6 medium carrots, sliced in
  1/2-inch rounds
4 stalks celery, sliced in 1/2-inch diagonals
1/4 cup tomato paste
1 1/2 cups chicken broth
1 cup good red wine
1 pound large mushrooms, cleaned and
  quartered
1 tablespoon arrowroot in 1/4 cup water

1. Heat 1 tablespoon olive oil in a large Dutch oven and brown the onions and Canadian bacon.

2. In a large bag, shake the flour, chicken, garlic powder, rosemary, thyme, and black pepper.

3. Remove the onion and Canadian bacon from the pan, add 1 tablespoon oil, and heat. Add the chicken and brown on both sides.

4. Add the cognac to the pan and stir to remove brown bits and cook until it all has evaporated.

5. Add the onions, Canadian bacon, potatoes, carrots, and celery.

Continued on page 144

Continued from page 143

Coq au Vin

6. Mix the tomato paste and chicken broth and pour over the chicken and vegetables. Bring to a boil.

7. Add the red wine, reduce to simmer. Cover and simmer for 1½ hours.

8. Add the mushrooms and simmer ½ hour more.

9. Mix 1 tablespoon arrowroot in the water and stir into the mixture. Cover until ready to serve.

Nutritional analysis per serving:

CALORIES	PROTEIN, GM.	CARBOHYDRATE, GM.	FAT, GM.	SATURATED FAT, GM.
731	40.2	95.1	15.1	3.4

SODIUM, MG.	CHOLESTEROL, MG.	FIBER, GM.	CALCIUM, MG.	CALORIES FROM FAT
343.1	94.5	14.4	145	19%

Mustard Chicken

Resealable bags are wonderful for marinating because they seal the flavor in the chicken. Be sure to throw out the marinade after use.

SERVES 6

½ cup Dijon mustard
¼ cup white wine vinegar
1 clove garlic, crushed
¼ teaspoon crushed thyme
6 chicken breast halves, skin removed

Sauce

1 tablespoon cornstarch
1 cup chicken broth
½ cup low-fat sour cream
¼ cup Dijon mustard

1. Combine the mustard, wine vinegar, garlic, and thyme. Pour over the chicken and marinate for 2 to 6 hours.

2. Grill or broil the chicken until done. Place on a serving platter and keep warm.

3. Make the sauce by mixing cornstarch into the chicken broth. Heat until thickened.

4. Stir in the sour cream and mustard.

5. Spoon the sauce over the chicken.

Nutritional analysis per serving:

CALORIES	PROTEIN, GM.	CARBOHYDRATE, GM.	FAT, GM.	SATURATED FAT, GM.
195	28.7	4.3	6.5	2.2

SODIUM, MG.	CHOLESTEROL, MG.	FIBER, GM.	CALCIUM, MG.	CALORIES FROM FAT
425	77	0.8	53	30%

Beef Provençal

This great one-dish meal is often referred to as Farmer's Stew in France.

SERVES 10

1 teaspoon dried orange rind
1½ cups dry red wine
1½ tablespoons dried thyme leaves
3 pounds boneless chuck, trimmed of all
   fat and cut in 1-inch cubes
¾ cup all-purpose flour
½ teaspoon ground black pepper
1 tablespoon olive oil
1 leek, washed, trimmed of root and top
   green, cut in rings
8 small white onions, peeled and cut in
   half
16 small new potatoes, scrubbed
1 clove garlic, crushed
1 can (1 pound 12 ounce) tomatoes,
   undrained
2 bay leaves
½ cup water
4 medium zucchini, cut in 1-inch slices
Chopped parsley

1. Mix the orange rind, wine, and thyme in a large bowl. Place the beef cubes in the bowl and toss to coat well. Marinate in the refrigerator for 2 to 3 hours.

2. Drain the marinade from the meat. Reserve the marinade.

3. Place ½ cup of the flour and the pepper in a plastic bag. Shake the beef cubes in the bag until they are covered.

4. Heat the olive oil in a large Dutch oven and brown the meat.

5. Place the leeks, onions, and potatoes in the Dutch oven and sauté for about 2 minutes. Stir constantly.

6. Mix the garlic, marinade, and tomatoes. Add the bay leaves and pour over the meat and vegetables.

7. Bake in a preheated oven at 300°F for 3 hours.

8. Mix ¼ cup flour with ½ cup water. Set aside.

Continued on page 147

Continued from page 146

Beef Provençal

9. Remove the Dutch oven from the oven. Add the flour mixture, and stir to thicken.

10. Stir the zucchini into the meat mixture. Bake for 30 minutes covered. Uncover and bake for another 10 minutes.

11. Sprinkle with chopped parsley.

Nutritional analysis per serving:

Calories	Protein, gm.	Carbohydrate, gm.	Fat, gm.	Saturated Fat, gm.
566	30.8	60.6	20.2	7.3

Sodium, mg.	Cholesterol, mg.	Fiber, gm.	Calcium, mg.	Calories from Fat
150.7	86.9	7.4	88	32%

Beef Stroganoff

This is quick, easy to prepare, and always a favorite when company comes to dinner. Serve with rice or noodles.

SERVES 6

1 pound beef sirloin steak, trimmed and cut in strips
1 cup low-salt beef broth
1/2 medium onion, thinly sliced
1 pound mushrooms, sliced
1/4 cup dry white vermouth
3 teaspoons cornstarch
1/4 teaspoon ground black pepper
1 cup low-fat sour cream

1. In a skillet sprayed with nonstick cooking spray, brown the meat on all sides on a high heat. Remove from the skillet, and set aside.

2. Heat 1/4 cup beef broth in the skillet. Add the onions. Cook until soft on a medium heat. Add the mushrooms. Cover and simmer for 5 minutes. Remove the cover and continue cooking until all of the liquid is absorbed, stirring constantly.

3. Add the vermouth. Bring quickly to boil, then reduce heat to simmer.

4. Mix the cornstarch in the beef broth. Add to the skillet, and stir until thickened.

5. Add the beef and black pepper, and gently stir in the sour cream.

Nutritional analysis per serving:

CALORIES	PROTEIN, GM.	CARBOHYDRATE, GM.	FAT, GM.	SATURATED FAT, GM.
222	15.4	7	13.8	6.2

SODIUM, MG.	CHOLESTEROL, MG.	FIBER, GM.	CALCIUM, MG.	CALORIES FROM FAT
173.5	53.8	1.1	36	11%

Pepper Steak

This sirloin steak can be barbecued for a casual Sunday afternoon or broiled and sliced for a formal Saturday dinner.

SERVES 6

2 pounds boneless sirloin steak
2 teaspoons coarsely ground black pepper
Parsley to garnish

1. Sprinkle both sides of the steak with pepper. Using a rolling pin, press it in well.

2. Barbecue or broil the steak until the desired doneness.

3. Let stand 10 minutes. Slice in thin slices. Garnish with parsley.

Nutritional analysis per serving:

CALORIES	PROTEIN, GM.	CARBOHYDRATE, GM.	FAT, GM.	SATURATED FAT, GM.
278	25.3	0.4	18.7	7.3

SODIUM, MG.	CHOLESTEROL, MG.	FIBER, GM.	CALCIUM, MG.	CALORIES FROM FAT
57.4	90.5	0.1	13	61%

Almond Cream

Almond Cream is a light, elegant dessert—and it's lovely served in wine glasses.

SERVES 6

1½ cups 1% milk
3 tablespoons cornstarch
1½ teaspoons pure vanilla extract
1½ teaspoons almond extract
2 egg whites
2 tablespoons sugar
¼ teaspoon cream of tartar
1½ teaspoons ground almonds

1. Combine the milk and cornstarch in a medium saucepan and cook over medium heat. Stir constantly until the mixture comes to a boil and thickens. Remove from the heat.

2. Stir in the vanilla, almond extract, and sugar.

3. Beat the egg whites, slowly adding the cream of tartar until stiff. Fold them into the milk mixture.

4. Divide the cream into six 4-ounce dessert dishes and sprinkle each one with ¼ teaspoon ground almonds.

Nutritional analysis per serving:

CALORIES	PROTEIN, GM.	CARBOHYDRATE, GM.	FAT, GM.	SATURATED FAT, GM.
73	3.3	11.2	1	0.4

SODIUM, MG.	CHOLESTEROL, MG.	FIBER, GM.	CALCIUM, MG.	CALORIES FROM FAT
49.4	2.5	0.1	78	12%

Crêpes

Almost anything can go into a crêpe and become an attractive, nourishing main course—sort of a French burrito. This basic recipe will make twelve 6-inch crêpes. You can make them ahead of time and freeze them. Put a sheet of wax paper between each one.

MAKES 12 CRÊPES

2 cups nonfat milk, cold
2 eggs
4 egg whites
2 cups unbleached white flour

1. Put the ingredients into a blender and blend at top speed for 1 minute, scraping down the sides of the blender. Cover and refrigerate for at least 2 hours.

2. Spray a 6½-to-7-inch skillet with a nonstick coating, and heat.

3. Pour ¼ cup batter into the skillet. Pick up the skillet and roll it around until the batter covers the bottom. Return the skillet to the heat for about 60 to 80 seconds. Then jerk and toss the skillet sharply back and forth to loosen the crêpe. Turn or flip the crêpe over and cook for 30 seconds. (If the crêpe seems too thick, add water, 1 tablespoon at a time.)

Nutritional analysis per serving:

CALORIES	PROTEIN, GM.	CARBOHYDRATE, GM.	FAT, GM.	SATURATED FAT, GM.
102	5.6	16.8	1.1	0.3

SODIUM, MG.	CHOLESTEROL, MG.	FIBER, GM.	CALCIUM, MG.	CALORIES FROM FAT
49.8	35.8	0.5	58	10%

Floating Island

The Floating Island is an elegant dessert, yet it is very light and low in calories. So enjoy it the Guiltless way.

SERVES 6

Custard

1½ cups 1% milk
1 tablespoon sugar
1 tablespoon cornstarch
½ teaspoon orange rind
1 teaspoon pure orange extract
½ teaspoon pure vanilla extract

1. Heat the milk, sugar, and cornstarch in a saucepan over a medium heat until it comes to a boil. Remove from the heat.

2. Stir in the orange rind, orange extract, and vanilla. Chill.

Continued on page 153

Continued from page 152

Floating Island

Meringue

4 egg whites (at room temperature)
1/8 teaspoon cream of tartar
1/4 cup sugar
1 can (10 1/2 ounces) mandarin oranges,
  packed in water
Fresh mint to garnish
Custard

1. Beat the egg whites with the cream of tartar until foamy. Continue beating at high speed. Slowly add the sugar until stiff peaks form when the beater is raised slowly.

2. Spoon the mixture into a 5-cup mold that has been sprayed with vegetable spray. Press down to remove air pockets.

3. Place the mold in a water bath (a baking pan with boiling water 2 inches deep) and bake in a preheated oven at 350°F for 25 minutes, or until a knife inserted in the center comes out clean.

4. Cool on a rack for 5 minutes.

5. Spoon the chilled custard into a serving bowl. Loosen the edge of the mold with a spatula and unmold the meringue on the custard.

6. Place orange slices around the meringue. Garnish with fresh mint, and serve.

Nutritional analysis per serving:

CALORIES	PROTEIN, GM.	CARBOHYDRATE, GM.	FAT, GM.	SATURATED FAT, GM.
101	4.7	19.6	0.7	0.4

SODIUM, MG.	CHOLESTEROL, MG.	FIBER, GM.	CALCIUM, MG.	CALORIES FROM FAT
69.8	2.5	0.4	83	6%

Pears à la Cream

You can use any fruit preserve of purée in this, or you could even place some chocolate sauce in the center of the pear.

SERVES 8

8 canned pear halves, packed in water
4 teaspoons raspberry preserves
Almond Cream (omit the chopped
  almonds) (page 150)

1. In a dessert dish, place each pear half with ½ teaspoon preserves in the center.

2. Spoon the Almond Cream over each one.

3. Chill until ready to serve.

Nutritional analysis per serving:

CALORIES	PROTEIN, GM.	CARBOHYDRATE, GM.	FAT, GM.	SATURATED FAT, GM.
158	3.1	35.6	1.2	0.3

SODIUM, MG.	CHOLESTEROL, MG.	FIBER, GM.	CALCIUM, MG.	CALORIES FROM FAT
38.4	1.8	4.3	76	7%

Strawberry Crêpes

Frozen strawberries or any other frozen berries will work nicely as well. Add a tablespoon of a fruit liqueur or cognac for a very French taste!

SERVES 4

2 tablespoons sugar
2 teaspoons cornstarch
1 quart fresh strawberries, hulled and halved
½ cup water
4 crêpes (page 151)

1. Mix the sugar, cornstarch, and water. Cook over a medium heat until bubbly and thickened. Cool slightly.

2. Pour the mixture over the strawberries and mix carefully.

3. Place each crêpe on a serving dish. Place a quarter of the strawberry mixture in the middle of each crêpe. Fold over each side, and then turn the crêpe over so the seam is down.

4. Garnish with a little strawberry filling over the center of the crêpe.

Nutritional analysis per serving:

CALORIES	PROTEIN, GM.	CARBOHYDRATE, GM.	FAT, GM.	SATURATED FAT, GM.
63	1.7	14.2	0.2	0.04

SODIUM, MG.	CHOLESTEROL, MG.	FIBER, GM.	CALCIUM, MG.	CALORIES FROM FAT
20.4	3.2	1.2	15	2%

German Cuisine

Introduction

The German people enjoy an exciting cuisine. The northern Germans eat different fare than the Bavarians, but they all enjoy potatoes and bread cooked or baked in various ways. Sausages and sauerkraut are common, but I avoided them in this section because of their fat and sodium content. Some specialty companies make delicious lower fat, lower salt versions, so look around and you may find some treats to accompany your potato pancakes, spaetzle, or dumplings.

Germans love celebrations, especially the famous fall Oktoberfest. People from villages, towns, and cities gather to enjoy good food, good music, and lots of beer. Plan your own Oktoberfest party. Put on some oompah music, some polkas, and have a ball. Be sure to serve beer (regular, light, or nonalcoholic). Here's a sample menu.

Soup
> Split-Pea Soup

Main Course
> Sauerbraten
>
> Potato Dumplings
>
> Red Cabbage with Apples
>
> Fresh Rye Bread (from your bakery)

Side Dishes
> Cabbage Rolls
>
> Wiener Schnitzel

Dessert
> Homemade Applesauce

And, don't forget the music!

Cabbage Soup with Meatballs

This is a great first course or a meal for two. You can also add cubed potatoes.

SERVES 6

4 cups low-salt beef broth
1/2 head green cabbage, coarsely chopped
3 carrots, washed and scraped, cut into 1/4-inch slices
1 turnip, peeled and cut into small chunks
1 leek, white part only, thinly sliced
1 can (5 1/2 ounces) vegetable juice
1/2 recipe Swedish Meatballs (page 323)

1. In a large pot combine the beef broth, cabbage, carrots, turnip, leek, and vegetable juice. Bring to a boil, then reduce heat and simmer.

2. Add the meatballs to the simmering pot and heat through.

3. Serve in large soup bowls, over rice or noodles if desired.

Nutritional analysis per serving:

CALORIES	PROTEIN, GM.	CARBOHYDRATE, GM.	FAT, GM.	SATURATED FAT, GM.
131	11.9	12.6	3.7	1.4

SODIUM, MG.	CHOLESTEROL, MG.	FIBER, GM.	CALCIUM, MG.	CALORIES FROM FAT
391.2	26.2	2.6	54	25%

Chicken and Barley Soup

On a cold winter night serve up a big bowl of this soup as you sit by the fire. It is truly comfort food.

SERVES 6

4 chicken breasts, skinless, bone in
3 quarts cold water
2 carrots, coarsely chopped
2 celery stalks with leaves, coarsely
  chopped
1 parsnip, coarsely chopped
1 onion, peeled and pierced with whole
  cloves
Ground fresh pepper
1 pound mushrooms, quartered
½ cup pearl barley, rinsed
1 teaspoon low-salt chicken paste
½ cup boiling water
2 tablespoons parsley, finely chopped

1. Combine the chicken breasts, cold water, carrots, celery, parsnip, onion, and a few grinds of fresh pepper in a large pot.

2. Bring to a boil, then reduce to a simmer. Let it simmer, partially covered, for about 30 minutes.

3. Add the mushrooms and barley to the pot. Mix the chicken paste in the hot water and stir into the soup. Stir occasionally and simmer half-covered for about 1 hour or until the barley and mushrooms are tender.

4. Remove the chicken breasts from the soup. Allow to cool slightly and remove meat from bones. Chop the meat coarsely and return it to the simmering soup. Discard the onion, stir in the parsley, and serve.

Nutritional analysis per serving:

CALORIES	PROTEIN, GM.	CARBOHYDRATE, GM.	FAT, GM.	SATURATED FAT, GM.
218	22	27.4	2.8	0.7

SODIUM, MG.	CHOLESTEROL, MG.	FIBER, GM.	CALCIUM, MG.	CALORIES FROM FAT
73.1	48.5	6.1	49	11%

Hot German Potato Salad

Yukon Gold potatoes also work very well in this potato salad. They are particularly nice because they are yellow in color and have a creamy texture.

SERVES 6

4 medium-size red potatoes, scrubbed
   but not peeled
2 tablespoons butter
1/2 cup onion, finely chopped
1/4 cup white vinegar
2 tablespoons cider vinegar
1/4 cup water
Freshly ground black pepper
2 tablespoons parsley, finely chopped
1/4 teaspoon celery seed

1. Boil or steam potatoes until just done; do not overcook. Drain. Allow the potatoes to cool slightly, then slice into 1/4-inch slices into a large serving bowl.

2. Heat the butter in a nonstick pan and add the onions. Cook just until soft and transparent.

3. Stir in both vinegars, the water, pepper, parsley, and celery seed. Stir and cook for about 2 more minutes.

4. Pour the sauce over the hot potatoes. Stir gently and serve.

Nutritional analysis per serving:

CALORIES	PROTEIN, GM.	CARBOHYDRATE, GM.	FAT, GM.	SATURATED FAT, GM.
106	1.6	16.5	4.2	2.5

SODIUM, MG.	CHOLESTEROL, MG.	FIBER, GM.	CALCIUM, MG.	CALORIES FROM FAT
46.4	10.9	1.7	15	36%

Leek Salad

Here is an interesting way to use leeks. The pickled beets add good flavor as well as color to the otherwise white salad.

SERVES 6

6 firm, fresh leeks, 1 to 1½ inches in
  diameter
¼ cup low-calorie sour cream
¼ cup cider vinegar
1 teaspoon German-style mustard
1 teaspoon bottled horseradish
Freshly ground black pepper
Lettuce
Pickled beets for garnish

1. To prepare the leeks, cut the roots off and strip away any old outer leaves. Line up the leeks and cut off the green tops until each leek is 6 to 7 inches long. Rinse well.

2. Lay the leeks flat in a steamer and steam for 3 to 5 minutes, or until they show a slight resistance when pierced with a fork. Do not overcook.

3. Drain leeks well, reserving ¼ cup of the liquid. Arrange them in a serving dish or deep platter.

4. Combine the cooking liquid with the sour cream, vinegar, mustard, horseradish, and pepper. Mix well, pour over the leeks, and chill.

5. To serve, arrange the leeks on a bed of lettuce and garnish with pickled beets.

Nutritional analysis per serving:

CALORIES	PROTEIN, GM.	CARBOHYDRATE, GM.	FAT, GM.	SATURATED FAT, GM.
78	1.9	15.8	1.5	0.7

SODIUM, MG.	CHOLESTEROL, MG.	FIBER, GM.	CALCIUM, MG.	CALORIES FROM FAT
36.7	2.3	1.9	71	17%

Split-Pea Soup

The always pleasing and healthful split-pea soup can be a meal in itself. Serve it with bread and a big salad, or serve it in small cups as a start to a great meal.

SERVES 6

1 pound split peas, green or yellow
5 cups water
1 onion, chopped
2 carrots, chopped
1/2 teaspoon marjoram
1/2 teaspoon thyme
Freshly ground black pepper

1. Rinse the peas in a strainer and put them into a soup kettle. Add the water and bring to a boil. Skim off any foam that rises to the top.

2. Boil the peas for 2 to 3 minutes. Then cover the pot, turn off the heat, and let stand for 1 hour.

3. Bring the peas back up to a simmer. Add the onions, carrots, and herbs. Stir in a few grinds of pepper. Bring to a boil, then reduce heat to simmer, covering partially.

4. Simmer for about 1 1/4 hours or until the peas are soft but not falling apart.

Nutritional analysis per serving:

CALORIES	PROTEIN, GM.	CARBOHYDRATE, GM.	FAT, GM.	SATURATED FAT, GM.
284	19.4	51.8	1	0.1

SODIUM, MG.	CHOLESTEROL, MG.	FIBER, GM.	CALCIUM, MG.	CALORIES FROM FAT
13.6	0.0	10.6	44	3%

Colcannon | *A great way to use up leftovers!*

SERVES 8

1 onion, minced
½ cup nonfat milk
2 medium potatoes, boiled
2 parsnips, boiled
2 tablespoons butter
Freshly ground pepper
1 cup cabbage, shredded and cooked
1 tablespoon parsley, minced

1. Cook the onions in the milk until tender.

2. Mash the potatoes and parsnips together; add butter and pepper.

3. Add onions and milk slowly, beating well.

4. Stir in the cabbage and garnish with parsley.

Nutritional analysis per serving:

CALORIES	PROTEIN, GM.	CARBOHYDRATE, GM.	FAT, GM.	SATURATED FAT, GM.
99	2	16.5	3.3	1.9

SODIUM, MG.	CHOLESTEROL, MG.	FIBER, GM.	CALCIUM, MG.	CALORIES FROM FAT
48.8	8.5	2.9	48	30%

Dilled Carrots in Beer

I like to slice the carrots on the diagonal so they're fairly thin or julienne them with a slicer.

SERVES 4

1 tablespoon brown sugar
¼ cup beer
¼ teaspoon dillweed
½ pound carrots, sliced, and steamed

1. Place the brown sugar in the bottom of a heavy saucepan. Allow it to melt slowly over medium heat, stirring constantly. Watch carefully until it just begins to caramelize or turn a light brown color.

2. Carefully add the beer to the pan. Stir in the dillweed and cooked carrots. Stir to coat the carrots and heat through.

Nutritional analysis per serving:

CALORIES	PROTEIN, GM.	CARBOHYDRATE, GM.	FAT, GM.	SATURATED FAT, GM.
48	0.7	10.3	0.1	0.02

SODIUM, MG.	CHOLESTEROL, MG.	FIBER, GM.	CALCIUM, MG.	CALORIES FROM FAT
22.5	0.0	1.9	21	2%

Garlic Vegetable Medley

Steam the vegetables to crisp-tender so they have a nice texture and hold their shape.

SERVES 4

1 clove garlic, minced
¼ cup chicken broth
½ head fresh cauliflower, broken into flowerets, steamed
1 large zucchini, sliced and steamed
2 carrots, sliced and steamed
2 tablespoons Parmesan cheese

1. Spray a skillet with nonstick cooking spray. Heat the skillet to medium-hot and add the garlic. Cook, stirring often, until the garlic just begins to brown.

2. Add the chicken broth to the skillet, then add the steamed vegetables.

3. Cover the pan and let the vegetables cook just long enough to heat through. Remove the cover and sprinkle on the Parmesan cheese. Cover again, just long enough to melt the cheese. Serve.

Nutritional analysis per serving:

CALORIES	PROTEIN, GM.	CARBOHYDRATE, GM.	FAT, GM.	SATURATED FAT, GM.
41	2.3	6.5	1	0.5

SODIUM, MG.	CHOLESTEROL, MG.	FIBER, GM.	CALCIUM, MG.	CALORIES FROM FAT
50.5	2	2.1	62	23%

Hungarian Noodle Bake

This noodle bake is a good side dish or a perfect main dish for a meatless meal.

SERVES 6

4 ounces noodles, dry
1 cup nonfat cottage cheese
½ cup reduced-calorie sour cream
½ cup nonfat yogurt
¼ cup onion, finely chopped
1 clove garlic, minced
½ teaspoon cayenne pepper
1 tablespoon poppy seeds
Freshly ground pepper
Paprika
2 tablespoons Parmesan cheese

1. Preheat the oven to 350°F.

2. Cook the noodles in boiling water until just tender. Drain.

3. Combine the cottage cheese, sour cream, yogurt, onion, garlic, cayenne pepper, and poppy seeds. Stir to mix and add a few grinds of black pepper.

4. Mix the noodles with the cottage cheese mixture. Pour into a square baking dish, sprinkle with paprika, and bake uncovered for 25 to 30 minutes.

5. Just before removing from the oven, sprinkle with Parmesan cheese. Serve.

Nutritional analysis per serving:

CALORIES	PROTEIN, GM.	CARBOHYDRATE, GM.	FAT, GM.	SATURATED FAT, GM.
96	7.9	7.6	2.5	1.9

SODIUM, MG.	CHOLESTEROL, MG.	FIBER, GM.	CALCIUM, MG.	CALORIES FROM FAT
206.3	11.9	0.7	124	36%

Potato Dumplings

These are great served with Chicken and Barley Soup (page 162). You can poach them in the soup instead of steaming them; just add about 1 extra cup of chicken broth to the soup.

SERVES 6

⅔ cup mashed potato
1 cup flour
4 teaspoons baking powder
2 teaspoons oil
½ cup milk (plus or minus 1 to
  2 tablespoons)

1. Combine all of the ingredients into a dough, the consistency of biscuit dough. Roll out the dough until it's about ½ inch thick.

2. Cut into 12 biscuit-shaped pieces using a 2-inch biscuit cutter.

3. Spray a large steamer basket with nonstick cooking spray and place over boiling water. Carefully lay the dumplings into the steamer basket.

4. Cover and steam about 12 minutes or until done.

Nutritional analysis per serving:

CALORIES	PROTEIN, GM.	CARBOHYDRATE, GM.	FAT, GM.	SATURATED FAT, GM.
120	3.1	19.8	3	0.6

SODIUM, MG.	CHOLESTEROL, MG.	FIBER, GM.	CALCIUM, MG.	CALORIES FROM FAT
359.2	1.2	0.8	202	23%

Potato Pancakes

These are good as a side dish or served with Homemade Applesauce (page 191).

SERVES 4

2 medium-size baking potatoes
2 egg whites
¼ cup onion, finely grated
¼ cup flour

1. Peel the potatoes, dropping each one into a bowl of cold water to prevent discoloring.

2. In a large mixing bowl, beat the egg whites. Add the onion and gradually beat in the flour.

3. Pat the potatoes dry and grate coarsely into a sieve or colander. Press each potato down firmly into the sieve to squeeze out as much moisture as possible. Add immediately to the egg and onion batter.

4. Preheat the oven to 250°F. Spray nonstick cooking spray into a heavy skillet, heat until very hot, then pour ¼ cup of the potato mixture into the skillet. Flatten the mixture with a spatula into a pancake about 5 inches in diameter. Cook for about 2 minutes on each side.

Continued on page 172

Continued from page 171

Potato Pancakes

5. When the pancake is golden brown and crisp around the edges, transfer it to an ovenproof dish and keep in the warm oven.

6. Continue making pancakes as described, adding a little more nonstick spray to the skillet as needed and allowing it to heat before adding more batter.

Nutritional analysis per serving:

CALORIES	PROTEIN, GM.	CARBOHYDRATE, GM.	FAT, GM.	SATURATED FAT, GM.
93	3.7	19.2	0.2	0.03

SODIUM, MG.	CHOLESTEROL, MG.	FIBER, GM.	CALCIUM, MG.	CALORIES FROM FAT
30.6	0.0	1.6	9	2%

Red Cabbage with Apples

This is pretty and tangy, and very low in calories. The fat calories come from the butter, so you can cut the butter back to 1 tablespoon or use butter buds.

SERVES 8

Small head red cabbage
2/3 cup red wine vinegar
2 tablespoons sugar
2 tablespoons butter
2 medium cooking apples, cored and cut into chunks
1/2 cup onion, finely chopped
1 whole onion, peeled and pierced with 2 whole cloves
1 bay leaf
1 cup boiling water
3 tablespoons dry red wine (optional)

1. Wash the cabbage well and remove any tough outer leaves. Cut the cabbage into quarters. Shred the cabbage into 1/8-inch-wide strips by hand or using a food processor.

2. Place the cabbage into a large mixing bowl. Add the vinegar and sugar, and toss evenly to coat the shreds.

3. In a heavy casserole heat the butter, and add the apples and chopped onion. Cook, stirring frequently, for 5 minutes or until the apples are lightly browned.

Continued on page 174

Continued from page 173

Red Cabbage with Apples

4. Add the cabbage, whole onion with cloves, bay leaf, and boiling water to the casserole. Stir to mix well. Bring it to a boil, then cover, reduce to a simmer, and cook for 1½ to 2 hours. Check occasionally to see if the cabbage is too dry. If it is, add a little hot water. When the cabbage is done, there should be almost no liquid left in the casserole.

5. Remove the whole onion and the bay leaf. Stir in the red wine, if desired. Serve.

Nutritional analysis per serving:

CALORIES	PROTEIN, GM.	CARBOHYDRATE, GM.	FAT, GM.	SATURATED FAT, GM.
77	0.5	12	3.2	1.9

SODIUM, MG.	CHOLESTEROL, MG.	FIBER, GM.	CALCIUM, MG.	CALORIES FROM FAT
33.9	8.2	1.4	15	38%

Spaetzle

Spaetzle is wonderful with stews and soups.

SERVES 6

1½ cups all-purpose flour
¼ teaspoon ground nutmeg
1 whole egg
2 egg whites
½ cup nonfat milk
2 quarts water

1. In a mixing bowl, combine the flour and nutmeg.

2. Beat the whole egg and egg whites together, pour them into the flour mixture, and stir to mix well.

3. Pour the milk into the mixture in a thin stream, stirring constantly with a large spoon. Stir until the dough is smooth.

4. Bring 2 quarts of water to a boil. Set a large colander over the pot. Slowly pour the dough into the colander, pressing it through the holes and into the water.

5. When all of the dough has dropped into the water, remove colander. Stir the dumplings gently to prevent them from sticking. Boil briskly until tender (5 to 8 minutes). Remove the spaetzle from the water with a slotted spoon.

Nutritional analysis per serving:

CALORIES	PROTEIN, GM.	CARBOHYDRATE, GM.	FAT, GM.	SATURATED FAT, GM.
131	5.9	23.2	1.2	0.4

SODIUM, MG.	CHOLESTEROL, MG.	FIBER, GM.	CALCIUM, MG.	CALORIES FROM FAT
39.5	35.4	0.7	35	8%

Sweet and Sour Red Cabbage

This dish is better made a day ahead and heated or served cold.

SERVES 4

4 cups fresh red cabbage, coarsely grated
1/2 cup chicken broth
1 small onion, chopped
1/4 cup lemon juice
1/2 cup fresh orange juice
2 tablespoons apple juice concentrate
1 tablespoon cornstarch or arrowroot

1. Steam the cabbage until tender, about 3 to 5 minutes.

2. In a nonstick skillet reduce 1/4 cup chicken broth to 1 tablespoon. Add the onion and sauté until tender.

3. Mix the lemon juice, orange juice, apple juice, remaining broth, and cornstarch until the cornstarch dissolves.

4. Pour the mixture into the skillet and stir until it comes to a boil and thickens.

5. Add the cabbage and toss until it is well coated.

6. Put into a covered container and refrigerate several hours or overnight if possible.

Nutritional analysis per serving:

CALORIES	PROTEIN, GM.	CARBOHYDRATE, GM.	FAT, GM.	SATURATED FAT, GM.
58	1.8	13.2	0.3	0.1

SODIUM, MG.	CHOLESTEROL, MG.	FIBER, GM.	CALCIUM, MG.	CALORIES FROM FAT
115.1	0.0	2.9	45	5%

Whitefish and Potatoes

Choose a firm, thick whitefish for this dish. If the fish is thin, it will cook more quickly, so be sure to keep an eye on it.

SERVES 6

4 medium or 8 small red potatoes, scrubbed, not peeled

1½ pounds firm, fresh whitefish fillets

Juice of 1 lemon

¼ cup vegetable or fish broth

1 cup onion, finely chopped

3 tablespoons German-style or prepared hot mustard

Fresh parsley to garnish

1 tablespoon chopped chives or green onion tops, minced

1. Preheat the oven to 350°F.

2. Place the potatoes in enough water to cover them. Boil until just cooked (do not overcook).

3. Rinse the fish fillets under running water and pat dry with paper towels. Sprinkle both sides with lemon juice and let rest for 10 minutes.

4. Dip the fillets into 2 tablespoons broth, turning to coat thoroughly. Arrange them side by side in a baking dish. Sprinkle the onions on top and bake for 12 to 15 minutes, or until the fish is firm and opaque.

Continued on page 178

Continued from page 177

Whitefish and Potatoes

5. Heat a deep serving platter. Drain and cool the potatoes slightly, then slice them crosswise into 1/4-inch-thick rounds. Arrange the potato slices, overlapping in a circular manner, on the heated serving platter.

6. Place the baked fish on top of the potatoes. Mix the remaining liquid from the fish with about 2 tablespoons broth and the mustard. Heat quickly and pour over the top of the fish and potatoes.

7. Garnish with parsley or chives. Serve immediately.

Nutritional analysis per serving:

CALORIES	PROTEIN, GM.	CARBOHYDRATE, GM.	FAT, GM.	SATURATED FAT, GM.
179	23.5	16.5	1.8	0.3

SODIUM, MG.	CHOLESTEROL, MG.	FIBER, GM.	CALCIUM, MG.	CALORIES FROM FAT
221.9	54.5	2	38	9%

Chicken Paprikash

If you want to spice this up a bit, use hot Hungarian paprika. This is excellent served with Spaetzle (page 175) instead of rice.

SERVES 4

2 tablespoons butter
1 onion, finely chopped
1 tablespoon paprika
1½ cups chicken broth
4 chicken breast halves, boned and skinned
1 tablespoon flour
1 cup reduced-calorie sour cream
2 cups rice, cooked

1. Spray a heavy skillet with nonstick cooking spray. Melt the butter, and add the onions. Sauté until the onions are cooked. Stir in the paprika.

2. Slowly add the chicken broth and heat to a boil. Immediately reduce heat to a simmer, add the chicken breasts. Cover, and simmer gently for about 20 minutes, or until the chicken is cooked through.

3. Mix the flour with the sour cream. Stir it slowly into the chicken mixture, never allowing it to boil. Stir until slightly thickened.

4. Serve over cooked rice.

Nutritional analysis per serving:

CALORIES	PROTEIN, GM.	CARBOHYDRATE, GM.	FAT, GM.	SATURATED FAT, GM.
412	31.8	33.6	15.8	8.6

SODIUM, MG.	CHOLESTEROL, MG.	FIBER, GM.	CALCIUM, MG.	CALORIES FROM FAT
237.4	101.8	1.1	72	34%

German Chicken

This chicken is perfect served with Spaetzle (page 175) or boiled red potatoes.

SERVES 4

4 chicken breasts, skinless
1 teaspoon paprika
1 small head green cabbage, cored and cut into 1/2-inch wedges
1 medium onion, sliced
2 cooking apples, cored and sliced into rings
2 teaspoons caraway seeds
1 tablespoon flour
1/2 cup reduced-calorie sour cream

1. Preheat the oven to 350°F.

2. Spray an ovenproof skillet with nonstick cooking spray. Sprinkle the chicken breasts with the paprika and brown on both sides in the heated skillet. Remove the chicken to a platter.

3. Add the cabbage, onion, apples, and caraway seeds to the skillet. Cook for several minutes until the vegetables are softened but not fully cooked.

4. Place the chicken breasts on top of the cabbage mixture, cover, and bake for 45 minutes. Remove from the oven.

5. Combine the flour with the sour cream. Remove the chicken to a warm platter, stir the sour cream mixture slowly into vegetables and juices. Heat gently if it needs to thicken slightly.

Nutritional analysis per serving:

CALORIES	PROTEIN, GM.	CARBOHYDRATE, GM.	FAT, GM.	SATURATED FAT, GM.
238	28.1	16.6	6.6	2.8

SODIUM, MG.	CHOLESTEROL, MG.	FIBER, GM.	CALCIUM, MG.	CALORIES FROM FAT
75.6	79.1	2.8	56	25%

Beef Roulade

Try serving this with a red cabbage dish and the Garlic Vegetable Medley (page 168) for interesting colors and flavors.

SERVES 6

1½ pounds flank steak, trimmed and pounded to ¼ inch thick
6 teaspoons German-style mustard
¼ cup onion, finely chopped
Celery stalks
2 cups water
1 cup celery, coarsely chopped
¼ cup leeks, white part only, thinly sliced
1 parsnip, small, scraped, finely chopped
3 sprigs parsley
2 tablespoons flour

1. Cut the pounded meat into rectangular pieces about 4 inches wide and 8 inches long. Spread each rectangle with mustard, sprinkle with onion, and lay a strip of celery across the narrow end.

2. Roll up each piece like a jelly roll. Secure each roll by piercing with a skewer or a toothpick or by tying with a piece of twine.

3. Spray a heavy skillet with nonstick cooking spray, and heat to a moderate heat. Add the beef rolls and slowly brown on all sides. Transfer the rolls to a plate.

4. Pour water into the skillet and bring to a boil. Add the chopped celery, leeks, parsnip, and parsley, and return the beef to the skillet.

5. Cover the skillet and reduce the heat. Simmer for 1 hour or until the meat seems very tender. Turn the rolls once or twice during the cooking period. Heat a platter. Transfer the rolls to the heated platter and cover while making the sauce.

6. Strain the cooking liquid through a fine sieve, pressing hard on the vegetables before discarding them. Measure the liquid, return it to skillet, and boil it briskly until it is reduced to 2 cups. Remove from the heat.

Continued on page 182

Continued from page 181

Beef Roulade

7. In a small bowl mix the flour and ¼ cup water. Gradually add the mixture to the hot liquid, stirring with a whisk until the sauce is smooth and thick. Strain if necessary.

8. Return the sauce and Roulade to the skillet. Simmer over a low heat just long enough for the rolls to heat through.

Nutritional analysis per serving:

CALORIES	PROTEIN, GM.	CARBOHYDRATE, GM.	FAT, GM.	SATURATED FAT, GM.
268	34.7	9.3	9.4	3.5

SODIUM, MG.	CHOLESTEROL, MG.	FIBER, GM.	CALCIUM, MG.	CALORIES FROM FAT
161.4	90.8	1.8	39	32%

Cabbage Rolls

Cabbage rolls are a popular dish. You can easily make these with ground turkey or chicken.

SERVES 4

1 head cabbage
1 pound extra-lean ground beef (or any
  lean ground meat)
½ cup onion, finely chopped
1 teaspoon chopped fresh parsley
1 teaspoon thyme
1 clove garlic, minced
Dash of cayenne pepper
½ cup reduced-salt beef stock, boiling

Sauce
4 fresh tomatoes, diced
¼ cup onion, finely chopped
½ teaspoon thyme
¼ cup carrot, grated (1 small carrot)

1. In a large pot bring several cups of water to a boil. Remove the stem portion from the head of cabbage and drop the entire head into the boiling water for a few seconds. Carefully remove one leaf at a time. After you have removed 8 leaves, take the rest of the cabbage out of the water. Return the 8 leaves to the boiling water and blanch for about 2 minutes.

2. Remove the leaves, drain, and plunge into cold water to stop the cooking process. When cooled, set the leaves aside to drain.

3. Preheat the oven to 350°F.

4. Combine the ground beef with the onion, parsley, thyme, garlic, and cayenne pepper. Mix well; then divide into 8 equal parts.

5. Place a cooked cabbage leaf on a flat surface. Place one portion of the raw meat mixture in the center and fold up the bottom part. Next, fold over the sides and top to make a neat package. Continue with the rest of the leaves and the meat mixture.

6. Place the cabbage rolls into a ovenproof casserole. Pour the boiling broth over the rolls and cover. Bake 50 to 60 minutes.

Continued on page 184

Continued from page 183

Cabbage Rolls

7. While the rolls are baking, prepare the sauce. Combine the sauce ingredients in a skillet sprayed with nonstick cooking spray. Cover, and let cook slowly while the rolls are in the oven.

8. For the last 10 minutes of baking, add the sauce to the rolls, cover, and finish baking. Serve.

Nutritional analysis per serving:

CALORIES	PROTEIN, GM.	CARBOHYDRATE, GM.	FAT, GM.	SATURATED FAT, GM.
226	25.7	10.3	9.2	3.3

SODIUM, MG.	CHOLESTEROL, MG.	FIBER, GM.	CALCIUM, MG.	CALORIES FROM FAT
86.1	77	2.9	33	36%

Fruited Pork Tenderloin

Cooking the tenderloin in a plastic cooking bag keeps the juices in and browns the meat.

SERVES 6

2 pounds pork tenderloin
Plastic cooking bag
1 apple, cored and cut into rings
8 dried prunes
8 dried apricot halves
1 teaspoon rosemary (sprig of fresh rosemary
¼ cup dry white wine (or dry vermouth)

1. Preheat the oven to 325°F.

2. Remove the tenderloin from the package, rinse, and pat dry. Follow the package directions for preparing the plastic cooking bag. Place the pork into the bag and put it into a medium-size roasting pan.

3. Place the apple rings, prunes, and apricots decoratively onto the pork. Sprinkle the rosemary on top. Add the wine if desired. Secure the bag and roast for about 1½ hours or until the pork reaches 185°F internal temperature.

4. Carefully remove the pork and fruit from the bag and set it onto a platter. Carve into thin slices and serve.

Nutritional analysis per serving:

CALORIES	PROTEIN, GM.	CARBOHYDRATE, GM.	FAT, GM.	SATURATED FAT, GM.
191	21.3	13.3	4.7	1.6

SODIUM, MG.	CHOLESTEROL, MG.	FIBER, GM.	CALCIUM, MG.	CALORIES FROM FAT
43	58.9	1.6	16	22%

Pork Chops with Potatoes

Using bone-in pork chops adds more flavor to this dish and keeps the meat moist.

SERVES 4

1 cup Basic White Sauce (page 109)
¼ cup vermouth
4 lean thick loin chops, trimmed, with
  bone
4 small to medium potatoes, scrubbed
  and sliced
Paprika
Chopped fresh parsley

1. Preheat the oven to 350°F.

2. Make the White Sauce according to directions, adding the vermouth
   at the end. Stir to mix well and set aside.

3. Spray a heavy skillet with nonstick cooking spray. Brown the chops on
   both sides, then layer the sliced potatoes on top. Pour the White
   Sauce over the potatoes. Cover and bake for 1 hour.

4. Sprinkle with the paprika and parsley to garnish.

Nutritional analysis per serving:

CALORIES	PROTEIN, GM.	CARBOHYDRATE, GM.	FAT, GM.	SATURATED FAT, GM.
301	23.2	25.4	9.8	4.4

SODIUM, MG.	CHOLESTEROL, MG.	FIBER, GM.	CALCIUM, MG.	CALORIES FROM FAT
111.6	61.9	1.9	98	29%

Sauerbraten

This traditional German recipe is often served on special occasions. You'll need 2 to 3 days to marinate the roast and about 2 hours to cook it. Sauerbraten is delicious served with Potato Dumplings (page 170) or boiled potatoes and red cabbage.

SERVES 6

2 pounds lean rump roast, trimmed of
  any fat
½ cup red wine vinegar
½ cup cider vinegar
1 medium onion, thinly sliced
Freshly ground black pepper
1 bay leaf
½ teaspoon ground allspice
4 whole cloves
1 carrot, sliced
1 stalk celery, sliced
6 gingersnaps, crushed

1. In a glass or ceramic bowl, combine the vinegars, onion, several grinds of pepper, bay leaf, allspice, cloves, carrot, and celery.

2. Rinse the roast, pat it dry, and add it to the marinade. Cover tightly and refrigerate for 2 to 3 days, turning once or twice a day.

3. Remove the meat and pat it dry. Strain the marinade and reserve it. Heat a Dutch oven or heavy kettle that has been sprayed with nonstick cooking spray. Add the roast and brown on all sides.

4. Pour in the reserved marinade and simmer, covered, for about 2 hours, or until roast is tender.

5. Remove the roast to a heated platter. Remove any fat from the liquid in Dutch oven. Bring the liquid to a boil.

Continued on page 188

Continued from page 187

Sauerbraten

6. Add the gingersnap crumbs to the liquid and boil gently for about 5 minutes until the liquid is slightly thickened.

7. To serve, cut the meat into very thin slices and place on individual plates or on a serving platter. Ladle the sauce on top.

Nutritional analysis per serving:

CALORIES	PROTEIN, GM.	CARBOHYDRATE, GM.	FAT, GM.	SATURATED FAT, GM.
428	42.5	9.7	23.4	9

SODIUM, MG.	CHOLESTEROL, MG.	FIBER, GM.	CALCIUM, MG.	CALORIES FROM FAT
144.7	125.7	1.1	39	49%

Wiener Schnitzel

There are many variations for schnitzel. Usually bread[ ]is the first step. This version gives a similar taste and ap[ ]without the added fat. You can also use pork tenderloin[ ]breast; just pound them out so they are thin.

SERVES 4

1 medium onion, thinly sliced
1 clove garlic, minced
1 to 2 teaspoons paprika
2 tablespoons flour
1 pound veal cutlets (scaloppini cut)

1. Spray a skillet with nonstick cooking spray and heat to a medium temperature. Sauté the onions and garlic until soft.

2. Combine the paprika and flour. Sprinkle over the veal cutlets and pound the cutlets with a meat mallet or the side of a cleaver.

3. Add the cutlets to the pan with the onions and garlic. Reduce heat slightly if necessary and brown cutlets well on both sides (cutlets cook quickly).

4. Serve on a plate with the onion and garlic mixture on top.

Nutritional analysis per serving:

CALORIES	PROTEIN, GM.	CARBOHYDRATE, GM.	FAT, GM.	SATURATED FAT, GM.
190	21.3	5.7	8.6	3.5

SODIUM, MG.	CHOLESTEROL, MG.	FIBER, GM.	CALCIUM, MG.	CALORIES FROM FAT
51.7	76.3	0.7	17	41%

Carrot Bread | *You may add raisins and chopped nuts for a little variety.*

SERVES 8

¾ cup brown sugar
¼ cup oil
½ cup plain nonfat yogurt
1 teaspoon vanilla
4 egg whites
1 cup carrots, grated
1 cup whole-wheat flour, sifted
1 cup unbleached flour, sifted
1½ teaspoons baking powder
1 teaspoon baking soda
1 teaspoon cinnamon

1. Preheat the oven to 350°F. Spray a 9-by-5-by-2½-inch bread pan with nonstick cooking spray.

2. In a medium-size bowl combine the brown sugar, molasses, oil, yogurt, vanilla, and egg whites. Stir to mix well; then stir in the grated carrots.

3. In a separate bowl, sift the flours with baking powder, baking soda, and cinnamon. Add the flour mixture to the carrot mixture a little at a time, stirring to mix. Do not beat or overstir.

4. Pour the batter into the prepared bread pan. Bake for 50 to 60 minutes or until done. Cool on a rack, removing from the pan as soon as it is cool enough to handle.

Nutritional analysis per serving:

CALORIES	PROTEIN, GM.	CARBOHYDRATE, GM.	FAT, GM.	SATURATED FAT, GM.
256	6.3	44.9	7.3	1.1

SODIUM, MG.	CHOLESTEROL, MG.	FIBER, GM.	CALCIUM, MG.	CALORIES FROM FAT
272.4	0.3	2.6	110	25%

Homemade Applesauce

There is nothing like fresh applesauce. I like to use Gala apples. You can also use apple juice concentrate for sweetness instead of the brown sugar.

SERVES 8

6 medium cooking apples, with peel
2 tablespoons water
1 tablespoon brown sugar

1. Wash the apples. Core, quarter, and cut them into bite-size pieces.

2. Put the apples into a medium-size saucepan. Add about 2 tablespoons water. Bring to a boil, then reduce heat. Add the brown sugar, stir, and cover.

3. Cook about 20 minutes, or until apples are very soft. Check occasionally to be sure they have enough liquid.

Nutritional analysis per serving:

CALORIES	PROTEIN, GM.	CARBOHYDRATE, GM.	FAT, GM.	SATURATED FAT, GM.
68	0.2	17.6	0.4	0.1

SODIUM, MG.	CHOLESTEROL, MG.	FIBER, GM.	CALCIUM, MG.	CALORIES FROM FAT
0.7	0.0	2.3	9	5%

Greek Cuisine

Introduction

The Greek people are among the friendliest in the world. They are warm and outgoing, with a great love of life that flows over into a great love of food. On a recent two-week cruise on the Royal Cruise Line, I spent over a week in the Greek Isles. The crew was Greek, so naturally I've chosen to share some of my favorite Greek foods.

The secret to Greek cooking is the subtle flavors, often from fresh herbs and spices. It's fairly easy to modify fat content without sacrificing flavor. You'll be surprised to see how low in fat and calories Greek dishes are. So read on and set up your kitchen for great Greek cooking. Here's a sample menu.

Appetizers
Eggplant Caviar on Pita Bread
Hummus on Pita Bread
Mugs of Lemon Chicken Soup
Buffet
Pear and Lettuce Salad
Greek Salad
Oven-Fried Eggplant with Cucumber
Yogurt Salad
Pastitsio
Turkey Breast Marinated with Lemon
and Herbs
Lamb Loin
Greek Easter Bread (from your bakery)
Dessert
Honey Yogurt Cake
Fresh Fruit
Coffee

GREEK EASTER BRUNCH

Greek Easter is one of the most celebrated of all holidays. In Greece, after going to church, the Greeks break a long fast with lots of wonderful food. What fun to change the pace from a more traditional American Easter brunch or dinner to a Greek-style festival of foods.

Start with your decor. Greek colors are blue and white—an easy combination to work with. Use your white dishes and serving pieces with blue table-cloths and napkins. Your centerpiece can be a fresh fruit basket. Place a loaf of Greek Easter Bread on a cutting board on the table. Most bakeries will have Greek Easter bread, but you may need to order it ahead. Also order fresh-baked pita bread.

Greek music is a must. It really creates the warm, fun-loving atmosphere. You can't miss with the soundtrack from Zorba the Greek, but your favorite record store probably has lots of suggestions. For a really festive event, contact a local Greek restaurant or Greek church for the names of musicians who might play for you.

The beverages for your Easter brunch could include the Greek wine, retsina, mixed with soda water and a twist of lemon. Mineral water with a twist of lemon is always appropriate. With dessert, serve a strong coffee and offer mataxa (Greek brandy) or ouzo (a licorice-flavored liqueur).

Cucumber Yogurt Salad

This can be served as a condiment or on a bed of lettuce as a salad.

SERVES 6

2 cups Yogurt Cheese (page 98)
1 large cucumber, peeled, seeded, and
  coarsely grated
3 cloves garlic, crushed
1 teaspoon dried dillweed (1 tablespoon
  fresh dill)
½ teaspoon ground white pepper
Thickly sliced cucumber
Fresh dill

1. Mix the first 5 ingredients together and chill for 2 hours.

2. Garnish with a cucumber slice and fresh dill.

Nutritional analysis per serving:

CALORIES	PROTEIN, GM.	CARBOHYDRATE, GM.	FAT, GM.	SATURATED FAT, GM.
100	9.7	14.5	0.4	0.2

SODIUM, MG.	CHOLESTEROL, MG.	FIBER, GM.	CALCIUM, MG.	CALORIES FROM FAT
126.3	2.9	0.2	337	3%

Eggplant Caviar

This is an excellent dish to have on hand. It's very low in calories and can be served as a dip with crackers at cocktail time, in pita bread for lunch, or on lettuce leaves and garnished with chopped tomatoes and cucumbers as a first course at dinner. You'll get the best results if you refrigerate the Eggplant Caviar overnight before serving.

SERVES 8

2 medium eggplants
1 teaspoon olive oil
1 medium onion, diced
2 cloves garlic, minced
1 red bell pepper, diced
1 tablespoon chopped fresh parsley
½ teaspoon ground black pepper
1 tablespoon fresh lemon juice
3 teaspoons capers

1. Preheat the oven to 400°F.

2. Bake the whole eggplants for 1 hour. Let them cool until you can handle them.

3. Heat the olive oil in a skillet, and sauté the onion, garlic, and red bell pepper until soft.

4. Cut the eggplants in half, scoop out the pulp, and put the pulp into a food processor with steel blade. Add the onion mixture and pulsate 4 times.

5. Add the parsley, black pepper, lemon juice, and capers, and pulsate 2 to 4 times, until the caviar is well mixed.

6. Place it in a covered container and refrigerate at least 6 hours before serving.

Nutritional analysis per serving:

CALORIES	PROTEIN, GM.	CARBOHYDRATE, GM.	FAT, GM.	SATURATED FAT, GM.
30	0.6	4.4	1.4	0.2

SODIUM, MG.	CHOLESTEROL, MG.	FIBER, GM.	CALCIUM, MG.	CALORIES FROM FAT
46	0.0	1	9	43%

Greek Salad

A Greek salad adds wonderful color to a meal, and its excellent flavor is enhanced by the feta cheese. You can also add Greek olives.

SERVES 6

1 head Boston lettuce
1 medium English cucumber, sliced
2 medium tomatoes, cut in wedges
2 medium green bell peppers, sliced
1 small red onion, thinly sliced
1 tablespoon minced fresh oregano
3 tablespoons red wine vinegar
1/2 teaspoon black pepper
4 ounces crumbled feta cheese

1. Wash and dry the lettuce, keeping the leaves whole. Line a platter or shallow bowl with the leaves.

2. Mix the cucumber, tomatoes, bell peppers, and onions.

3. Mix the oregano, vinegar, and pepper and toss it gently with the vegetable mixture.

4. Place the vegetables on top of the lettuce leaves and sprinkle with the feta cheese.

Nutritional analysis per serving:

CALORIES	PROTEIN, GM.	CARBOHYDRATE, GM.	FAT, GM.	SATURATED FAT, GM.
73	3.6	6.3	4.3	2.8

SODIUM, MG.	CHOLESTEROL, MG.	FIBER, GM.	CALCIUM, MG.	CALORIES FROM FAT
213.9	16.6	1.2	109	53%

Greek Salad Dressing

This dressing is also an excellent marinade for beef, lamb, or chicken. The recipe makes 1 cup.

SERVES 6

2 tablespoons olive oil
3 garlic cloves, minced
¼ cup lemon juice
½ teaspoon coriander
2 teaspoons oregano
⅔ cup white wine vinegar
Dash cayenne pepper

Combine all of the ingredients in a blender or covered container and blend well. Chill in a covered container.

Nutritional analysis per serving:

CALORIES	PROTEIN, GM.	CARBOHYDRATE, GM.	FAT, GM.	SATURATED FAT, GM.
51	0.2	2.9	4.8	0.6

SODIUM, MG.	CHOLESTEROL, MG.	FIBER, GM.	CALCIUM, MG.	CALORIES FROM FAT
2.7	0.0	0.2	12	84%

Greek Tomato Sauce

Imported canned Italian plum tomatoes are the secret ingredient in this special sauce. They are easily found in most supermarkets.

SERVES 6

2 teaspoons olive oil
3 cloves garlic, minced
2 onions, chopped
2 cans (32 ounces) whole Italian plum tomatoes
1 can (6 ounces) tomato paste
2 tablespoons chopped fresh oregano (2 teaspoons dried)
1/2 teaspoon ground black pepper
1 teaspoon sugar

1. Heat the olive oil in a large Dutch oven. Add the garlic and onions and sauté until soft.

2. Add the remaining ingredients. With a potato masher, mash the tomatoes slightly. Bring to a boil, stirring constantly.

3. Reduce heat and simmer, uncovered, for 1 hour, stirring frequently.

Nutritional analysis per serving:

CALORIES	PROTEIN, GM.	CARBOHYDRATE, GM.	FAT, GM.	SATURATED FAT, GM.
182	4.8	29.8	6.4	1.1

SODIUM, MG.	CHOLESTEROL, MG.	FIBER, GM.	CALCIUM, MG.	CALORIES FROM FAT
444.7	0.1	5.5	48	32%

Hummus

Hummus is an excellent source of protein, and it's very versatile as a dip with crackers and vegetables or as a sandwich spread.

SERVES 10

1 cup dried chickpeas
2 cloves garlic, peeled
3 tablespoons fresh lemon juice
½ cup tahini butter
½ teaspoon cayenne pepper
Fresh chopped parsley to garnish

1. Soak the chickpeas overnight, then rinse them.

2. In a large saucepan, cover the chickpeas with water and bring to a boil. Cover and simmer 1 hour, or until tender.

3. Drain the cooked chickpeas, reserving 1 cup of the liquid.

4. In a food processor with a steel blade, process the garlic cloves until they are stuck to the sides.

5. Add the remaining ingredients, except the parsley, to the food processor, and process until smooth.

6. Put the mixture in a covered bowl and refrigerate for at least 6 hours before serving. Garnish with the chopped parsley.

Nutritional analysis per serving:

CALORIES	PROTEIN, GM.	CARBOHYDRATE, GM.	FAT, GM.	SATURATED FAT, GM.
97	1	3.1	9.3	5.7

SODIUM, MG.	CHOLESTEROL, MG.	FIBER, GM.	CALCIUM, MG.	CALORIES FROM FAT
107.9	24.8	0.6	9	86%

Lemon Chicken Soup

This has always been one of my favorite soups. It is easy to make and a perfect first course because it is delicate and very low in calories. If you wanted to make it a bit heartier, add cut-up chicken breast and poach it right in the soup, or use leftover cooked chicken. Add a salad and dessert, and you have a tasty luncheon.

SERVES 6

6 cups low-salt chicken broth
2/3 cup white rice
1 egg
2 egg whites
Juice of 2 lemons

1. Bring the broth to boil. Add the rice, cover, and simmer for 20 minutes.

2. Beat the egg and egg whites together. Add a little of the hot broth and beat. Slowly add the eggs to hot broth and stir until thickened.

3. Stir in the lemon juice and serve.

Nutritional analysis per serving:

CALORIES	PROTEIN, GM.	CARBOHYDRATE, GM.	FAT, GM.	SATURATED FAT, GM.
51	5.3	3.7	1.5	0.5

SODIUM, MG.	CHOLESTEROL, MG.	FIBER, GM.	CALCIUM, MG.	CALORIES FROM FAT
430	35	0.1	21	26%

Pear and Lettuce Salad

This salad is so simple; yet its light, refreshing taste adds the perfect touch to a meal.

SERVES 6

1 head romaine lettuce
2 pears
1 tablespoon lemon juice in 1 cup water
¼ cup pear nectar
3 tablespoons pear vinegar or white wine vinegar

1. Wash the Romaine well, cut it into bite-size pieces, and spin it dry in a salad spinner.

2. Cut the pears in chunks and toss them in the lemon water to keep them from turning brown.

3. Mix the pear nectar and vinegar.

4. Toss the lettuce, pears, and dressing together.

Nutritional analysis per serving:

CALORIES	PROTEIN, GM.	CARBOHYDRATE, GM.	FAT, GM.	SATURATED FAT, GM.
42	0.4	10.9	0.3	0.02

SODIUM, MG.	CHOLESTEROL, MG.	FIBER, GM.	CALCIUM, MG.	CALORIES FROM FAT
3	0.0	1.7	13	5%

Spinach and Lentil Soup

If you have leftover chicken or meat, cut it up and add it to this soup for a tasty entrée.

SERVES 6

1 cup large brown lentils
7½ cups low-salt chicken broth
1 teaspoon olive oil
1 large onion, chopped
2 packages (10 ounces) frozen spinach,
   thawed, with water squeezed out
2 tablespoons tomato paste
¼ teaspoon cayenne pepper
1 tablespoon chopped fresh oregano

1. Put the lentils and chicken broth in a large saucepan. Bring to a boil, reduce heat, and simmer, uncovered, for 1 hour, or until the lentils are tender.

2. Heat the olive oil in a skillet. Add the onions and sauté until golden. Add the spinach and tomato paste. Mix them over a low heat until warm.

3. Add the mixture to the lentils. Add the cayenne pepper, and oregano. Cover and simmer for 20 minutes. If soup becomes too thick, add water.

Nutritional analysis per serving:

CALORIES	PROTEIN, GM.	CARBOHYDRATE, GM.	FAT, GM.	SATURATED FAT, GM.
88	8.8	10.9	1.8	0.4

SODIUM, MG.	CHOLESTEROL, MG.	FIBER, GM.	CALCIUM, MG.	CALORIES FROM FAT
521	0.0	4.6	158	18%

Spinach Cheese Pie (Spanakopita)

When you're working with phyllo dough, keep it covered with a damp cloth. It is very thin and will dry out quickly. Once you get the knack, you can create other dishes from your leftovers, wrapping them in the phyllo.

SERVES 6

1/2 cup low-salt chicken broth
1 package (10 ounces) frozen chopped
  spinach, thawed, with water squeezed out
3 ounces crumbled feta cheese
1 1/2 cups low-fat ricotta cheese
2 egg whites, slightly beaten
1 tablespoon minced fresh oregano (1
  teaspoon dried)
1/2 teaspoon ground black pepper
Pinch nutmeg
6 sheets frozen phyllo dough, thawed

1. Preheat the oven to 400°F. Spray a 9-inch pie pan or springform pan with a nonstick cooking spray.

2. Put the chicken broth into a spray bottle.

3. Mix the spinach, feta cheese, ricotta cheese, egg whites, oregano, pepper, and nutmeg.

4. Place 4 sheets of the phyllo dough in the bottom of the pie plate, spraying each with the chicken broth. Line up the dough with the sides of the pan; fold any excess dough into the bottom of the pan.

5. Spoon the spinach mixture into the pan. Cover with the remaining 2 sheets of phyllo, again spraying each with the chicken broth.

6. Bake for 40 minutes.

Nutritional analysis per serving:

CALORIES	PROTEIN, GM.	CARBOHYDRATE, GM.	FAT, GM.	SATURATED FAT, GM.
151	11.8	5.2	9.6	6.2

SODIUM, MG.	CHOLESTEROL, MG.	FIBER, GM.	CALCIUM, MG.	CALORIES FROM FAT
168	37.5	1.1	285	57%

Yogurt Soup

This is a perfect start to a summer evening meal. The flavors mingle so well, you would never guess the walnuts are there. But you don't want to make Yogurt Soup without them!

SERVES 8

2 cloves garlic, peeled
½ cup walnuts
1 tablespoon white wine vinegar
3 cups plain nonfat yogurt
1 cup 1% milk
½ teaspoon white pepper
1 cucumber, peeled, seeded, and diced
Chopped fresh parsley to garnish

1. Use a food processor with a steel blade to process the garlic. Drop in the cloves, and run it until all the garlic sticks to the sides.

2. Add the walnuts and vinegar, and process until the nuts are finely chopped.

3. Add the yogurt, milk, and white pepper. Blend until smooth.

4. Pour the mixture into a bowl, add the cucumbers, and refrigerate for at least 4 hours before serving.

5. Garnish with chopped parsley.

Nutritional analysis per serving:

CALORIES	PROTEIN, GM.	CARBOHYDRATE, GM.	FAT, GM.	SATURATED FAT, GM.
120	7.6	11.2	5.4	0.7

SODIUM, MG.	CHOLESTEROL, MG.	FIBER, GM.	CALCIUM, MG.	CALORIES FROM FAT
87.2	2.9	0.5	234	40%

Orzo Pilaf

Orzo is a rice-shaped pasta that is often used in Greek cooking.

SERVES 6

3 cups water
2 tablespoons low-salt chicken broth
granules
1 cup orzo
1 clove garlic, minced
1 small onion, chopped
2 medium carrots, grated
1/2 medium green bell pepper, chopped

1. Season the water with the chicken broth granules and then bring the water to a boil.

2. Add the orzo. Cook for 10 minutes, and drain.

3. In a sauté pan sprayed with a nonstick cooking spray, sauté the garlic and all of the vegetables together until soft.

4. Mix the orzo into the vegetables and transfer the mixture to a serving dish. This pilaf can be set aside and reheated in the microwave just before serving.

Nutritional analysis per serving:

CALORIES	PROTEIN, GM.	CARBOHYDRATE, GM.	FAT, GM.	SATURATED FAT, GM.
52	1.7	11.2	0.3	0.04

SODIUM, MG.	CHOLESTEROL, MG.	FIBER, GM.	CALCIUM, MG.	CALORIES FROM FAT
19	0.0	1.5	56	4%

Oven-Fried Eggplant

Here's a crispy, tender way to cook eggplant.

SERVES 4

1 medium-to-large eggplant,
  cut in ¼-inch rounds
2 cups plain bread crumbs
½ teaspoon dried oregano
½ teaspoon garlic powder
¼ teaspoon ground black pepper
½ cup unbleached flour
2 egg whites, slightly beaten with
  ¼ cup water

1. Preheat the oven to 350°F. Prepare a cookie sheet by spraying it with nonstick spray.

2. In a large pot of boiling water, blanch the eggplant for 3 minutes in small batches.

3. Combine the bread crumbs, oregano, garlic powder, and pepper.

4. Dip the eggplant first in the flour, then in the egg whites, and then in the bread-crumb mixture.

5. Place the dipped eggplant on a cookie sheet and bake for 15 minutes.

Nutritional analysis per serving:

CALORIES	PROTEIN, GM.	CARBOHYDRATE, GM.	FAT, GM.	SATURATED FAT, GM.
214	8.1	40.9	1.7	0.4

SODIUM, MG.	CHOLESTEROL, MG.	FIBER, GM.	CALCIUM, MG.	CALORIES FROM FAT
318.2	0.0	2.3	52	7%

Halibut on Skewers

This dish has a very delicate flavor; even people who don't normally eat fish like it! Be sure to serve it with the bay leaves—you don't eat them, but they make a more interesting presentation. Leftovers are great served cold in a salad.

SERVES 6

½ medium onion, finely chopped
1 tablespoon fresh lemon juice
2 tablespoons water
½ teaspoon ground white pepper
1½ pounds halibut, cut into 1-inch cubes
24 large bay leaves

1. Mix the onion, lemon juice, water, and pepper in a bowl.

2. Gently add the fish, coating all sides. Cover tightly and refrigerate for 4 hours.

3. Put the bay leaves in a pot of boiling water. Turn off the heat and let stand for 1 hour. Drain.

4. Thread the fish cubes and bay leaves alternately on skewers.

5. Barbecue on the grill or cook under the broiler for 10 to 15 minutes.

Nutritional analysis per serving:

CALORIES	PROTEIN, GM.	CARBOHYDRATE, GM.	FAT, GM.	SATURATED FAT, GM.
120	21.8	4.1	1.7	0.4

SODIUM, MG.	CHOLESTEROL, MG.	FIBER, GM.	CALCIUM, MG.	CALORIES FROM FAT
93.1	54.5	1.2	57	13%

Shrimp with Tomatoes and Feta Cheese

Rinse fresh shrimp well and devein them before cooking. If you are using frozen shrimp, thaw them under cold running water and add them right at the end, so you just heat them through (overcooking shrimp makes them tough).

SERVES 6

1½ pounds shrimp (16 to a pound)
1 tablespoon olive oil
1 medium onion, chopped
½ cup dry white wine (or vermouth)
1 can (27 ounces) diced tomatoes with juice
2 tablespoons chopped fresh parsley
½ teaspoon oregano
¼ teaspoon ground pepper
¼ pound crumbled feta cheese

1. Clean and rinse the shrimp, pat them dry, and set them aside.

2. Heat the olive oil in a large skillet and sauté the onion until soft.

3. Stir in the wine, tomatoes, parsley, oregano, and pepper. Bring to a boil and cook until the mixture thickens slightly.

4. Add the shrimp and cook over a medium heat until the shrimp are done, about 10 to 15 minutes.

5. Stir in the feta cheese.

Nutritional analysis per serving:

Calories	Protein, gm.	Carbohydrate, gm.	Fat, gm.	Saturated Fat, gm.
248	26.9	10.5	8.6	3.5

Sodium, mg.	Cholesterol, mg.	Fiber, gm.	Calcium, mg.	Calories from Fat
370.1	186.6	2.7	196	31%

Lemon Chicken

Start with the Lemon Chicken Soup (page 203) to keep with a lemon theme. Serve with green beans for added color.

SERVES 6

6 chicken breast halves, skinned and left on bone
1 small onion, cut in thin strips
2 sticks celery, cut in julienne strips
2 carrots, cut in julienne strips
1 tablespoon chopped fresh basil (1/2 teaspoon dried)
1 bay leaf
Juice and rind of 2 small lemons
1/2 cup water
1/2 teaspoon ground black pepper

1. In a large sauté pan sprayed with a nonstick cooking spray, brown the chicken breasts, meat side down. Remove and set aside.

2. Add the onions, celery, and carrots. Cook over a medium heat until soft.

3. Add the basil, bay leaf, lemon juice and rind, water, and pepper. Mix and bring to a boil.

4. Reduce the heat to simmer. Add the chicken, bone side down. Cover and cook until done, about 30 to 45 minutes.

5. Remove the chicken and vegetables to a serving platter. Bring the remaining sauce to a boil to thicken. Pour over the chicken.

Nutritional analysis per serving:

CALORIES	PROTEIN, GM.	CARBOHYDRATE, GM.	FAT, GM.	SATURATED FAT, GM.
162	27.1	4.9	3.2	0.8

SODIUM, MG.	CHOLESTEROL, MG.	FIBER, GM.	CALCIUM, MG.	CALORIES FROM FAT
85.9	72.7	1.3	40	18%

Moussaka

This traditional Greek dish is usually prepared with ground lamb or beef and covered with a thick white sauce. Here I've replaced the white sauce with my own low-fat version and used ground chicken to reduce the fat content even more. You can use beef or lamb in this recipe or a combination of red meat and chicken, but remember you will be increasing the fat calories.

SERVES 8

2 large eggplants, cut into ¼-inch round slices
1 teaspoon olive oil
2 medium onions, chopped
1½ pounds chicken breast meat, ground
1 can (27 ounces) diced tomatoes in juice
½ cup chopped fresh parsley
¼ teaspoon ground cinnamon
½ teaspoon ground nutmeg
1 tablespoon fresh oregano (½ teaspoon dried)
1 cup plain nonfat yogurt

1. Preheat the oven to 400°F. Spray a baking pan with nonstick spray.

2. Lay the eggplant slices on paper towels for 45 minutes, turning once. Place the eggplant on a cookie sheet and bake for 15 minutes. Remove the eggplant from the oven, and reduce the temperature to 350°F.

3. Heat the olive oil in a nonstick skillet. Add the onions and sauté until soft. Remove the onions from the pan and set them aside.

4. Sauté the chicken in the same skillet until it is almost cooked. Add the onions, tomatoes with juice, parsley, cinnamon, nutmeg, and oregano. Mix and simmer, uncovered, for 30 minutes.

Continued on page 214

Continued from page 213

Moussaka

Greek White Sauce
3 cups nonfat milk
2 teaspoons butter
1/2 teaspoon ground white pepper
3/4 cup Cream of Rice cereal
1/4 cup Parmesan cheese

5. Stir in the yogurt.

6. Layer the eggplant on the bottom of the baking pan. Top with the chicken mixture.

7. Put the milk, butter, and white pepper in a saucepan. Bring to a boil. Slowly add the Cream of Rice cereal, stirring constantly. Add the Parmesan cheese. When the sauce is thick, pour it over the Moussaka.

8. Bake for 45 minutes. Let stand 10 minutes before serving.

Nutritional analysis per serving:

Calories	Protein, gm.	Carbohydrate, gm.	Fat, gm.	Saturated Fat, gm.
232	26.1	18.6	6	2.7

Sodium, mg.	Cholesterol, mg.	Fiber, gm.	Calcium, mg.	Calories from Fat
301.8	54.1	2.9	329	23%

Turkey Breast Marinated with Lemon and Herbs

This is also excellent cooked on the grill.

SERVES 6

2 pounds boneless, skinless turkey breast
Juice and grated rind of 2 lemons
1 teaspoon oregano
Pinch cumin
1 tablespoon chopped fresh parsley
½ teaspoon thyme
½ teaspoon ground white pepper

1. Rinse and pat the turkey breast dry.

2. Mix the remaining ingredients.

3. Coat all sides of the turkey breast with the marinade. Cover and refrigerate overnight, if possible, or no less than 4 hours.

4. Preheat the oven to 325°F.

5. Roast, covered, for 35 minutes per pound (70 minutes for a 2-pound breast). Roast uncovered for the last 10 minutes, or until the temperature inside the turkey reaches 170°F.

Nutritional analysis per serving:

CALORIES	PROTEIN, GM.	CARBOHYDRATE, GM.	FAT, GM.	SATURATED FAT, GM.
185	35	0.5	3.8	1.2

SODIUM, MG.	CHOLESTEROL, MG.	FIBER, GM.	CALCIUM, MG.	CALORIES FROM FAT
76	80.5	0.1	28	18%

Lamb Loin

Whenever you can, grill your meat. It's a healthful way to cook and your guests will love it. This lamb dish is perfect for the outdoor grill.

SERVES 4

2 tablespoons fresh lemon juice
2 cloves garlic, crushed
1½ teaspoons fresh oregano
  (½ teaspoon dried)
1½ teaspoons fresh thyme
  (½ teaspoon dried)
¼ teaspoon pepper
1½ pounds loin of lamb, boned, trimmed,
  and tied

1. Mix the first 5 ingredients and rub on the lamb. Wrap it tightly and refrigerate the lamb for 4 to 6 hours.

2. Grill or roast at 350°F to desired doneness. (Medium rare is about 11 minutes on each side.)

Nutritional analysis per serving:

CALORIES	PROTEIN, GM.	CARBOHYDRATE, GM.	FAT, GM.	SATURATED FAT, GM.
299	29.3	1.2	18.9	7.8

SODIUM, MG.	CHOLESTEROL, MG.	FIBER, GM.	CALCIUM, MG.	CALORIES FROM FAT
75.8	106	0.1	18	57%

Pastitsio

You can make this dish a day ahead of time, but the Pastitsio tastes better if the Greek White Sauce is put on right before cooking.

SERVES 8

1 pound lean ground beef
1 small onion, chopped
1 can (27 ounces) diced tomatoes in juice
3 tablespoons chopped fresh parsley
1/2 teaspoon cinnamon
1/2 teaspoon ground black pepper
1 pound ziti
4 egg whites
1/2 cup Parmesan cheese
Greek White Sauce (page 214)

1. Preheat the oven to 350°F. Spray a baking pan with nonstick cooking spray.

2. In a nonstick skillet, brown the ground beef. Remove it from the pan and set it aside on paper towels to drain the excess fat. In the skillet, sauté the onion until soft. Return the meat to the pan and mix it with the onion.

3. Add the tomatoes with juice, parsley, cinnamon, and pepper. Mix and simmer 15 minutes, uncovered.

4. Cook the ziti in boiling water until slightly underdone. Drain well.

5. Slightly whip the egg whites and mix them into the ziti, along with 1/4 cup Parmesan cheese.

Continued on page 218

Continued from page 217

Pastitsio

6. Spread the ziti mixture in the baking pan and press it down with a wooden spoon or your hand.

7. Top with the meat mixture, then with the Greek White Sauce. Sprinkle with remaining cheese.

8. Bake for 45 minutes. Let stand 10 to 15 minutes before serving.

Nutritional analysis per serving:

CALORIES	PROTEIN, GM.	CARBOHYDRATE, GM.	FAT, GM.	SATURATED FAT, GM.
558	32.3	57.9	21.4	10

SODIUM, MG.	CHOLESTEROL, MG.	FIBER, GM.	CALCIUM, MG.	CALORIES FROM FAT
565.3	64.7	4.6	457	34%

Shish Kebab

The traditional meat in the ever popular Shish Kebab is lamb, but you may use beef, chicken or turkey—just marinate it in the same way.

SERVES 6

Marinade

1 medium clove garlic, minced
1 tablespoon minced fresh oregano (1 teaspoon dried)
1 teaspoon minced fresh rosemary (1/4 teaspoon dried)
1/3 cup dry white wine (or dry vermouth)
1/2 teaspoon freshly ground pepper
2 tablespoons red wine vinegar

Kebabs

1 1/2 pounds very lean lamb, cut in 1-inch cubes
2 medium onions cut in half (separate wedges in layers of 2 each)
3 bell peppers (green, yellow, and red), cut in fourths
16 mushrooms, washed

1. To make marinade, mix all of the ingredients together.

2. Soak the lamb cubes in the marinade for 2 to 6 hours.

3. On a skewer, alternate the lamb, onion, peppers, and mushrooms.

4. Grill or cook under a broiler to the desired doneness.

Nutritional analysis per serving:

CALORIES	PROTEIN, GM.	CARBOHYDRATE, GM.	FAT, GM.	SATURATED FAT, GM.
254	21.9	10.3	13	5.3

SODIUM, MG.	CHOLESTEROL, MG.	FIBER, GM.	CALCIUM, MG.	CALORIES FROM FAT
56.2	70.7	2.2	29	46%

Stuffed Peppers

Use peppers in all three colors to add eye appeal—you can freeze these to have on hand for a quick lunch.

SERVES 6

6 medium red, yellow, or green bell peppers
1 medium onion, chopped
12 ounces lean ground beef or lamb
1 tablespoon chopped fresh dill (1 teaspoon dried)
2 tablespoons fresh lemon juice
1 teaspoon ground black pepper
1 cup cooked brown rice
3 cups Greek Tomato Sauce (page 201)

1. Preheat the oven to 350°F.

2. Wash the peppers and blanch them in boiling water for 3 minutes. Remove them from the water and cool.

3. Cut 1 inch off the top of each pepper. Remove the core and seeds. Trim the bottom so the pepper will stand up.

4. In a skillet sprayed with a nonstick cooking spray, cook the onion until soft. Remove it from the pan and set aside.

5. In the skillet, brown the meat well and drain it in a colander lined with paper towels to remove the excess fat.

6. Add the onions, meat, and the remaining ingredients (except for the Greek Tomato Sauce) to the skillet. Mix well.

Continued on page 221

Continued from page 220

Stuffed Peppers

7. Fill the peppers with the meat mixture and put the tops on. Place them in a baking dish half filled with water. Cover loosely with foil. Bake for 45 minutes.

8. Remove the peppers with a slotted spoon to a serving platter. Top each pepper with ½ cup Greek Tomato Sauce that has been heated.

Nutritional analysis per serving:

CALORIES	PROTEIN, GM.	CARBOHYDRATE, GM.	FAT, GM.	SATURATED FAT, GM.
417	20	45.3	18.9	5.7

SODIUM, MG.	CHOLESTEROL, MG.	FIBER, GM.	CALCIUM, MG.	CALORIES FROM FAT
495.4	50.1	7.6	78	41%

Greek Rice Pudding

Rice pudding also makes a very nice breakfast!

SERVES 8

5 cups nonfat milk
1 cup short-grain white rice
1 slice lemon peel, about 1 inch long
3/4 cup brown sugar
3 teaspoons cornstarch
1 teaspoon vanilla
1/2 teaspoon almond extract
Cinnamon

1. Heat the milk to boiling. Add the rice and lemon peel. Lower heat and cook 30 minutes, stirring often.

2. Add the brown sugar and cook for 15 minutes more. Add the cornstarch to the mixture and cook 5 minutes longer.

3. Remove from the heat. Discard the lemon peel. Stir in the vanilla and almond extract.

4. Pour into 8 individual dessert dishes. Let them cool to room temperature. Sprinkle with cinnamon.

Nutritional analysis per serving:

CALORIES	PROTEIN, GM.	CARBOHYDRATE, GM.	FAT, GM.	SATURATED FAT, GM.
203	6.6	42.8	0.4	0.2

SODIUM, MG.	CHOLESTEROL, MG.	FIBER, GM.	CALCIUM, MG.	CALORIES FROM FAT
88	2.8	0.3	213	2%

Honey Cakes

To give the walnuts a more intense flavor, toast them in the oven or in a skillet, just until brown. Be careful not to burn them.

SERVES 12

3 cups all-purpose flour, sifted
1 teaspoon baking powder
1 teaspoon baking soda
1 cup plain nonfat yogurt
1/2 cup sugar
1/2 cup cognac
4 tablespoons orange juice
1 tablespoon orange rind
1/2 cup honey
1/2 cup finely chopped walnuts
1 teaspoon ground cinnamon

1. Preheat the oven to 350°F. Spray a cookie sheet with a nonstick spray.

2. Sift the flour, baking powder, and baking soda together.

3. Combine the yogurt, sugar, cognac, orange juice, and orange rind.

4. Slowly add the flour mixture to the yogurt mixture, and mix well.

5. Shape the dough into 24 balls. Place them on the prepared cookie sheet and press down with a spoon. Bake for 20 minutes, and cool.

6. In a small bowl, slightly warm the honey in the microwave (to make it less sticky). Mix the walnuts and cinnamon and put them on a plate. Dip the cakes into the honey, and then into the walnuts.

Nutritional analysis per serving:

CALORIES	PROTEIN, GM.	CARBOHYDRATE, GM.	FAT, GM.	SATURATED FAT, GM.
248	5	44.9	3.6	0.3

SODIUM, MG.	CHOLESTEROL, MG.	FIBER, GM.	CALCIUM, MG.	CALORIES FROM FAT
146.9	0.4	1.1	75	13%

Honey Yogurt Cake

This all-purpose cake is nice to have around for tea.

SERVES 10

4 tablespoons butter
½ cup honey
6 egg whites
¾ cup plain nonfat yogurt
2 cups all-purpose flour, sifted
1 teaspoon baking powder
¼ cup finely chopped walnuts

1. Preheat the oven to 350°F. Spray a loaf pan with nonstick baking spray.

2. Cream the butter and honey together.

3. Add the egg whites, 2 at a time, beating after each addition.

4. Fold in the yogurt, flour, baking powder and walnuts.

5. Spoon the mixture into the prepared loaf pan, and bake for 1 hour.

Nutritional analysis per serving:

CALORIES	PROTEIN, GM.	CARBOHYDRATE, GM.	FAT, GM.	SATURATED FAT, GM.
219	6.1	33.8	7.1	3.2

SODIUM, MG.	CHOLESTEROL, MG.	FIBER, GM.	CALCIUM, MG.	CALORIES FROM FAT
140.4	13.4	0.8	72	29%

Peach Pudding

If you have a pretty Jell-O mold, use it for this pudding. It will present well and make a nice centerpiece. You can also divide it among 8 dessert dishes or small ramekins before putting it in to set.

SERVES 8

3 cans (1 pound) water-packed peaches
2 envelopes unflavored gelatin
¼ cup orange juice
¼ cup brown sugar
½ cup finely chopped walnuts

1. Drain the peaches, reserving 1 cup liquid.

2. Place the gelatin in a bowl. Heat the peach liquid to boiling and pour it over the gelatin. Stir until gelatin dissolves.

3. Mix the orange juice and brown sugar, and add to the peaches. Place the mixture in a food processor with a metal blade or into a blender. Purée.

4. Add the gelatin mixture to the purée and mix well.

5. Pour the pudding into a mold or bowl and chill until halfway set.

6. Mix the walnuts into the pudding and let set.

7. To serve, unmold the pudding, or spoon it into small bowls.

Nutritional analysis per serving:

CALORIES	PROTEIN, GM.	CARBOHYDRATE, GM.	FAT, GM.	SATURATED FAT, GM.
183	2.4	36.6	4.9	0.4

SODIUM, MG.	CHOLESTEROL, MG.	FIBER, GM.	CALCIUM, MG.	CALORIES FROM FAT
27.8	0.0	2.3	20	24%

Italian Cuisine

Introduction

The Italian cuisine adapts easily to a low-fat, high-complex carbohydrate diet. The Italian kitchen is always warm and friendly—it's the heart of the house. Italians love to cook; it is a pleasure. They take their food seriously, but also celebrate the joy of both cooking and eating.

Italian foods are prepared simply with simple ingredients. Pasta is served at almost every meal, and the freshest ingredients are always used. Use fresh herbs whenever possible. When buying dried herbs, buy them in small quantities and keep them in airtight containers in a cool place. One part dried herbs is equivalent to three parts fresh.

Olive oil is considered one of the healthiest oils for you. The best to buy is extra-virgin oil, which is made from the first cold pressing. It has a very delicate flavor and is suitable for all of the recipes here. It's more expensive than other oils, but well worth it. And since I use very little oil in these recipes, it will last a long time. You can keep olive oil for up to one year in a cool, dark place. You may want to decant it in a small ceramic or glass container for handy use. (Don't use plastic, it will change the flavor.)

AN ITALIAN DINNER PARTY

If you've ever been to an Italian home for Sunday dinner, you'll remember that the food keeps coming and coming. Try this suggested menu and treat your friends to a family-style Italian meal!

Appetizer
   Antipasto

Soup
   Minestrone

Pasta

   Linguine with Clam Sauce

Main Course

   Chicken Cacciatore

   Risotto

Dessert

   Almond Cake

   Espresso

Here's an idea for an informal Italian dinner.

Tomato and Cucumber Salad

Pasta and Bean Soup

Bread Sticks

Bowl of Fresh Fruit

Minestrone

This familiar Italian soup is a meal in itself! Get some good Italian bread, spray it with a garlic-infused olive oil, and grill it. It is perfect!

SERVES 8

1 pound dry beans
1 tablespoon olive oil
1 medium onion, chopped
1 clove garlic, chopped
1 teaspoon oregano
1 teaspoon basil
1½ cups celery, sliced
    in ¼-inch pieces
2 cups carrots, chopped
2 cups zucchini, sliced in ¼-inch pieces
1 cup cabbage, thinly sliced
1 pound mushrooms, washed and sliced
2 cans (28 ounces), diced tomatoes in juice
6 cups water
2 teaspoons beef bouillon paste
½ pound elbow macaroni, cooked
½ cup fresh parsley, chopped

1. Soak the beans overnight. Rinse.

2. Heat the olive oil in a large Dutch oven. Add the onion and garlic, and sauté until soft. Add the oregano and basil. Sauté 30 seconds.

3. Add the celery, carrots, zucchini, cabbage, mushrooms, tomatoes in juice, water, and bouillon paste. Bring to a simmer.

4. Simmer 2 to 3 hours, or until the beans are tender.*

5. Add the cooked macaroni and parsley.

  *Minestrone can be made in a slow cooker at step 4. Put all of the ingredients in a slow cooker. Cook on High all day. Add the pasta and parsley right before serving.

Nutritional analysis per serving:

CALORIES	PROTEIN, GM.	CARBOHYDRATE, GM.	FAT, GM.	SATURATED FAT, GM.
330	18.6	59.9	3.3	0.5

SODIUM, MG.	CHOLESTEROL, MG.	FIBER, GM.	CALCIUM, MG.	CALORIES FROM FAT
228.5	0.0	14.1	151	9%

Pasta and Bean Soup

To make this soup very quickly, you can use canned white beans. The soup will be ready in a snap.

SERVES 8

1 pound small white beans
1 tablespoon olive oil
1 medium onion, chopped
1 clove garlic, minced
1 teaspoon Italian Blend seasoning
2 tablespoons chopped fresh parsley
2 celery stalks, chopped
2 medium carrots, sliced in ¼-inch
  rounds
3 rosemary leaves, chopped
5 cups chicken broth
1 can (23 ounces) diced tomatoes in juice
Black pepper to taste
½ pound cooked pasta shells

1. Soak the beans overnight. Rinse.

2. In a large Dutch oven, heat the olive oil. Sauté the onion and garlic until soft. Add the Italian seasoning and chopped parsley. Sauté for 30 seconds.

3. Add the celery, carrots, rosemary, chicken broth, diced tomatoes with juice, and black pepper. Heat to simmer.

4. Add the beans. Cover and simmer 2 to 3 hours, or until beans are tender.*

5. Add cooked pasta and serve.

* This can be made in a slow cooker at step 4. Put all of the ingredients into the slow cooker and cook all day on High, adding the pasta right before serving.

Nutritional analysis per serving:

Calories	Protein, gm.	Carbohydrate, gm.	Fat, gm.	Saturated Fat, gm.
301	17.9	51.9	3.2	0.6

Sodium, mg.	Cholesterol, mg.	Fiber, gm.	Calcium, mg.	Calories from Fat
257	0.0	11.6	118	9%

Antipasto

You can spread this out on a platter to serve with cocktails before the meal. Add sliced Italian meats and cheeses if you want to make the Antipasto more substantial. This dressing is also an excellent marinade for beef, lamb, or chicken.

SERVES 6

1 package (9 ounces) frozen artichoke hearts (steamed for 2 minutes)
1 cucumber, cut in half lengthwise, seeded and sliced
¼ pound fresh mushrooms, sliced
2 cups green beans, cut into 3-inch pieces (steamed for 5 minutes)
1 green or red sweet pepper, sliced (steamed for 2 minutes)

Antipasto Dressing (Makes 1 cup)

2 tablespoons olive oil
3 garlic cloves, minced
¼ cup lemon juice
2 teaspoons oregano
⅔ cup white wine vinegar
Dash cayenne pepper

1. To make the dressing, combine all of the ingredients in a blender or covered container and blend well.

2. Store in a covered container and chill while preparing the antipasto.

3. Add the dressing and toss, cover, and chill for several hours, stirring occasionally before serving.

Nutritional analysis per serving:

CALORIES	PROTEIN, GM.	CARBOHYDRATE, GM.	FAT, GM.	SATURATED FAT, GM.
94	2.8	12.4	5.1	0.7

SODIUM, MG.	CHOLESTEROL, MG.	FIBER, GM.	CALCIUM, MG.	CALORIES FROM FAT
100.1	0.0	2.8	52	49%

Caesar Salad

Caesar Salads have become very popular. You can top it with sliced steak, grilled chicken, or grilled shrimp to make it a substantial entrée.

SERVES 4

1 large head romaine lettuce
1 cup croutons
2 tablespoons Parmesan cheese,
   freshly grated
Freshly grated black pepper to taste

Caesar Dressing
½ cup Vinaigrette Dressing (page 22)
2 tablespoons Parmesan cheese, grated
¼ cup egg substitute

1. To make the dressing, combine ingredients and chill1.

2. Wash the romaine lettuce well, drain, and tear into bite-size pieces. Spin or pat dry.

3. Add the dressing and toss well. Add the croutons and toss lightly.

4. Place on 4 salad plates and sprinkle each with ½ tablespoon Parmesan cheese and the black pepper.

Nutritional analysis per serving:

CALORIES	PROTEIN, GM.	CARBOHYDRATE, GM.	FAT, GM.	SATURATED FAT, GM.
130	5.2	10.5	8	3.6

SODIUM, MG.	CHOLESTEROL, MG.	FIBER, GM.	CALCIUM, MG.	CALORIES FROM FAT
450.3	4.2	0.8	101	54%

Eggplant, Peppers, Tomatoes, and Ziti

This dish is colorful, healthful, and very low in calories.

SERVES 6

1 pound eggplant peeled, and cut in ½-inch cubes
1 tablespoon olive oil
2 cloves garlic
2 large red or yellow peppers, cut in half, then in ¼-inch strips
2 teaspoons capers
1 can (28 ounces) diced tomatoes in juice
2 teaspoons fresh basil, thinly sliced
Ground black pepper to taste
1 pound ziti
⅓ cup grated Parmesan cheese

1. Lightly salt the eggplant and set it in a colander in the sink. Rinse and dry on paper towels.

2. Heat the oil in a skillet. Add the garlic and sauté until golden brown. Remove the garlic and discard.

3. Add the eggplant and sauté until soft.

4. Add the peppers, capers, tomatoes with juice, basil, and pepper. Bring to a simmer. Cover and cook 30 minutes, stirring occasionally.

5. Cook the pasta and drain it. Add the sauce to the pasta and toss with Parmesan cheese.

Nutritional analysis per serving:

CALORIES	PROTEIN, GM.	CARBOHYDRATE, GM.	FAT, GM.	SATURATED FAT, GM.
357	12.2	66.1	4.8	1

SODIUM, MG.	CHOLESTEROL, MG.	FIBER, GM.	CALCIUM, MG.	CALORIES FROM FAT
103.1	2	5.9	84	12%

Lasagna | *Consider making two and freezing one for later.*

SERVES 8

1 pound lasagna noodles
6 cups Meat Sauce (page 248)
2 cups low-fat cottage cheese, blended in
   blender or food processor until smooth
2 cups Zucchini Filling (page 246)
⅓ cup grated Parmesan cheese
1 cup grated mozzarella cheese

1. Cook lasagna noodles in a large pot of boiling water until slightly underdone. Drain and rinse in cold water.

2. Preheat the oven to 350°F. Spray a lasagna pan well with a nonstick spray.

3. Put a layer of noodles in the pan. Top with 4 cups of Meat Sauce, then with the cottage cheese. Sprinkle with the Parmesan cheese. Top with another layer of noodles, and then spread the Zucchini Filling over them. Top with the remaining noodles. Spread the remaining 2 cups of Meat Sauce next. Sprinkle the mozzarella cheese over the top.

4. Cover the pan and bake for 45 minutes. Let stand 10 minutes before cutting.

Nutritional analysis per serving:

CALORIES	PROTEIN, GM.	CARBOHYDRATE, GM.	FAT, GM.	SATURATED FAT, GM.
579	39.9	67.9	17.3	7.2

SODIUM, MG.	CHOLESTEROL, MG.	FIBER, GM.	CALCIUM, MG.	CALORIES FROM FAT
790.6	62	8.9	360	27%

Lasagna Roll-Ups

This is a fun way to make lasagna. It's more formal [...] for a dinner party. And the roll-ups can be frozen i[...] quick meal when there is no time to cook. Like piz[...] ways to make roll-ups.

SERVES 6

1 pound lasagna noodles (16 noodles)
Meat Sauce recipe (page 248)
8 ounces mozzarella cheese, grated

1. In a large pot, cook the noodles until slightly underdone. Drain and rinse.

2. Preheat the oven to 350°F.

3. Lay out each noodle, put 1/3 cup sauce down the center, and roll it up. Place 2 rolls in individual bake-and-serve dishes, or line them up in one large bake-and-serve dish. Top with 1/3 cup sauce and 1 ounce cheese.

4. Bake, covered, for 30 minutes.

Nutritional analysis per serving:

CALORIES	PROTEIN, GM.	CARBOHYDRATE, GM.	FAT, GM.	SATURATED FAT, GM.
612	38.2	73.3	18.4	8.2

SODIUM, MG.	CHOLESTEROL, MG.	FIBER, GM.	CALCIUM, MG.	CALORIES FROM FAT
683.6	77.5	7	343	27%

Linguine with Clam Sauce

This is one of those dishes you can whip up in less than 30 minutes.

SERVES 4

1 teaspoon olive oil
1 clove garlic, minced
2 tablespoons capers
1 can (15 ounces) diced tomatoes in juice
3 tablespoons chopped fresh parsley
1/2 teaspoon freshly ground black pepper
1 can (6 1/2 ounces) chopped clams
1/2 pound pasta, cooked and drained

1. Heat the olive oil in a large nonstick skillet.

2. Sauté the garlic and capers for 1 minute.

3. Add the tomatoes, parsley, pepper, and clams. Simmer for 5 minutes, uncovered.

4. Toss with the pasta and serve.

Nutritional analysis per serving:

CALORIES	PROTEIN, GM.	CARBOHYDRATE, GM.	FAT, GM.	SATURATED FAT, GM.
273	11.3	51	2.6	0.3

SODIUM, MG.	CHOLESTEROL, MG.	FIBER, GM.	CALCIUM, MG.	CALORIES FROM FAT
207	6.8	4.9	65	9%

Manicotti

You can make this dish ahead of time. If you have held it in the refrigerator, bake it for 1 hour. Or if you have already baked it, just heat it through again.

SERVES 6

1 tablespoon olive oil
1 medium onion, chopped
1 garlic clove, minced
1 package (10 ounces) chopped, frozen spinach, cooked, drained, and squeezed dry
1 pound skimmed ricotta cheese
1 pound mushrooms, sliced and cooked
1 cup grated mozzarella cheese
1 teaspoon Italian Blend seasoning
12 manicotti shells, cooked al dente
3 cups Basic Marinara Sauce (page 247)

1. Preheat the oven to 350°F.

2. Heat the olive oil in a skillet. Add the onion and garlic, and sauté until soft.

3. Mix all of the ingredients in a bowl, including the onion and garlic, excluding the shells and sauce.

4. Divide into 12 portions, and fill each manicotti shell with 1 portion.

5. Line up the filled shells in a ovenproof serving dish. Spoon the Marinara Sauce over the top. Cover and bake for 45 minutes.

Nutritional analysis per serving:

CALORIES	PROTEIN, GM.	CARBOHYDRATE, GM.	FAT, GM.	SATURATED FAT, GM.
728	39.6	80.4	28.5	13.1

SODIUM, MG.	CHOLESTEROL, MG.	FIBER, GM.	CALCIUM, MG.	CALORIES FROM FAT
866.7	78	7.4	553	35%

Pasta Primavera

What a delicious way to eat your vegetables! Another dish that is great for vegetarians.

SERVES 4

½ cup carrots, grated
1 cup zucchini, grated or diced
3 large green onions, diced, green part only
½ teaspoon minced garlic
2 teaspoons cornstarch
1 cup nonfat milk
1 tablespoon butter
¼ cup low-fat sour cream
1 tablespoon chopped parsley
½ teaspoon Italian Blend seasoning
1 cup broccoli flowerets (steamed 3 to 5 minutes)
½ cup small peas (steamed 3 to 5 minutes)
4 cups cooked pasta
½ cup grated Parmesan cheese
Pepper to taste

1. Spray a large skillet with a nonstick coating. Sauté the carrots, zucchini, onions, and garlic until tender.

2. Add the cornstarch to the milk and mix until dissolved. Add the butter to the milk mixture.

3. Stir the milk mixture into the sautéed vegetables. Cook over a medium heat, stirring until the sauce thickens.

4. Stir in the sour cream, parsley, and seasonings.

5. Add the broccoli and peas. Stir in gently.

6. Place well-drained pasta into a bowl.

7. Pour the sauce over the pasta. Add Parmesan cheese and pepper. Toss thoroughly, and serve immediately.

Nutritional analysis per serving:

CALORIES	PROTEIN, GM.	CARBOHYDRATE, GM.	FAT, GM.	SATURATED FAT, GM.
387	17.2	60.5	9.1	4.9

SODIUM, MG.	CHOLESTEROL, MG.	FIBER, GM.	CALCIUM, MG.	CALORIES FROM FAT
260.6	20.1	6.4	296	21%

Ricotta Spinach Roll-Ups

This variation on the Lasagna Roll Ups is meatless.

SERVES 6

1 pound lasagna noodles
1 recipe Manicotti Filling (page 239)
4 cups Basic Marinara Sauce (page 247)

Prepare these roll-ups just as you did the Lasagna Roll-Ups (page 237), except use ⅙ of the Manicotti Filling for each noodle and top each roll with ¼ cup Marinara Sauce.

Nutritional analysis per serving:

CALORIES	PROTEIN, GM.	CARBOHYDRATE, GM.	FAT, GM.	SATURATED FAT, GM.
713	34.5	87	26.9	11.9

SODIUM, MG.	CHOLESTEROL, MG.	FIBER, GM.	CALCIUM, MG.	CALORIES FROM FAT
1179	56.9	8.7	565	34%

Ratatouille

The servings are large and full of low-calorie vegetables. You may serve Ratatouille hot or cold.

SERVES 6

1 large onion, sliced
4 medium zucchini, sliced
1 green or red sweet pepper, seeded and sliced
1 eggplant, peeled and cubed
4 tomatoes, chopped in large pieces
¼ cup tomato paste
½ teaspoon minced garlic
¼ cup chopped fresh parsley
2 teaspoons sweet basil
1 teaspoon oregano
¼ teaspoon black pepper

1. Combine all of the ingredients in a large saucepan.

2. Cook over a medium heat until all the vegetables are tender. Stir frequently.

3. Reduce heat, cover, and simmer for 10 to 15 minutes.

4. Remove the cover and continue cooking until the liquid has evaporated and the mixture has thickened.

Nutritional analysis per serving:

CALORIES	PROTEIN, GM.	CARBOHYDRATE, GM.	FAT, GM.	SATURATED FAT, GM.
80	2.9	15.2	0.9	0.1

SODIUM, MG.	CHOLESTEROL, MG.	FIBER, GM.	CALCIUM, MG.	CALORIES FROM FAT
20.2	0.0	4.2	66	12%

Risotto

Risotto, the Italian version of rice, can be made in many variations—from a side dish to a main course. The traditional way is to brown the rice and then keep adding liquid until it is absorbed and the rice is cooked. I have kept part of the tradition but have made it a bit easier and healthier.

SERVES 4

2 teaspoons olive oil
1 medium onion, chopped
1 cup arborio* rice
1/2 cup dry vermouth
2 cups chicken broth
1/4 cup grated Parmesan cheese

*I used arborio, a hard-grain rice that is quite good. You may also use a short-grain brown rice in these recipes. If you have a rice cooker, put the ingredients in it after you have completed the sautéing steps. It works perfectly and will keep the rice warm until you are ready to serve it.

1. In a saucepan, heat the olive oil on medium-high heat. Add the onion and sauté until soft. Add the rice and sauté until all of the rice is coated.

2. Add the vermouth and stir until all of the liquid is absorbed. Then, add 1/2 cup chicken broth and cook until the broth is absorbed.

3. Add the remaining chicken broth. Bring to a boil, then simmer. Cover and cook until all of the liquid is absorbed.

4. Stir in the Parmesan cheese.

Nutritional analysis per serving:

CALORIES	PROTEIN, GM.	CARBOHYDRATE, GM.	FAT, GM.	SATURATED FAT, GM.
247	8.9	18.8	11.7	3.7

SODIUM, MG.	CHOLESTEROL, MG.	FIBER, GM.	CALCIUM, MG.	CALORIES FROM FAT
328	11	0.7	214	42%

Rolled Eggplant

Although this dish is time-consuming, it presents very well, and can be made a day ahead. Try it when vegetarian friends come to dinner.

SERVES 4

2 medium eggplants, peeled and sliced
lengthwise 1/4 inch thick (8 slices)
1 1/2 cups Zucchini Filling (page 246)
3 cups Basic Marinara Sauce (page 247)
2 cups low-fat ricotta cheese
1/2 teaspoon ground garlic
2 tablespoons grated Parmesan cheese
2 teaspoons chopped fresh parsley
1/4 cup sliced ripe olives

1. Lightly salt the eggplant and let it sit for 30 minutes. Rinse and pat dry. (This process removes any bitterness)

2. On a cookie sheet sprayed with a nonstick spray, bake the eggplant at 350°F for 10 minutes.

3. Place a large spoonful of the Zucchini Filling in each slice of eggplant and roll it up. Place the rolls seam-side down in a bake-and-serve dish, making two rolls per serving.

4. Spoon the Marinara Sauce down the center of each roll.

5. Place the ricotta cheese in a food processor or blender with the garlic and Parmesan cheese. Blend it until it is smooth and creamy.

Continued on page 245

Continued from page 244

Rolled Eggplant

6. Spoon the mixture down the center of each roll. Sprinkle parsley down the center of the cheese and place olives down center of the parsley.

7. Cover and bake for 45 minutes. Let the rolls rest for 10 minutes before serving.

Nutritional analysis per serving:

CALORIES	PROTEIN, GM.	CARBOHYDRATE, GM.	FAT, GM.	SATURATED FAT, GM.
545	26.9	56.1	26.9	10.5

SODIUM, MG.	CHOLESTEROL, MG.	FIBER, GM.	CALCIUM, MG.	CALORIES FROM FAT
1272	52	14.5	507	45%

Zucchini Filling

This all-around great filling is very low in calories!

SERVES 6

1 tablespoon olive oil
2 medium onions, chopped
1 clove garlic, chopped
1/2 teaspoon basil
1/2 teaspoon oregano
1/4 teaspoon ground red chili pepper
1 green pepper, chopped
2 pounds zucchini, sliced 1/4 inch thick
1 pound mushrooms, sliced
1 can (28 ounces) diced tomatoes in juice

1. In a Dutch oven, heat the olive oil. Add the onions and garlic. Sauté until tender. Add the herbs and sauté for 30 seconds.

2. Add the remaining ingredients. Cover and simmer for 15 minutes.

3. Uncover and cook on a medium heat until the liquid is reduced.

Nutritional analysis per serving:

CALORIES	PROTEIN, GM.	CARBOHYDRATE, GM.	FAT, GM.	SATURATED FAT, GM.
108	5.2	18.2	3.3	0.5

SODIUM, MG.	CHOLESTEROL, MG.	FIBER, GM.	CALCIUM, MG.	CALORIES FROM FAT
27.3	0.0	6.1	75	28%

Basic Marinara Sauce

This very simple sauce can be made and frozen in 2-cups containers so you can grab it at the last minute to use in a multitude of ways.

SERVES 8

1 tablespoon olive oil
2 cloves garlic, chopped
1 medium onion, sliced
1 teaspoon Italian Blend seasoning
2 cans (28 ounces) diced tomatoes in juice
1 can (28 ounces) tomato purée
2 tablespoons chopped fresh parsley

1. Heat the olive oil in large Dutch oven. Add the garlic and onion. Sauté until tender.

2. Add the Italian seasoning. Cook for 30 seconds.

3. Add the diced tomatoes with juice, tomato purée, and parsley, Stir. Turn heat to low and simmer for 1 hour.

Nutritional analysis per serving:

CALORIES	PROTEIN, GM.	CARBOHYDRATE, GM.	FAT, GM.	SATURATED FAT, GM.
86	3.2	15.2	2.6	0.3

SODIUM, MG.	CHOLESTEROL, MG.	FIBER, GM.	CALCIUM, MG.	CALORIES FROM FAT
200.1	0.0	5.5	92	27%

Meat Sauce

You can use ground turkey or chicken in this sauce if you prefer. Try mixing it into rigatoni or rice and baking for a good one-dish meal.

SERVES 8

1 tablespoon olive oil
1 medium onion, chopped
1 clove garlic, minced
2 medium carrots, chopped
1 medium green pepper, chopped
1 teaspoon Italian Blend seasoning
2 tablespoons chopped fresh parsley
1 pound extra-lean ground beef
1 can (28 ounces) diced tomatoes in juice
1 can (28 ounces) tomato sauce
1 bay leaf

1. In a large Dutch oven, heat the olive oil. Sauté the onion, garlic, carrots, and green pepper until soft.

2. Add the Italian seasoning and sauté for 30 seconds. Add the parsley.

3. In a nonstick skillet, sauté the ground beef until done. Drain on paper towels to remove the excess fat.

4. Add the beef to the Dutch oven. Add the tomatoes in juice and the tomato sauce and bring to a simmer. Add the bay leaf. Cover and simmer for 2 hours.

Nutritional analysis per serving:

Calories	Protein, gm.	Carbohydrate, gm.	Fat, gm.	Saturated Fat, gm.
175	14.7	16.2	6.6	1.9

Sodium, mg.	Cholesterol, mg.	Fiber, gm.	Calcium, mg.	Calories from Fat
693.1	38.5	4.5	62	34%

Mushroom Sauce

Adding raw mushrooms to the sauce retains their texture and gives more substance to the sauce.

SERVES 8

1 tablespoon olive oil
2 cloves garlic, chopped
1 medium onion, chopped
1 teaspoon basil
1/2 teaspoon oregano
1/2 teaspoon ground red pepper
1 can (28 ounces) diced tomatoes in juice
1 can (28 ounces) whole Italian plum
   tomatoes with basil
1 can (28 ounces) tomato sauce
1 tablespoon fresh chopped parsley
1 pound mushrooms, sliced

1. Heat the olive oil in a large Dutch oven. Add the garlic and onion. Sauté until soft.

2. Add the basil, oregano, and red pepper. Sauté for 30 seconds.

3. Add all of the cans of tomatoes, the tomato sauce, and fresh parsley. Bring to a simmer.

4. Add the mushrooms. Simmer, uncovered, for 1 hour.

Nutritional analysis per serving:

CALORIES	PROTEIN, GM.	CARBOHYDRATE, GM.	FAT, GM.	SATURATED FAT, GM.
169	5.9	29.1	5.3	0.8

SODIUM, MG.	CHOLESTEROL, MG.	FIBER, GM.	CALCIUM, MG.	CALORIES FROM FAT
939.9	0.0	6.8	71	28%

Chicken Cacciatore

You may use any parts of the chicken in this recipe—just be sure to remove the skin.

SERVES 6

1 tablespoon olive oil
6 chicken breast halves, skin removed
1 medium onion, sliced
2 cloves garlic, minced
1 teaspoon oregano
1 pound mushrooms, sliced
1 bell pepper, sliced
1 can (28 ounces) diced tomatoes in juice
1 can (28 ounces) tomato sauce
½ teaspoon black pepper
2 tablespoons chopped fresh parsley
1 pound pasta, cooked al dente

1. Heat the olive oil in a Dutch oven. Brown the chicken breast halves and remove them from the pan.

2. Add the onion and garlic, and sauté until soft. Add the oregano and sauté for 30 seconds.

3. Add the mushrooms and bell pepper. Cover and simmer for 5 minutes. Uncover and cook until the liquid is reduced.

4. Add the tomatoes, tomato sauce, black pepper, and parsley. Bring to a simmer.

5. Add the chicken breasts, cover, and simmer for 45 minutes.

6. Serve over pasta.

Nutritional analysis per serving:

Calories	Protein, gm.	Carbohydrate, gm.	Fat, gm.	Saturated Fat, gm.
557	41.7	81.4	7.8	1.5

Sodium, mg.	Cholesterol, mg.	Fiber, gm.	Calcium, mg.	Calories from Fat
950.6	72.7	9.5	103	13%

Halibut Cacciatore

You will be amazed at how good this is—and how easy!

SERVES 4

1 green bell pepper, sliced
3 cups Mushroom Sauce (page 249)
1 pound halibut, cut into 12 pieces

1. In a large skillet sprayed with a nonstick cooking spray, sauté the green pepper until soft.

2. Add the Mushroom Sauce and bring to a simmer.

3. Add the halibut. Cover and simmer 20 minutes or until the halibut is cooked.

Nutritional analysis per serving:

CALORIES	PROTEIN, GM.	CARBOHYDRATE, GM.	FAT, GM.	SATURATED FAT, GM.
247	33.3	40	8	2.1

SODIUM, MG.	CHOLESTEROL, MG.	FIBER, GM.	CALCIUM, MG.	CALORIES FROM FAT
1972	54.6	14	165	14%

Meatballs Marinara

Spaghetti and meatballs are always a hit with young and old.

SERVES 4

½ pound very lean ground beef
1 egg white
½ teaspoon garlic powder
¼ teaspoon black pepper
2 teaspoons chopped fresh parsley
1 tablespoon Parmesan cheese
¼ cup bread crumbs
2 cups Basic Marinara Sauce (page 247)

1. Mix all of the ingredients except the Marinara Sauce, in a bowl.

2. Form the mixture into 16 walnut-size meatballs.

3. Brown the meatballs on all sides in a nonstick pan sprayed with a nonstick spray.

4. Add the Marinara Sauce. Cover and simmer for 30 minutes.

Nutritional analysis per serving:

Calories	Protein, gm.	Carbohydrate, gm.	Fat, gm.	Saturated Fat, gm.
213	16.1	17.2	9.6	2.5

Sodium, mg.	Cholesterol, mg.	Fiber, gm.	Calcium, mg.	Calories from Fat
756.3	39.5	2.7	62	40%

Scampi

This scampi is great tossed with pasta.

SERVES 4

1 tablespoon olive oil
1 medium onion, chopped
2 cloves garlic, minced
1 green pepper, chopped
¼ teaspoon ground red chili pepper
½ cup dry vermouth
1 can (15 ounces) diced tomatoes, drained
1 pound raw shrimp, shell removed and cleaned

1. Heat the olive oil in a large skillet. Add the onion, garlic, and green pepper. Sauté until tender.

2. Add the ground red pepper and vermouth. Cook until the liquid is almost all absorbed.

3. Add the tomatoes. Cook on medium until hot, almost to a boil.

4. Add the shrimp and cook until done, about 3 minutes.

Nutritional analysis per serving:

CALORIES	PROTEIN, GM.	CARBOHYDRATE, GM.	FAT, GM.	SATURATED FAT, GM.
229	24.5	12	5.8	0.9

SODIUM, MG.	CHOLESTEROL, MG.	FIBER, GM.	CALCIUM, MG.	CALORIES FROM FAT
160.5	170	2.9	102	23%

Almond Cake

To liven the cake up at bit, try this: After baking, poke holes in the top and drizzle Frangelico liqueur aver the cake. The Hazelnut flavor is a lovely complement.

SERVES 10

4 teaspoons butter
1½ cups sugar
1 cup egg substitute
1 teaspoon vanilla extract
¼ teaspoon almond extract
¾ cup plain nonfat yogurt
2 cups self-rising flour
½ cup chopped almonds

1. Preheat the oven to 325°F. Spray a loaf pan with a nonstick spray.

2. Cream the butter and sugar until light and fluffy.

3. Add the egg substitute ½ cup at time, beating after each addition.

4. Fold in the vanilla and almond extract, yogurt, flour, and almonds.

5. Spoon the mixture into the prepared loaf pan and bake for 1 hour.

Nutritional analysis per serving:

CALORIES	PROTEIN, GM.	CARBOHYDRATE, GM.	FAT, GM.	SATURATED FAT, GM.
299	7.3	49.9	8.1	2.1

SODIUM, MG.	CHOLESTEROL, MG.	FIBER, GM.	CALCIUM, MG.	CALORIES FROM FAT
82.4	6.2	1	74	24%

Mexican Cuisine

Introduction

Ever popular Mexican food traces its roots to both the Spanish and Native Americans. The cuisine embraces staples like corn, rice, beans, and tomatoes and a host of flavorings including garlic, chilies of all varieties, cilantro, and cumin. Various regions of Mexico influence the cooking and seasoning style, particularly in the Southwest where California, Arizona, New Mexico, and Texas all border Mexico. Sonoran style, Santa Fe style, Tex-Mex, and California style are all regional variations in methods of preparation, seasoning, and serving.

Mexican food is traditionally high in complex carbohydrates, but the cooking techniques often use lard or other fats. By limiting fats, Mexican food can add exciting variety, flavor, and appeal to your food plan.

SALSA

Salsa is a general term that means "a sauce." Salsa or "chili" is used as a condiment or ingredient in virtually all Mexican-style meals including breakfast. Salsas may be fresh (raw) or cooked and vary from mild to very hot. They are usually very low in calories and may be used as desired. Store-bought salsas, although convenient, may be higher in salt or sodium. To prepare a salsa, you can use a food processor, blender, or chop the ingredients by hand. Salsas can be chunky or smooth. Make it whatever consistency you like.

MEXICAN FIESTA

May 5th, "Cinco de Mayo," is the perfect time to have a Mexican Fiesta.

Serve buffet style, decorate with bright colors, and play mariachi music. If you're having a big party, hire a live band. A piñata filled with goodies adds a festive touch.

Start with a margarita. Use a good-quality gold tequila, but use very little per drink—or have virgin margaritas. Here's a sample menu.

Appetizers
- Oven-Baked Tortilla Chips
- Bean Dip
- Guacamole
- Three-Layer Cheese Appetizer
- Salsa

Serve Buffet Style
- Jicama Salad
- Tamale Pie
- Chicken Enchiladas
- Black Bean and Corn Relish

Dessert
- Fresh Fruit
- Mexican Coffee

For a delicious Mexican luncheon, try these dishes:

- Salad
- Chilies Rellenos
- Guiltless Refried Beans
- Mexican Rice
- Flan

Albondigas (Meatball Soup)

Spray corn tortillas lightly with a chili-infused oil, slice them into strips, and bake at 500°F for about 10 minutes, until they are crispy. They complement the Albondigas nicely.

SERVES 8

8 cups chicken broth
2 carrots, peeled and sliced
2 zucchini, scrubbed and sliced
1/2 head cabbage, chopped coarsely
1 pound raw ground turkey
1 slice bread, ground into crumbs
2 egg whites
1 teaspoon oregano leaves

1. Pour the chicken broth into a large pot. Bring it to a simmer, adding the carrots, zucchini, and cabbage.

2. Mix the raw turkey with bread the crumbs. Add the egg whites and oregano, and mix thoroughly. Make the mixture into 16 meatballs.

3. Drop the meatballs, one at a time, into the soup, allowing the broth to return to a slow simmer.

4. Simmer the soup about 15 minutes, or until the meatballs are cooked through.

Nutritional analysis per serving:

CALORIES	PROTEIN, GM.	CARBOHYDRATE, GM.	FAT, GM.	SATURATED FAT, GM.
111	13	5.9	3.8	1.2

SODIUM, MG.	CHOLESTEROL, MG.	FIBER, GM.	CALCIUM, MG.	CALORIES FROM FAT
421	24.8	1.4	48	31%

Black Bean Soup

This soup can be frozen in batches or individual servings. It makes a hearty meal or a first course. Some people prefer this type of soup to have a very smooth texture. You may want to blend or purée small batches in a blender or food processor to desired consistency. Garnish with a dollop of light sour cream.

SERVES 6

2 cups black beans (soaked 8 hours)
2 medium onions, coarsely chopped
2 cloves garlic, chopped
2 carrots, coarsely chopped
4 stalks celery, coarsely chopped
1 tablespoon cumin
2 bay leaves
2 tablespoons chopped fresh parsley
1 teaspoon fresh ground pepper
1/2 cup dry sherry (optional)

1. Place the beans in a large pot and cover with water. Bring to a boil. Reduce heat, cover, and simmer for 1 hour removing any froth or foam.

2. Spray a skillet with nonstick spray. Sauté the onions for about 4 minutes. Add the garlic, carrots, celery, and cumin. Sauté until the vegetables are soft or tender.

3. Add the bay leaves, parsley, and pepper to the bean mixture. Add sherry, if desired.

4. Cover and cook 2 to 3 hours or until the beans are tender. Remove the bay leaves before serving.

Nutritional analysis per serving:

CALORIES	PROTEIN, GM.	CARBOHYDRATE, GM.	FAT, GM.	SATURATED FAT, GM.
328	17.8	58	1.5	0.3

SODIUM, MG.	CHOLESTEROL, MG.	FIBER, GM.	CALCIUM, MG.	CALORIES FROM FAT
46.2	0.0	13.6	134	4%

Black Bean and Corn Relish

If you want to cut the calories on this dish, serve it wrapped in large crisp lettuce leaves.

SERVES 8

2 cups cooked black beans, cooled to
   room temperature
1 cup fresh corn kernels (or frozen)
½ cup red salsa (use your favorite!)

1. Combine the beans and corn in a large bowl. Add the salsa and mix well.

2. Allow it to marinate a few hours before serving.

3. Serve as a side dish or wrapped in a tortilla.

Nutritional analysis per serving:

CALORIES	PROTEIN, GM.	CARBOHYDRATE, GM.	FAT, GM.	SATURATED FAT, GM.
76	4	14.3	0.5	0.1

SODIUM, MG.	CHOLESTEROL, MG.	FIBER, GM.	CALCIUM, MG.	CALORIES FROM FAT
7	0.0	3.1	20	6%

Gazpacho

You may use the canned roasted green chilies, if you prefer. Remember when you work with fresh chilies, keep your hands away from your eyes.

SERVES 4

1 clove garlic, minced
½ onion, minced
2 tablespoons green chilies, roasted, peeled, and chopped
1 can (16 ounces) tomatoes, no salt added
½ cucumber, chopped
2 fresh tomatoes, chopped
Juice of ½ lime
Dash hot pepper sauce

1. Start food processor or blender. Carefully add the garlic through the top opening. Add the onion and roasted chilies.

2. Stop the food processor or blender. Add the canned tomatoes and blend well.

3. Pour the mixture into a bowl and stir in the cucumber and fresh tomato.

4. Add the lime juice and hot pepper sauce. Chill and serve as a cold soup for an appetizer or as a condiment.

Nutritional analysis per serving:

CALORIES	PROTEIN, GM.	CARBOHYDRATE, GM.	FAT, GM.	SATURATED FAT, GM.
49	2.1	10.8	0.6	0.1

SODIUM, MG.	CHOLESTEROL, MG.	FIBER, GM.	CALCIUM, MG.	CALORIES FROM FAT
202.3	0.0	2.9	44	11%

Guacamole

This is a very smooth dip or spread. If you prefer a chunky version just mix all the ingredients by hand instead of using the food processor.

SERVES 6

1 cup nonfat cottage cheese
1 medium avocado
2 tablespoons salsa

1. Place the cottage cheese in a food processor with a steel blade and blend until very smooth.

2. Cut the avocado in half, remove the seed, and scoop out the meat into the food processor with the cottage cheese. Blend until smooth.

3. Add the salsa and quickly blend. Place into a serving bowl. Cover and refrigerate until ready to eat.

Nutritional analysis per serving:

CALORIES	PROTEIN, GM.	CARBOHYDRATE, GM.	FAT, GM.	SATURATED FAT, GM.
71	5.4	3.7	3	1.1

SODIUM, MG.	CHOLESTEROL, MG.	FIBER, GM.	CALCIUM, MG.	CALORIES FROM FAT
156.9	1.7	0.9	28	44%

Jicama Salad

Jicama is very refreshing and adds a wonderful texture to your meal.

SERVES 4

4 cups jicama, shredded or julienne cut
¼ cup lime juice
¼ to ½ teaspoon chili powder
1 clove garlic, pressed for juice only
1 to 2 tablespoons cilantro, finely chopped
Dash sugar

1. Put the shredded jicama into a bowl.

2. In another small bowl, combine the lime juice, chili powder, garlic juice, cilantro, and sweetener. Mix well.

3. Pour the dressing over the jicama, and mix to combine the ingredients.

4. Cover and let marinate for several hours in the refrigerator. Serve as a side dish, salad, or garnish.

Nutritional analysis per serving:

CALORIES	PROTEIN, GM.	CARBOHYDRATE, GM.	FAT, GM.	SATURATED FAT, GM.
56	1.1	13.1	0.3	0.03

SODIUM, MG.	CHOLESTEROL, MG.	FIBER, GM.	CALCIUM, MG.	CALORIES FROM FAT
13.8	0.0	6.5	19	4%

Lima Bean Soup

To make a nice garnish, put sour cream into a plastic squeeze bottle with a pointed top and squiggle across the soup right before serving.

SERVES 8

1 pound dry baby lima beans, about 6
  cups cooked
8 cups chicken broth
1 can (16 ounces) whole tomatoes
1 small onion, minced
2 teaspoons marjoram
¼ teaspoon black pepper
1 cup carrots, sliced
1 cup celery, sliced

1. Place the lima beans in a soup pot. Cover with boiling water and let sit for 1 hour. Drain off the liquid.

2. Add the chicken broth to the beans. Break up the tomatoes and add to the mixture.

3. Spray a heavy skillet with nonstick spray and sauté the onion until tender. Add the marjoram and stir to mix. Add this mixture to the beans along with the pepper, carrots, and celery.

4. Simmer the soup, partially covered, for about 1 hour or until the beans are tender.

5. Remove 2 cups of soup and purée it in a food processor or blender, then add it back to the soup.

Nutritional analysis per serving:

CALORIES	PROTEIN, GM.	CARBOHYDRATE, GM.	FAT, GM.	SATURATED FAT, GM.
236	16.8	41	1.4	0.4

SODIUM, MG.	CHOLESTEROL, MG.	FIBER, GM.	CALCIUM, MG.	CALORIES FROM FAT
450.5	0.0	13.8	76	5%

Mexican Lentil Soup

Use a combination of red and green or brown lentils to add more color.

SERVES 6

1 pound lentils (6 to 7 cups cooked)
2 bay leaves
6 garlic cloves, roasted
1 tomato, chopped
1 medium red onion, chopped
2 large carrots, peeled and chopped
2 teaspoons cumin
1 teaspoon oregano
¼ cup chili purée
6 cups chicken broth
Fresh cilantro
Lime juice

1. Wash or rinse the lentils and drain. Place them in a large pot and cover with cold water. Add the bay leaves and bring to a boil. Reduce heat and simmer until tender, approximately 30 minutes. Remove the bay leaves.

2. Cut the tops off each of the garlic cloves. Place them on a piece of foil or in a small ovenproof dish. Spray lightly with nonstick spray and roast in a 325°F until tender, approximately 30 minutes. Remove from the oven and let cool.

3. Squeeze the garlic out of husks into a blender. Add the chopped tomato, cumin, oregano, and chili, and purée until smooth.

4. Spray a skillet with nonstick spray and sauté the onions and carrots until tender.

Continued on page 267

Continued from page 266

Mexican Lentil Soup

5. Add the tomato-garlic purée and the cooked vegetables to the lentils. Add the chicken broth. Simmer for about 30 minutes.

6. Serve the soup with sprigs of cilantro and a squeeze of fresh lime juice.

Nutritional analysis per serving:

CALORIES	PROTEIN, GM.	CARBOHYDRATE, GM.	FAT, GM.	SATURATED FAT, GM.
312	21.2	47.9	5.3	1.1

SODIUM, MG.	CHOLESTEROL, MG.	FIBER, GM.	CALCIUM, MG.	CALORIES FROM FAT
476.5	0.0	18.2	83	15%

Mexican-Style Chicken Soup

This is a perfect one dish meal, served with warm corn tortillas.

SERVES 4

1 whole chicken, about 3 pounds
1 teaspoon cumin seeds
1 bunch cilantro, washed
1⅓ cups brown rice, cooked
2 fresh tomatoes, diced
4 thin slices avocado
½ cup red salsa, if desired

1. Rinse the chicken thoroughly, removing the innards and extra fat. Place it in a soup pot and cover with water. Add the cumin seeds and the entire bunch of cilantro. Bring to a boil. Then simmer until done, usually about 2 hours.

2. Remove the chicken from the broth and allow it to cool slightly. Strain the broth to remove the cumin and cilantro. Then allow the broth to chill and remove the fat layer before using.

3. Meanwhile, remove the meat from chicken bones, and chill until ready to use.

4. To serve, reheat the broth with the chicken in it. Place ⅓ cup rice into each of 4 soup dishes, ladle the broth and chicken on top. Then garnish with diced tomatoes and a slice of avocado. Serve salsa on the side for extra spiciness.

Nutritional analysis per serving:

CALORIES	PROTEIN, GM.	CARBOHYDRATE, GM.	FAT, GM.	SATURATED FAT, GM.
285	25.1	23	10.7	2

SODIUM, MG.	CHOLESTEROL, MG.	FIBER, GM.	CALCIUM, MG.	CALORIES FROM FAT
62.5	58.2	3.1	31	34%

Ranchero Sauce

Here's a simple sauce to serve over Chilies Rellenos (page 276) Burritos (page 272), or enchiladas.

SERVES 4

1 onion, peeled, thinly sliced
1 clove garlic, minced
1 medium tomato, chopped
1 cup chicken broth
1 teaspoon flour

1. Spray a heavy skillet with nonstick spray and heat. Sauté the onion and garlic until soft but not brown.

2. Add the tomato and cook for a few minutes. Add about 4 tablespoons chicken broth.

3. Cook until the liquid is slightly reduced, then sprinkle the flour on top of the sauce and quickly blend in.

4. Simmer until the desired consistency is achieved.

Nutritional analysis per serving:

CALORIES	PROTEIN, GM.	CARBOHYDRATE, GM.	FAT, GM.	SATURATED FAT, GM.
24	1.4	4.5	0.3	0.1

SODIUM, MG.	CHOLESTEROL, MG.	FIBER, GM.	CALCIUM, MG.	CALORIES FROM FAT
99.5	0.0	0.8	12	11%

Three-Layer Cheese Appetizer

A great appetizer to serve a gathering of friends—add margaritas, Mexican beer with slices of lime, or sangria to start off.

SERVES 10

½ cup onion, finely chopped
1 clove garlic, finely chopped
1 pound low-fat ricotta cheese
4 ounces low-fat cream cheese
2 tablespoons pine nuts, toasted
1 jar (4 ounces) pimentos, drained well
  and puréed
½ teaspoon ground cumin
1 tablespoon finely chopped jalapeño pepper
3 tablespoons cilantro leaves, chopped

1. Spray a heavy skillet with nonstick spray and sauté the onion and garlic until tender.

2. Using a blender or food processor, combine the ricotta cheese and cream cheese until well blended. Add the garlic and onion, mix well, and divide into three small bowls.

3. Mix the pine nuts into one bowl.

4. To another bowl, add the puréed pimento mixed with the cumin.

5. To last bowl, add the jalapeño and approximately 2 tablespoons cilantro.

Continued on page 271

Continued from page 270

Three-Layer Cheese Appetizer

6. Prepare a 5- to 6-cup mold by lining it with plastic wrap or cheesecloth. Carefully spoon the pine nut mixture into the bottom of the mold. Spoon the pimento mixture on top and follow with the pepper/cilantro mixture.

7. Fold the ends of the plastic wrap or cheese cloth over the top of the mold and press down lightly to compact. Chill overnight.

8. To serve, invert the mold onto a platter and carefully remove the wrapping. Garnish with the remaining cilantro, and serve with raw vegetables or baked corn tortilla chips.

Nutritional analysis per serving:

Calories	Protein, gm.	Carbohydrate, gm.	Fat, gm.	Saturated Fat, gm.
115	7.1	4.6	7.9	4.4

Sodium, mg.	Cholesterol, mg.	Fiber, gm.	Calcium, mg.	Calories from Fat
84.1	54.8	0.4	126	61%

Burritos

This finger food is a great way to use leftovers. Try adding leftover potatoes or rice to the beans. You may also add 8 ounces of cooked beef or chicken or ⅔ cup beans and 4 ounces trimmed sirloin steak or skinless chicken.

SERVES 4

1⅓ cups Guiltless Refried Beans
   (page 285)
4 flour tortillas
Salsa

1. Heat the beans until hot.

2. Heat the tortillas, one at a time, on a griddle or in a skillet on top of the stove.

3. Place ¼ of the hot beans onto tortilla.

4. Add the salsa and fold or roll to resemble a large cigar.

Nutritional analysis per serving:

CALORIES	PROTEIN, GM.	CARBOHYDRATE, GM.	FAT, GM.	SATURATED FAT, GM.
136	11.6	18	1.6	0.3

SODIUM, MG.	CHOLESTEROL, MG.	FIBER, GM.	CALCIUM, MG.	CALORIES FROM FAT
21	18.2	3.2	56	10%

Ceviche

This colorful, different dish is great drained and stuffed into a pita pocket with lettuce or on a warm tortilla.

SERVES 4

¼ cup lemon juice
¼ cup lime juice
1 tablespoon olive oil
1 tablespoon cilantro, fresh or dried
2 cloves garlic, pressed
1 jalapeño pepper, peeled, seeded, and chopped
½ teaspoon sweet basil
½ teaspoon ground black pepper
½ cup celery, chopped
1 medium red onion, chopped
2 medium tomatoes, chopped with juice and seeds
1 medium green or red sweet pepper, diced
1 medium cucumber, peeled and chopped
1 pound fresh whitefish, diced

1. Combine the lemon juice, lime juice, oil, cilantro, garlic, jalapeño, basil, and black pepper in a blender and chop.

2. Put the chopped vegetables and diced fish into a bowl, and pour the lemon juice mixture over it. Toss.

3. Cover tightly and refrigerate for 24 hours. The acid in the juice "cooks" the fish. Ceviche is spicy, but there is no fishy taste.

Nutritional analysis per serving:

CALORIES	PROTEIN, GM.	CARBOHYDRATE, GM.	FAT, GM.	SATURATED FAT, GM.
194	23.8	14	5.4	0.8

SODIUM, MG.	CHOLESTEROL, MG.	FIBER, GM.	CALCIUM, MG.	CALORIES FROM FAT
118	54.5	2.7	60	25%

Chicken Enchiladas

You can make these a bit more fancy by topping them with a dollop of Guacamole (page 263), a dollop of light sour cream, and sliced ripe olives.

SERVES 6

2 cups Quick Enchilada Sauce
12 corn tortillas
6 ounces cooked chicken, shredded or
  diced
6 ounces low-fat jack or cheddar cheese
  (reserve a little for top of casserole)
1/2 onion, minced
Cilantro leaves

1. Preheat the oven to 350°F.

2. Heat the Enchilada Sauce in a skillet until hot.

3. Dip a tortilla into the sauce, then remove it to a clean, flat surface. Place 1/2 ounce each of the chicken and cheese in the middle of the tortilla and top with a sprinkle of minced onion. Fold the tortilla into thirds and place it seam-side down into a baking dish large enough to hold the full dozen.

4. Repeat this process until all of the tortillas are filled. Spoon the remaining Enchilada Sauce over the tortillas. Top with a little reserved cheese.

5. Cover and bake for about 30 minutes, or until hot and bubbly.

Continued on page 275

Continued from page 274

Chicken Enchiladas

Quick Enchilada Sauce

1 cup chicken broth
1 cup tomato sauce
1 tablespoon tomato paste
1 tablespoon chili powder
2 cloves garlic, pressed
½ teaspoon oregano
¼ teaspoon cumin

6. Combine all of the ingredients in a saucepan. Bring to a boil; then reduce to a simmer for about 20 minutes.

Nutritional analysis per serving:

CALORIES	PROTEIN, GM.	CARBOHYDRATE, GM.	FAT, GM.	SATURATED FAT, GM.
220	18.8	19.4	8	6.3

SODIUM, MG.	CHOLESTEROL, MG.	FIBER, GM.	CALCIUM, MG.	CALORIES FROM FAT
328	53.1	2.1	284	33%

Chilies Rellenos

To save a bit of time you can use canned whole green chilies.

SERVES 4

8 large fresh green chilies
8 ounce low-fat jack cheese
4 egg whites
2 tablespoons flour
Ranchero Sauce (page 269)

1. Roast the chilies over an open flame on a gas range or in the broiler. Chilies should be blackened and the skin should bubble.

2. Place the chilies in a paper bag or on a dish cloth to steam for a few minutes. Then carefully scrape off the blackened skin. Make a slit lengthwise in each chili and carefully remove the seeds.

3. Preheat the oven to 375°F

4. Cut the cheese into 8 long equal pieces and place each cheese stick into the chili, being careful not to tear the pepper.

5. Whip the egg whites until they form soft peaks. Then whip in the flour.

Continued on page 277

Continued from page 276

Chilies Rellenos

6. Dip each cheese-stuffed chili into the egg mixture and roll to cover it thoroughly.

7. Place the chilies in a baking dish and bake for about 30 minutes, or until the egg mixture browns and the cheese is melted. Remove to a serving plate and top with Ranchero Sauce.

Nutritional analysis per serving:

CALORIES	PROTEIN, GM.	CARBOHYDRATE, GM.	FAT, GM.	SATURATED FAT, GM.
210	19.6	12.2	10	11.8

SODIUM, MG.	CHOLESTEROL, MG.	FIBER, GM.	CALCIUM, MG.	CALORIES FROM FAT
407.6	58.8	1.4	422	43%

Fajitas

Create a Fajitas bar with all of the items in bowls or skillets so your guests can create their own Fajitas. Add a bowl of Guacamole (page 263) and one of light sour cream too.

SERVES 4

1 pound lean chicken or beef
1/2 cup lime or lemon juice
2 tablespoons low-sodium soy sauce
2 tablespoons water
2 tablespoons tequila (optional)
1/2 teaspoon oregano
1/4 teaspoon cumin
1 clove garlic, crushed
1 small onion, thinly sliced
1 green pepper, stem and seeds removed, thinly sliced
1 red or yellow pepper, stem and seeds removed, thinly sliced
8 tortillas
Salsa
Cilantro

1. Cut the beef or chicken into chunks or strips and place in a glass dish.

2. Combine the lime or lemon juice, soy sauce, water, tequila, oregano, cumin, and garlic in a small bowl.

3. Pour the mixture over the meat. Add the sliced onions and stir to mix.

4. Cover and marinate in the refrigerator—no more than 4 hours for chicken, longer for beef.

5. Spray a heavy skillet with nonstick spray and heat. Drain the meat and add it to the skillet. Add the sliced peppers and cook just until the meat is done and the peppers are soft.

6. Divide the mixture into 4 serving dishes.

Nutritional analysis per serving:

CALORIES	PROTEIN, GM.	CARBOHYDRATE, GM.	FAT, GM.	SATURATED FAT, GM.
301	26.8	22.3	9.9	3.4

SODIUM, MG.	CHOLESTEROL, MG.	FIBER, GM.	CALCIUM, MG.	CALORIES FROM FAT
579.9	77	2.2	90	30%

Fiesta Fish

Good choices for this dish are, sea bass, halibut, or red snapper. Shrimp would also work, if you have some in your freezer and are looking for something different to do with them.

SERVES 6

1 tablespoon olive oil
1 whole green pepper, chopped
2 tablespoons red onion, chopped
1 cup chopped tomatoes
3 tablespoons lemon juice
1 teaspoon basil
1/2 teaspoon freshly ground black pepper
1/4 teaspoon chili powder
2 pounds fresh whitefish

1. Preheat the oven to 350°F. Prepare a baking dish by spraying it with a nonstick spray.

2. Heat the olive oil in a nonstick skillet and sauté the green pepper, onion, and tomatoes for 1 to 2 minutes to soften.

3. Remove from the heat, add lemon juice, basil, black pepper, and chili powder.

4. Place the fish in the prepared dish, and spoon the vegetable mixture over it. Cover and bake for 25 to 30 minutes, or until the fish flakes with a fork.

Nutritional analysis per serving:

CALORIES	PROTEIN, GM.	CARBOHYDRATE, GM.	FAT, GM.	SATURATED FAT, GM.
178	28.8	3.6	5	0.7

SODIUM, MG.	CHOLESTEROL, MG.	FIBER, GM.	CALCIUM, MG.	CALORIES FROM FAT
120.9	63.6	1.1	179	25%

Guiltless Chorizo

For a breakfast treat, cook chorizo, and then scramble eggs with it. Serve with corn or flour tortillas.

SERVES 6

1 pound lean ground turkey
1 tablespoon chili powder
2 to 3 cloves garlic, crushed
1 to 2 tablespoons tequila (optional)
1 teaspoon oregano
1/2 teaspoon cumin
2 egg whites
1 tablespoon oil

1. Combine the ground turkey, chili powder, garlic, tequila, oregano, cumin, and egg whites. Mix thoroughly and shape into 12 meatballs or sausages.

2. Spray a heavy skillet with nonstick spray, add the oil and heat. Brown the chorizo—a few at a time—until done.

3. Chorizo can be used in any dish calling for a spicy sausage. They will keep in the refrigerator 3 to 5 days if fully cooked.

Nutritional analysis per serving:

CALORIES	PROTEIN, GM.	CARBOHYDRATE, GM.	FAT, GM.	SATURATED FAT, GM.
109	12.8	1.4	4.4	1.2

SODIUM, MG.	CHOLESTEROL, MG.	FIBER, GM.	CALCIUM, MG.	CALORIES FROM FAT
59.6	33	0.3	18	36%

Mexican Pizza

This is a Friday night hit with the family—kids and adults both love this.

SERVES 4

4 flour tortillas
1 cup low-fat cheese, shredded
4 ounces cooked ground meat or 2
   Guiltless Chorizos (page 280)
1 small tomato, chopped
1/2 onion, peeled and chopped
1 tablespoon chopped olives (optional)
Fresh cilantro

1. Preheat the oven to 450°F.

2. Place the tortillas on a cookie sheet. Evenly divide the cheese, meat or chorizos, tomatoes, onions, and olives (if desired).

3. Bake for 4 to 5 minutes, or until the cheese is melted and bubbly.

4. Remove from the oven and place on a serving dish. Garnish with cilantro and cut into wedges, if desired.

Nutritional analysis per serving:

CALORIES	PROTEIN, GM.	CARBOHYDRATE, GM.	FAT, GM.	SATURATED FAT, GM.
134	14.2	11.1	3.7	1.3

SODIUM, MG.	CHOLESTEROL, MG.	FIBER, GM.	CALCIUM, MG.	CALORIES FROM FAT
264.5	21.7	1.1	74	25%

Quesadillas

Quesadillas are usually served open-faced or folded. Flour tortillas are probably more traditional, but corn tortillas may be used as well. Use your microwave oven, toaster oven, or oven/broiler. Just watch them carefully because the cheese melts quickly and the Quesadillas can become overdone and hard.

SERVES 4.

4 tortillas
1 cup low-fat cheese*, shredded

*Cheese is often the only ingredient used and it is high in fat. I recommend using fat-reduced cheeses, like Monterey jack, cheddar or a combination. Go easy on the cheese. Use more salsa or other low-calorie additions like freshly chopped tomatoes, fresh or imitation crabmeat, cooked chicken or beef, or beans.

1. Preheat the oven to 450°F.

2. Place the tortillas on a cookie sheet and sprinkle with ¼ cup cheese each.

3. Bake in the oven (or broil) just until the cheese melts.

4. Serve open-faced or folded, plain or with assorted condiments. Serve whole or cut into wedges.

Nutritional analysis per serving:

CALORIES	PROTEIN, GM.	CARBOHYDRATE, GM.	FAT, GM.	SATURATED FAT, GM.
75	7.9	8.4	1.1	0.4

SODIUM, MG.	CHOLESTEROL, MG.	FIBER, GM.	CALCIUM, MG.	CALORIES FROM FAT
232.4	2.5	0.4	66	13%

Rolled Tacos

When you're in the mood for Mexican food, these are fun, easy, and satisfy the craving! Try topping them with Guacamole (page 263).

SERVES 6

2 pounds chicken breasts, boned,
   skinned, and split
2 cups green chili salsa
1 dozen corn tortillas, warm
Shredded lettuce

1. Preheat the oven to 300°F.

2. Rinse the chicken breasts and place them in a casserole. Pour the salsa over the chicken, cover, and bake for 1½ hours. Cool.

3. Shred the chicken and put it back in the sauce. Reheat when ready to use.

4. Place ¹⁄₁₂ mixture in 1 warm corn tortilla and roll it up. Serve on a bed of shredded lettuce.

Nutritional analysis per serving:

CALORIES	PROTEIN, GM.	CARBOHYDRATE, GM.	FAT, GM.	SATURATED FAT, GM.
221	30.9	13.7	4.1	0.9

SODIUM, MG.	CHOLESTEROL, MG.	FIBER, GM.	CALCIUM, MG.	CALORIES FROM FAT
69.8	77.6	0.9	77	17%

Tamale Pie

This dish is perfect for your vegetarian friends or if you are just cutting back on the amount of meat you eat.

SERVES 6

Cornbread

1 cup cornmeal
1 cup whole-wheat flour
1 tablespoon baking powder
1 tablespoon sugar
1 cup corn kernels
1 cup nonfat milk
2 egg whites
2 tablespoons corn oil

Topping

2 cups cooked pinto beans
1 cup green chili salsa
1 cup reduced-fat jack cheese, grated

1. Preheat the oven to 350°F. Spray a 9-inch baking pan with a nonstick spray.

2. Combine the cornmeal, flour, baking powder, sugar, and corn in a large bowl.

3. Mix the nonfat milk, egg whites, and corn oil. Add to the dry ingredients and mix well.

4. Pour into the prepared pan, and spread the pinto beans, salsa, and cheese evenly over the top.

5. Bake for 35 minutes.

Nutritional analysis per serving:

CALORIES	PROTEIN, GM.	CARBOHYDRATE, GM.	FAT, GM.	SATURATED FAT, GM.
384	21.2	55.9	8.7	2.5

SODIUM, MG.	CHOLESTEROL, MG.	FIBER, GM.	CALCIUM, MG.	CALORIES FROM FAT
672.9	8.6	9.1	469	20%

Guiltless Refried Beans

These are so easy and so good and all without fat! You can also put the bean mixture in the food processor to speed up the process.

SERVES 4

2 cups cooked pinto beans
1/4 cup chicken broth
1/2 teaspoon chili powder

1. Spray a heavy skillet with nonstick spray and heat. Add the beans and chicken broth, mashing and stirring the beans until the desired consistency.

2. Add the chili powder and stir to mix.

Nutritional analysis per serving:

CALORIES	PROTEIN, GM.	CARBOHYDRATE, GM.	FAT, GM.	SATURATED FAT, GM.
103	6.2	17.3	0.4	0.1

SODIUM, MG.	CHOLESTEROL, MG.	FIBER, GM.	CALCIUM, MG.	CALORIES FROM FAT
164	0.0	6.6	32	4%

Mexican Rice

This is an excellent side dish with Chicken Enchiladas (page 274). The fresh cilantro gives it a great taste.

SERVES 4

2 tomatoes, chopped into large chunks
1/2 onion, chopped into large chunks
2 cloves garlic, peeled and cut in half
1/4 teaspoon chili powder
1 tablespoon canola oil
1 cup brown rice
1 1/2 cups chicken broth
Small bunch of cilantro, chopped

1. Combine the tomatoes, onion, and garlic in a blender and purée.

2. Strain the mixture into a small bowl and add the chili powder.

3. Heat the oil in a heavy pan or skillet. Brown the rice in the hot oil, stirring constantly so it will not burn.

4. When the rice is browned, add the tomato mixture and broth or water. Bring to a boil, then reduce heat to simmer

5. Cover and cook for approximately 45 minutes, or until the rice is done and all of the liquid is absorbed.

6. Add the chopped fresh cilantro, stir slightly, and serve.

Nutritional analysis per serving:

CALORIES	PROTEIN, GM.	CARBOHYDRATE, GM.	FAT, GM.	SATURATED FAT, GM.
230	3.1	47	4.3	0.4

SODIUM, MG.	CHOLESTEROL, MG.	FIBER, GM.	CALCIUM, MG.	CALORIES FROM FAT
152	0.0	1.9	20	17%

Mexican-Style Cornbread

Here's a twist on traditional cornbread. Use creamed corn if you want a very moist cornbread.

SERVES 10

3/4 cup egg substitute
3/4 cup 1% milk
1 tablespoon pimento, chopped
1 to 2 chilies, roasted and chopped
  (about 1/2 cup)
1 cup cornmeal
1 cup flour
4 teaspoons baking powder
4 ounces low-fat shredded cheddar cheese
1 cup frozen corn kernels, thawed

1. Preheat the oven to 400°F. Prepare a 9-by-9-by-2-inch baking dish with nonstick spray.

2. In a bowl, combine the egg substitute and milk. Stir in the pimento and chopped chilies.

3. In a large bowl, combine the cornmeal, flour, and baking powder. Stir in the cheese and corn kernels.

4. Add the liquid ingredients and beat about 1 minute.

5. Spread evenly in the prepared baking dish and bake for 35 to 40 minutes. Cool and cut into 10 servings.

Nutritional analysis per serving:

CALORIES	PROTEIN, GM.	CARBOHYDRATE, GM.	FAT, GM.	SATURATED FAT, GM.
157	8.6	26.1	2.2	0.8

SODIUM, MG.	CHOLESTEROL, MG.	FIBER, GM.	CALCIUM, MG.	CALORIES FROM FAT
285.5	3.3	1.7	216	12%

Baked Grapefruit

This very light and refreshing dessert is perfect after a heavier meal.

SERVES 4

2 grapefruit
2 tablespoons orange juice, fresh preferred
1 tablespoon sugar
2 teaspoons tequila (optional)
¼ teaspoon cinnamon

1. Preheat the oven to 475°F, or the broiler.

2. Cut each grapefruit in half. Section each half, then place in an ovenproof dish.

3. Mix the remaining ingredients and spoon equally over the grapefruit halves.

4. Bake for approximately 10 minutes or broil for about 4 minutes until bubbly.

Nutritional analysis per serving:

CALORIES	PROTEIN, GM.	CARBOHYDRATE, GM.	FAT, GM.	SATURATED FAT, GM.
62	0.9	14.3	0.1	0.02

SODIUM, MG.	CHOLESTEROL, MG.	FIBER, GM.	CALCIUM, MG.	CALORIES FROM FAT
0.1	0.0	0.8	18	2%

Russian Cuisine

Introduction

Russian cuisine is similar to German and Scandinavian cuisine. Russia has a very cold climate, so the natives often use root vegetables because they store well or can be pickled. Sour cream is fundamental in Russian cooking. Russians love to entertain in their homes and will prepare dishes in advance so they can enjoy their guests.

Even though the Russian diet is rather heavy, it is easy to lighten those fat calories with the help of low-fat sour cream. I devised a delicious sauce for our Russian dishes by adding low-fat sour cream to the Basic White Sauce.

In Russia no party is complete without vodka. Most Russians will drink it straight, but I mix it with some soda or a squeeze of lime. Caviar is also a favorite, if your pocketbook and your sodium intake can handle it. There are some palatable caviars on the market that are within reason. A little caviar can go a long way, so try it at least once!

A RUSSIAN WINTER PARTY

Some parts of Russia have severe winters, so it seems appropriate to plan a Taste-of-Russia party in winter. Make it casual with a showing of *Silk Stockings* on your video. Here's a sample menu.

Appetizer
Blini with Caviar
Vodka and Soda

Soup
Hot Borscht in mugs
Russian Rye Bread (from your bakery)

Main Course
Chicken Cutlet
Vegetable Salad
Braised Carrots

Dessert
Cheese Curd Pudding
Tea

Blini (Buckwheat Pancakes)

Blini are served at the end of winter as a sign of sun and spring. They are accompanied by sour cream, caviar, and Russian vodka.

SERVES 6

2 cups nonfat milk, warmed
1 tablespoon yeast
1⅓ cups flour
½ cup buckwheat flour
1 teaspoon sugar
4 egg whites
2 tablespoons melted butter
¼ cup Yogurt Cheese (page 98)
¼ cup low-fat sour cream
¼ cup black caviar

1. In 1 cup milk dissolve the yeast and add 1 teaspoon flour. Place the mixture in a warm place until it rises to double its size.

2. Add the rest of the warmed milk. Sift in the remaining flour; add the sugar, 2 egg whites, and butter. Beat until smooth. Set the dough aside to rise until doubles in size. Knead it lightly, and let it rise again.

3. Whisk the remaining 2 egg whites until frothy and add them to the mixture.

4. Heat a nonstick skillet sprayed with nonstick spray and make 12 pancakes. (They will be thicker than normal pancakes.)

5. Mix the Yogurt Cheese and sour cream, and place 2 teaspoons on each pancake. Top with the caviar.

Nutritional analysis per serving:

CALORIES	PROTEIN, GM.	CARBOHYDRATE, GM.	FAT, GM.	SATURATED FAT, GM.
215	11.6	25.9	7.4	3.7

SODIUM, MG.	CHOLESTEROL, MG.	FIBER, GM.	CALCIUM, MG.	CALORIES FROM FAT
291	77.3	1.1	163	31%

Borscht

It is much easier to peel the beets if you blanch them first for about 10 minutes in boiling water. If you use canned beets, you can reduce the cooking time to 30 minutes.

SERVES 6

5 large beets, peeled and grated
1 medium onion, chopped
6 cups low-salt chicken broth
1 cup tomato puree
1 tablespoon lemon juice
1/2 teaspoon freshly ground black pepper
1 teaspoon sugar
1 cup low-fat sour cream

1. Combine the beets, onion, and chicken broth in a Dutch oven. Bring to a boil, reduce heat, cover, and simmer for 45 minutes.

2. Add the tomato purée, lemon juice, pepper, and sugar. Simmer for another 45 minutes.

3. Pour the soup into a blender and purée until smooth. Serve hot or cold, topped with sour cream.

Nutritional analysis per serving:

CALORIES	PROTEIN, GM.	CARBOHYDRATE, GM.	FAT, GM.	SATURATED FAT, GM.
140	5.5	17.8	5.8	2.9

SODIUM, MG.	CHOLESTEROL, MG.	FIBER, GM.	CALCIUM, MG.	CALORIES FROM FAT
430	8.5	2.7	67	37%

Braised Carrots

This dish adds great color and a nice sweetness.

SERVES 6

2 tablespoons butter
1/2 cup water
1 teaspoon sugar
1 pound carrots, sliced diagonally or cut
  into 1 1/2-inch strips

1. In a saucepan mix the butter, water, and sugar together. Bring to a boil.

2. Add the carrots. Reduce heat to simmer, cover, and cook for 5 minutes. Uncover and bring back to a boil and cook until all of the liquid is absorbed.

Nutritional analysis per serving:

CALORIES	PROTEIN, GM.	CARBOHYDRATE, GM.	FAT, GM.	SATURATED FAT, GM.
71	0.8	8.3	4.2	2.54

SODIUM, MG.	CHOLESTEROL, MG.	FIBER, GM.	CALCIUM, MG.	CALORIES FROM FAT
69.4	10.9	2.4	29	53%

Potato Cakes with Mushroom Sauce

Serve this dish with a tossed green salad for lunch or a light supper.

SERVES 6

1 pound russet potatoes, cubed with skin
2 tablespoons butter
2 egg whites
1/2 cup flour
Mushroom Sauce

1. Cook the potatoes and drain. Add the butter and mash them.

2. Mix in the egg whites and form into 6 balls. Flatten the balls in flour to coat them.

3. In a skillet sprayed with nonstick spray, fry the potato cakes. Top with the Mushroom Sauce.

Continued on page 297

Continued from page 296

Potato Cakes with Mushroom Sauce

Mushroom Sauce

6 ounces mushrooms, sliced
1 onion, chopped
1½ cups vegetable stock
1 tablespoon flour

1. Sauté the mushrooms and onion in a saucepan sprayed with a nonstick spray. Set aside.

2. Mix the vegetable stock and flour together in the skillet and heat, stirring constantly until thickened. Add the mushrooms and onions to the sauce and heat through.

Nutritional analysis per serving:

Calories	Protein, gm.	Carbohydrate, gm.	Fat, gm.	Saturated Fat, gm.
234	7.5	44.6	4.7	2.7

Sodium, mg.	Cholesterol, mg.	Fiber, gm.	Calcium, mg.	Calories from Fat
140	10.9	5	19	18%

Russian Red Cabbage

This will add some color to your plate!

SERVES 6

1 medium onion, chopped
1 medium red cabbage, shredded
2 tablespoons vinegar
1 tablespoon molasses
2 green apples, cored and grated
1/2 teaspoon ground black pepper
1 cup water

1. Sauté the onion in a Dutch oven sprayed with nonstick spray.

2. Add the remaining ingredients and bring to a boil. Reduce heat, cover, and simmer for 1 1/2 hours.

Nutritional analysis per serving:

CALORIES	PROTEIN, GM.	CARBOHYDRATE, GM.	FAT, GM.	SATURATED FAT, GM.
47	0.5	11.9	0.2	0.04

SODIUM, MG.	CHOLESTEROL, MG.	FIBER, GM.	CALCIUM, MG.	CALORIES FROM FAT
7.3	0.0	1.7	35	4%

Chicken Cutlet

This is very good served with Russian Red Cabbage (page 298).

SERVES 6

12 ounces ground chicken breast
1/4 teaspoon grated nutmeg
1/2 teaspoon ground white pepper
4 egg whites
2 tablespoons water
1 teaspoon olive oil
1/2 cup flour
1 1/2 cups bread crumbs

Sauce

1 recipe Basic White Sauce (page 109)
2 teaspoons paprika
1/4 cup low-fat sour cream
1 teaspoon cognac

1. Mix the ground chicken, nutmeg, pepper, and 2 egg whites together, and chill for half an hour.

2. Preheat the oven to 375°F. Spray a cookie sheet with nonstick spray.

3. Mix the remaining egg whites with the water and olive oil in a pie plate. Place the flour on one paper plate and the bread crumbs on another.

4. Make 6 balls from the chilled chicken mixture. Roll each ball first in flour, then in the egg mixture, and then in the bread crumbs.

5. Flatten the balls out to ovals. Place them on the cookie sheet and bake for 30 minutes, or until done.

Continued on page 300

Continued from page 299

Chicken Cutlet

6. Make the White Sauce and mix in the paprika, sour cream, and cognac.

7. Spoon the sauce over each cutlet and serve.

Nutritional analysis per serving:

CALORIES	PROTEIN, GM.	CARBOHYDRATE, GM.	FAT, GM.	SATURATED FAT, GM.
237	18.4	25.9	5.9	2.5

SODIUM, MG.	CHOLESTEROL, MG.	FIBER, GM.	CALCIUM, MG.	CALORIES FROM FAT
249.7	37.3	1.2	89	22%

Pancake Pie
This is a bit unusual, but very good.

SERVES 4

Pancakes
4 egg whites
1 teaspoon sugar
1½ cups nonfat milk
1 cup flour
1 tablespoon melted butter

Filling
12 ounces lean ground beef
1 medium onion, chopped
6 ounces mushrooms, sliced
1 recipe Basic White Sauce (page 109)
½ cup low-fat sour cream

1. Mix all of the pancake batter ingredients in a bowl and set aside.

2. Preheat the oven to 300°F. Prepare an 8-inch round deep-dish pan by spraying it with a nonstick spray.

3. Cook the meat in a nonstick skillet, and then remove to a paper plate lined with paper towels to absorb the excess fat.

4. Sauté the onion in the skillet sprayed with nonstick spray. Remove the onion to the plate with the ground beef.

5. Sauté the mushrooms in the skillet. Add the meat and onion. Stir in the White Sauce and sour cream.

Continued on page 302

Continued from page 301

Pancake Pie

6. Make six 8-inch pancakes with the batter. In an 8-inch round deep dish pan, layer the pancakes and meat mixture, starting and ending with a pancake.

7. Bake for 15 minutes. Turn it upside down on a round plate.

Nutritional analysis per serving:

Calories	Protein, gm.	Carbohydrate, gm.	Fat, gm.	Saturated Fat, gm.
544	34.6	68	16.6	8.4

Sodium, mg.	Cholesterol, mg.	Fiber, gm.	Calcium, mg.	Calories from Fat
247.6	83.2	6.1	230	27%

Russian Cutlets

You could use only beef or only chicken in this if you prefer.

SERVES 6

12 ounces lean ground beef
12 ounces ground chicken breast
1½ cups bread crumbs
1 medium onion, minced
2 tablespoons chopped fresh parsley
2 egg whites
¼ teaspoon ground black pepper
1 recipe Basic White Sauce (page 109)
¼ cup low-fat sour cream
Chopped fresh parsley for garnish

1. Preheat the oven to 350°F. Spray a cookie sheet with nonstick spray.

2. Mix the ground beef, ground chicken, ½ cup bread crumbs, onion, parsley, egg whites, and pepper.

3. Form 6 balls and roll them in 1 cup bread crumbs. Form the balls into ovals. Place on the cookie sheet. Bake for 45 minutes.

4. Make the White Sauce and add the sour cream to it.

5. Serve the cutlets with the sauce spooned over them. Sprinkle with chopped parsley.

Nutritional analysis per serving:

CALORIES	PROTEIN, GM.	CARBOHYDRATE, GM.	FAT, GM.	SATURATED FAT, GM.
283	28.3	19.7	9.3	4

SODIUM, MG.	CHOLESTEROL, MG.	FIBER, GM.	CALCIUM, MG.	CALORIES FROM FAT
258.7	75.8	1.1	98	30%

Cheese Curd Pudding

This pudding is full of protein and could also be a good breakfast choice.

SERVES 6

1 pound cheese curd (use dry curd
  cottage cheese)
3 egg whites
¼ cup sugar
2 tablespoons sour cream
2 teaspoons vanilla
6 teaspoons sugar-free jam

1. Preheat the oven to 350°F. Spray 6 custard cups with nonstick spray.

2. Place all of the ingredients, except the jam, in a food processor with a steel blade and process until smooth.

3. Divide the mixture into the custard cups and top each cup with 1 teaspoon jam.

4. Bake for 15 minutes. Serve cold.

Nutritional analysis per serving:

CALORIES	PROTEIN, GM.	CARBOHYDRATE, GM.	FAT, GM.	SATURATED FAT, GM.
113	11.2	13.3	1.3	0.7

SODIUM, MG.	CHOLESTEROL, MG.	FIBER, GM.	CALCIUM, MG.	CALORIES FROM FAT
335.7	4.4	0.1	51	10%

Scandinavian Cuisine

Introduction

Our fair-haired, fair-skinned friends in northern Europe are known for their fresh and preserved or pickled foods. Each Scandinavian country has its own specialties. Dairy products, especially cheese, are popular. Pickled vegetables and fish, especially herring, are often used as a base for hot and cold dishes. Bread and potatoes are popular, as in the rest of Europe. Fresh breads and a variety of unleavened breads are used as a base for open-faced sandwiches.

Perhaps one of the more common associations we make with Scandinavian cuisine is the smorgasbord display of cold foods that rivals any salad bar. It is a centuries' old precursor to grazing. Try a smorgasbord for your next gathering. It's a great idea for an outdoor affair or even a picnic. Here's a typical menu.

Smorgasbord
Cold Poached Salmon with Mustard-Dill Sauce
Fish Salad
Pickled Fish
Pickled Beet Salad
Cucumbers in Sour Cream
Mushroom Salad
Swedish Rye or Caraway Rye
    (from your bakery)
Unleavened Flat Bread Crackers
    (Rye Krisp or Kavli)
Platter of Crisp Lettuce Leaves and Tomato Wedges
Platter of Fresh Fruit

Cucumbers in Sour Cream

This light refreshing dish is perfect on a warm spring or summer day.

SERVES 4

2 cups cucumber, thinly sliced (about 2 medium cucumbers)
1/4 cup reduced-calorie sour cream
2 tablespoons Dijon-style mustard
2 tablespoons white vinegar
1/2 to 1 teaspoon sugar
Freshly ground pepper
1 teaspoon fresh dillweed, minced (1/2 teaspoon dried)

1. Place the sliced cucumbers into a bowl.

2. In another bowl combine the rest of the ingredients, and mix well. Pour over the cucumbers and stir to mix.

3. Chill and serve.

Nutritional analysis per serving:

CALORIES	PROTEIN, GM.	CARBOHYDRATE, GM.	FAT, GM.	SATURATED FAT, GM.
56	2.2	5.4	3.3	1

SODIUM, MG.	CHOLESTEROL, MG.	FIBER, GM.	CALCIUM, MG.	CALORIES FROM FAT
5.8	3.1	0.7	54	53%

Fish Salad

If serving this dish on a buffet, make sure you have nice lettuce cups to serve it in.

SERVES 6

½ recipe Pickled Fish (page 315)
4 small red potatoes, cooked with skins
   on, then diced
2 tablespoons onion, finely chopped
1 tablespoon horseradish sauce
1 teaspoon juice from Pickled Fish
3 tablespoons reduced-calorie sour cream
3 tablespoons plain nonfat yogurt
2 tablespoons fresh dill, chopped
Freshly ground pepper
6 lettuce leaves
2 hard-boiled eggs, whites only, sliced
2 fresh tomatoes, cut into wedges

1. With your hands, lightly crumble Pickled Fish into small chunks. Place with potatoes in a serving bowl.

2. In another bowl combine the onions, horseradish, pickling juice, sour cream, yogurt, dill, and a few grinds of pepper. Stir to mix well.

3. Pour the dressing over the fish and potatoes. Cover and chill in the refrigerator for at least 30 minutes before serving.

4. To serve, place 6 lettuce leaves on separate plates and spoon some Fish Salad on top of each leaf. Garnish with sliced egg whites and tomato wedges.

Nutritional analysis per serving:

CALORIES	PROTEIN, GM.	CARBOHYDRATE, GM.	FAT, GM.	SATURATED FAT, GM.
159	12	20.2	3.7	1.4

SODIUM, MG.	CHOLESTEROL, MG.	FIBER, GM.	CALCIUM, MG.	CALORIES FROM FAT
77.9	90.9	2.5	70	21%

Fresh Green Bean Salad

Choose thin, long green beans for this. If you use frozen beans, defrost them under cold water. If you want to bring up the color in the frozen beans, dunk them quickly—first in boiling water then in cold water. You want the beans to stay a bit crisp and not be overcooked.

SERVES 6

3 tablespoons red wine vinegar
1 tablespoon olive oil
1/2 cup chicken broth
Freshly ground black pepper
1 tablespoon fresh dill, finely chopped
1 tablespoon fresh parsley, finely chopped
1/2 teaspoon dried summer savory
1 pound fresh green beans

1. In a small bowl combine the vinegar, oil, chicken broth, and a few grinds of pepper. Beat well with a whisk to blend thoroughly.

2. Stir in the dill, parsley, and savory. Cover the bowl and set aside.

3. Trim the ends off the beans, then steam for 3 to 5 minutes over boiling water until the beans are crisp-tender. Remove from the heat at once and plunge them into very cold water or ice water. As the beans cool, drain them well or pat dry.

4. Transfer the beans to a large mixing bowl and pour the dressing over them, stirring to coat. Chill for at least 1 hour before serving.

Nutritional analysis per serving:

CALORIES	PROTEIN, GM.	CARBOHYDRATE, GM.	FAT, GM.	SATURATED FAT, GM.
40	1.2	4.2	2.5	0.3

SODIUM, MG.	CHOLESTEROL, MG.	FIBER, GM.	CALCIUM, MG.	CALORIES FROM FAT
67.8	0.0	0.6	28	57%

Fresh Spinach Soup

You can use frozen spinach for this, but fresh is much better.

SERVES 6

8 cups chicken broth
2 bunches fresh spinach, washed, large
  stems removed
2 tablespoons flour
2 tablespoons butter
1/8 teaspoon nutmeg

1. Bring the chicken broth to a boil in a large Dutch oven.

2. Chop the spinach coarsely and place in the pot with the broth. Simmer uncovered for 6 to 8 minutes.

3. Pour the broth and spinach into a sieve set over a large bowl. Press down on the spinach to remove moisture. Set aside 1/4 cup broth to cool. Return remaining broth to the pot and bring to a boil.

4. Combine the flour and butter with the 1/4 cup room-temperature broth. Mix until smooth. Pour slowly into hot broth, stirring constantly with a whisk. Simmer for a few minutes.

5. Chop the cooked spinach until fine and return it to the soup pot. Add the nutmeg, heat, and serve.

Nutritional analysis per serving:

CALORIES	PROTEIN, GM.	CARBOHYDRATE, GM.	FAT, GM.	SATURATED FAT, GM.
73	5.6	2.5	4.9	2.9

SODIUM, MG.	CHOLESTEROL, MG.	FIBER, GM.	CALCIUM, MG.	CALORIES FROM FAT
564	10.9	1.4	106	60%

Mushroom Salad

Make sure you have very fresh mushrooms for this.

SERVES 4

1 cup water
Juice of 1/2 lemon
1/2 pound fresh mushrooms, cleaned
  and sliced

Dressing

3 tablespoons reduced-calorie sour cream
1 tablespoon plain nonfat yogurt
1 tablespoon onion, finely minced
1 tablespoon white wine

1. In a small pot bring the water and lemon juice to a boil. Add the sliced mushrooms, reduce heat, cover, and cook about 3 minutes. Drain the mushrooms, then pat them dry with paper towels. Place in a serving dish.

2. Combine the dressing ingredients in a small dish and mix well. Gently stir the dressing into mushrooms. Serve as a garnish or salad.

Nutritional analysis per serving:

CALORIES	PROTEIN, GM.	CARBOHYDRATE, GM.	FAT, GM.	SATURATED FAT, GM.
39	1.7	5.3	1.4	0.7

SODIUM, MG.	CHOLESTEROL, MG.	FIBER, GM.	CALCIUM, MG.	CALORIES FROM FAT
11	2.3	1.2	36	32%

Pickled Beet Salad

Use fresh beets with tops. Remove the tops before preparing the beets. Wash and steam the tops for a few minutes. Beet greens or beet tops are a delicious and different green vegetable. Serve with a little vinegar mixed in.

SERVES 6

8 fresh beets
½ cup red wine vinegar
½ cup cider vinegar
1 onion, peeled and thinly sliced
4 whole cloves
½ teaspoon ground coriander seeds
6 whole black peppercorns
1 tablespoon horseradish (optional)

1. Scrub the beets and cut off the ends. Steam them over boiling water until just done. Remove them from the steamer and plunge them into cold water. Remove skins and drain.

2. Slice the beets into ⅛-inch slices and place them into a deep ceramic or glass bowl.

3. In a medium-size steel or enamel saucepan, bring the red and cider vinegars, onion, cloves, coriander, and peppercorns to a boil over a high heat. Pour the mixture over the beets. Be sure the beets are fully covered by the marinade. If not, add a little more vinegar. Cover and refrigerate for 24 hours to marinate.

4. Just before serving, remove the cloves and peppercorns. Mix the horseradish with 2 tablespoons of beet juice, then pour over the beets and stir gently to mix. Serve on a lettuce leaf or as a garnish.

Nutritional analysis per serving:

CALORIES	PROTEIN, GM.	CARBOHYDRATE, GM.	FAT, GM.	SATURATED FAT, GM.
91	2.4	20.9	1	0.4

SODIUM, MG.	CHOLESTEROL, MG.	FIBER, GM.	CALCIUM, MG.	CALORIES FROM FAT
115.8	1	3.1	55	10%

Pickled Fish

A delicious substitute for salted fish like pickled herring, use this fish as an appetizer on a toothpick for your smorgasbord or in any recipes calling for pickled fish.

SERVES 6

1 pound firm whitefish, about ½-inch thick
1 onion, sliced into rings
1 carrot, sliced
⅔ cup white vinegar
¼ cup water
3 bay leaves

1. Bring a pot of water to a boil. Rinse the fish well, then pat dry. Cut into 1-inch cubes. Drop a few cubes of fish one at a time into the boiling water. Remove pieces with a slotted spoon after about 10 seconds. Continue until all of the fish has been blanched. Drain the fish pieces and place them into a shallow glass or ceramic dish.

2. Spray another pan with nonstick spray, and lightly sauté the onions and carrots until the onions just begin to turn translucent. Do not brown.

3. Add the vinegar, water, and bay leaf and bring to a boil. Reduce the heat and simmer about 5 minutes.

4. Pour the hot vinegar mixture over the fish cubes, allowing the onions and carrots to lay decoratively on top. Cover and refrigerate for 24 hours.

Nutritional analysis per serving:

CALORIES	PROTEIN, GM.	CARBOHYDRATE, GM.	FAT, GM.	SATURATED FAT, GM.
86	14.6	4.6	1	0.2

SODIUM, MG.	CHOLESTEROL, MG.	FIBER, GM.	CALCIUM, MG.	CALORIES FROM FAT
67.2	36.3	0.8	30	10%

Potato-Leek Soup

I prefer to scrub the potatoes and leave the skin on; this keeps vitamins and minerals and adds more fiber, but if you want a more elegant look to your soup, peel them.

SERVES 6

3 leeks, white part only
2 tablespoons butter
2 stalks celery, chopped
3 medium potatoes
3 cups low-salt chicken broth
2 cups 1% milk
Parsley

1. Wash leeks well and slice thinly. Place the butter in a large Dutch oven. Add the sliced leeks and celery. Cook and stir for several minutes, taking care not to burn them.

2. Peel the potatoes (if desired). Cut them lengthwise into quarters, then dice into medium-size chunks. Add them to the soup pot.

3. Pour in the chicken broth and simmer for 20 to 30 minutes, or until the potatoes seem tender. Slowly pour in the milk and heat the soup, but do not boil it.

4. Serve the soup as is, or process it in a food processor to give it a smooth, creamy consistency. Garnish with parsley.

Nutritional analysis per serving:

CALORIES	PROTEIN, GM.	CARBOHYDRATE, GM.	FAT, GM.	SATURATED FAT, GM.
164	6	23.9	5.4	3.2

SODIUM, MG.	CHOLESTEROL, MG.	FIBER, GM.	CALCIUM, MG.	CALORIES FROM FAT
249	14.2	2.3	150	30%

Rice Casserole

Here is a delicious way to use leftover brown or white rice.

SERVES 6

2 cups cooked rice
¼ pound mushrooms, sliced
1 small onion, chopped
2 medium tomatoes, chopped
2 teaspoons marjoram (or any herb for
   seasoning)
Freshly ground pepper
1 ounce goat cheese (or any reduced-
   calorie cheese)
Parsley

1. Preheat the oven to 350°F.

2. Place the rice in a casserole dish.

3. Spray a frying pan with nonstick spray. Sauté the mushrooms and onions until tender. Stir in the tomatoes, marjoram, and pepper. Stir and cook just enough to heat through.

4. Pour the vegetable mixture over the rice and stir to mix. Crumble or grate the cheese over the top.

5. Cover and bake for 20 to 30 minutes, just until heated through. Garnish with parsley.

Nutritional analysis per serving:

CALORIES	PROTEIN, GM.	CARBOHYDRATE, GM.	FAT, GM.	SATURATED FAT, GM.
121	3.5	23.7	1.5	0.8

SODIUM, MG.	CHOLESTEROL, MG.	FIBER, GM.	CALCIUM, MG.	CALORIES FROM FAT
58.7	4.2	1.4	44	11%

Scandinavian Cabbage

This quick, easy recipe provides generous portions.

SERVES 6

1 small head cabbage, coarsely shredded
1 cup reduced-calorie sour cream
1 teaspoon caraway seed
¼ teaspoon freshly ground pepper

1. Steam the cabbage until it is crisp-tender. Remove to another pan.

2. Stir the rest of the ingredients into the cabbage and heat carefully just enough to heat it through. Serve.

Nutritional analysis per serving:

CALORIES	PROTEIN, GM.	CARBOHYDRATE, GM.	FAT, GM.	SATURATED FAT, GM.
45	0.8	1.7	4.1	2.5

SODIUM, MG.	CHOLESTEROL, MG.	FIBER, GM.	CALCIUM, MG.	CALORIES FROM FAT
12.4	8.5	0.4	30	82%

Sour Cream Potato Salad

This is a little different from our traditional American potato salad, and very good.

SERVES 6

4 medium potatoes, cooked and diced
1/2 cup cucumber, diced
1 tablespoon onion, minced
3/4 teaspoon celery seed
1/4 teaspoon pepper
2 hard-boiled eggs, whites only
1/4 cup reduced-calorie sour cream
1/4 cup plain nonfat yogurt
2 tablespoons vinegar
1/2 teaspoon dry mustard

1. Combine the potatoes, cucumber, onion, celery seed, pepper, and egg whites in a mixing bowl.

2. In another small bowl combine the sour cream and yogurt. Stir in the vinegar and dry mustard and mix very well.

3. Pour over the potato mixture and stir just enough to mix or coat the potatoes. Serve.

Nutritional analysis per serving:

CALORIES	PROTEIN, GM.	CARBOHYDRATE, GM.	FAT, GM.	SATURATED FAT, GM.
103	3.7	19.8	1.3	0.6

SODIUM, MG.	CHOLESTEROL, MG.	FIBER, GM.	CALCIUM, MG.	CALORIES FROM FAT
33.7	2.2	2	46	11%

Baked Fish with Cucumber Sauce

I prefer using a firmer fish like halibut in this recipe.

SERVES 4

1 pound fresh whitefish fillets or steaks
¼ cup cucumber, peeled and finely chopped
2 tablespoons reduced-calorie sour cream
2 tablespoons plain nonfat yogurt
1 tablespoon onion, freshly minced
1 tablespoon fresh dill, chopped

1. Preheat the oven to 350°F.

2. Rinse the fish and pat it dry. Place the fish in a baking dish and bake until done. (The baking time will vary according to the thickness of the fish.)

3. Combine the rest of the ingredients in a small bowl and mix thoroughly.

4. When the fish is done, divide it onto 4 plates and garnish each with about 2 tablespoons of the sauce.

Nutritional analysis per serving:

CALORIES	PROTEIN, GM.	CARBOHYDRATE, GM.	FAT, GM.	SATURATED FAT, GM.
121	22.2	2.3	2.2	0.8

SODIUM, MG.	CHOLESTEROL, MG.	FIBER, GM.	CALCIUM, MG.	CALORIES FROM FAT
101.4	56.2	0.2	57	16%

Baked Fish with Fresh Tomato Sauce

Sea bass or red snapper is excellent for this dish.

SERVES 4

1 pound fresh or frozen fish steaks
  or fillets
2 tablespoons melted butter
Freshly ground black pepper
4 tomatoes
1/2 onion, chopped
1 tablespoon capers
1 bay leaf

1. Preheat the oven to 350°F.

2. Rinse the fish, pat it dry, and place it in a baking dish. Season with the butter and pepper. Bake until done.

3. Meanwhile, fill a saucepan with water and bring it to a boil. Dip the tomatoes into the boiling water, then immediately plunge them into cold water in order to remove the skins. Cut the tomatoes in half and remove the seeds. Dice the tomatoes and set aside.

4. Spray a small skillet with nonstick spray. Sauté the onions until soft and just beginning to brown. Stir in the tomatoes, capers, and bay leaf. Cover and simmer about 15 minutes.

5. When the fish is cooked, place each serving on a plate and top with about 1/4 cup of tomato sauce.

Nutritional analysis per serving:

CALORIES	PROTEIN, GM.	CARBOHYDRATE, GM.	FAT, GM.	SATURATED FAT, GM.
190	22.7	7.4	7.9	4.1

SODIUM, MG.	CHOLESTEROL, MG.	FIBER, GM.	CALCIUM, MG.	CALORIES FROM FAT
252.9	70.8	1.9	33	37%

Poached Salmon with Mustard Dill Sauce

This salmon is also great served cold with a green salad by its side.

SERVES 4

1½ cups water
½ cup white wine
1 stalk celery, chopped
¼ cup chopped fresh parsley
1 pound fresh salmon steaks or fillets

Sauce
2 tablespoons Dijon-style mustard
1 tablespoon white wine
¼ cup reduced-calorie sour cream
1 tablespoon fresh dill, chopped

1. Combine the water, wine, celery, and parsley in a pan, and bring to a boil. Reduce to a simmer, and place the rinsed salmon into this poaching liquid. Cover and poach until done, about 10 minutes, depending on the thickness of the fish.

2. Combine the sauce ingredients in a small bowl and mix well. When the fish is done, carefully remove it to a platter or serving dish with a slotted spoon or spatula. Serve the sauce as a garnish or on the side.

Nutritional analysis per serving:

CALORIES	PROTEIN, GM.	CARBOHYDRATE, GM.	FAT, GM.	SATURATED FAT, GM.
241	25.3	2.6	11.6	2.6

SODIUM, MG.	CHOLESTEROL, MG.	FIBER, GM.	CALCIUM, MG.	CALORIES FROM FAT
175.6	73.4	0.5	88	43%

Swedish Meatballs

These are a great addition to any party!

SERVES 6

1 pound lean ground meat (beef, pork, veal, or a combination)
1/2 onion, finely chopped
1 large potato, boiled and mashed (about 1 cup)
3 tablespoons fine dry bread crumbs
2 tablespoons reduced-calorie sour cream
2 tablespoons plain nonfat yogurt
2 egg whites
1 tablespoon finely chopped parsley

1. Combine all of the ingredients and mix thoroughly. Shape into 32 small meatballs. Place them onto a flat tray, cover, and refrigerate for at least 1 hour before cooking.

2. When ready to cook, spray a heavy skillet with nonstick spray and heat it to a moderate temperature. Add about half the meatballs and cook them until well browned on all sides and cooked through. Repeat this process with the rest of the meatballs until all are cooked.

Nutritional analysis per serving:

CALORIES	PROTEIN, GM.	CARBOHYDRATE, GM.	FAT, GM.	SATURATED FAT, GM.
205	22.4	13.1	6.5	2.5

SODIUM, MG.	CHOLESTEROL, MG.	FIBER, GM.	CALCIUM, MG.	CALORIES FROM FAT
135.1	53.8	0.6	180	28%

Filled Apple Muffins

These are a bit time-consuming, but the effort makes a nice surprise center!

SERVES 8

2 tablespoons butter
⅓ cup sugar
2 egg whites
1½ cups flour
¼ teaspoon baking powder
½ teaspoon cinnamon
¼ teaspoon allspice
1 cup applesauce, unsweetened

1. Cream together the butter and sugar. Stir in the egg whites.

2. Sift the flour and baking powder together, and add the egg white mixture. Blend into a dough. Shape the dough into a ball, wrap it in plastic wrap, and chill for at least 1 hour.

3. Preheat the oven to 350°F. Spray a muffin tin with nonstick spray. The cups in the tin should measure about 2 inches in diameter.

4. Cut off ⅓ of the dough, rewrap it, and return it to the refrigerator. Divide the remaining dough into 8 pieces and firmly press each piece onto the bottom and sides of each cup in the muffin tin.

5. Combine the cinnamon and allspice with the applesauce. Fill each muffin with 2 tablespoons of the applesauce mixture.

Continued on page 325

Continued from page 324

Filled Apple Muffins

6. Remove the rest of the dough from the refrigerator and roll it out until it's very thin. Cut with a 2- to 2½-inch biscuit cutter and place each round on top of the applesauce. Pinch or crimp the top piece to the sides of each muffin in order to seal the edges.

7. Bake 30 to 35 minutes. The muffins should be nicely browned. Allow them to cool in the muffin tins, then remove them carefully.

Nutritional analysis per serving:

Calories	Protein, gm.	Carbohydrate, gm.	Fat, gm.	Saturated Fat, gm.
151	3.2	27.4	3.3	1.9

Sodium, mg.	Cholesterol, mg.	Fiber, gm.	Calcium, mg.	Calories from Fat
59.1	8.2	1.1	15	20%

Rum Fruitcake

Plan in advance to make this cake. It needs a week to marinate. Make several for great holiday gifts.

SERVES 24

1 cup rum
1 can (6 ounces) frozen orange juice
  concentrate, thawed
1 cup cranberries, chopped
1 package (8 ounces) dates, pitted and
  chopped
1/2 cup walnuts, chopped
1 tablespoon orange rind, grated
1 tablespoon vanilla
4 egg whites
1 can (8 ounces) pineapple tidbits,
  unsweetened, drained
2 1/4 cups flour
1 1/4 teaspoons baking soda
1/2 teaspoon cinnamon
1/2 teaspoon nutmeg
1/4 teaspoon allspice
1/2 cup fresh orange juice

1. Preheat the oven to 325°F. Prepare a Bundt pan with nonstick cooking spray.

2. Combine 1/2 cup rum, the orange juice concentrate, and cranberries in a bowl, and set aside for 1 hour.

3. Combine the dates, walnuts, orange rind, vanilla, egg whites, and pineapple. Add to the cranberry mixture and stir to mix.

4. In another bowl combine the dry ingredients. Add to the fruit mixture and stir well.

5. Spoon the batter into the prepared pan and bake for 45 minutes, or until done in the center. Let cool about 20 minutes, then remove from the pan.

Continued on page 327

Continued from page 326

Rum Fruitcake

6. Combine the remaining rum and the fresh orange juice.

7. Place the cake on a platter or plate. Place several layers of cheesecloth over the top of cake. Pour the rum-orange juice mixture over the cheesecloth. Wrap the cake and cheesecloth in waxed paper or plastic wrap, then in foil.

8. Place the cake in a dry place and let it sit for one week. Unwrap, slice, and serve.

Nutritional analysis per serving:

CALORIES	PROTEIN, GM.	CARBOHYDRATE, GM.	FAT, GM.	SATURATED FAT, GM.
105	2.4	18.1	1.8	0.2

SODIUM, MG.	CHOLESTEROL, MG.	FIBER, GM.	CALCIUM, MG.	CALORIES FROM FAT
68.5	0.0	1.5	10	16%

Scandinavian Fruit Soup

A classic soup that is tasty and different.

SERVES 6

½ cup dried pitted prunes (about 10)
½ cup dried apricot halves (about 16)
¼ cup raisins
½ lemon, sliced
3 (4-inch) cinnamon sticks
1 tablespoon sugar
1½ tablespoons quick-cooking tapioca
1 small apple, cubed

1. Combine all of the ingredients, except the apple, in a saucepan. Add 3 cups water and bring to a boil. Reduce heat, cover, and simmer for 20 minutes, stirring occasionally.

2. Add the apple. Cover and simmer about 5 minutes. Turn off the heat, remove the cinnamon sticks, and cool. Serve warm or cold.

Nutritional analysis per serving:

CALORIES	PROTEIN, GM.	CARBOHYDRATE, GM.	FAT, GM.	SATURATED FAT, GM.
99	1.1	25.8	0.4	0.1

SODIUM, MG.	CHOLESTEROL, MG.	FIBER, GM.	CALCIUM, MG.	CALORIES FROM FAT
6.4	0.3	2.8	31	3%

Sour Cream Waffles

Sour Cream Waffles make a wonderful dessert topped with fruit and whipped topping—or a scoop of chocolate sorbet.

SERVES 6

2 eggs
4 egg whites
1 tablespoon sugar
$\frac{1}{2}$ teaspoon cinnamon
1 teaspoon cardamom
1 cup flour
1 cup reduced-calorie sour cream
1 tablespoon oil

1. Mix the eggs and egg whites until combined. Add the sugar.

2. Add cinnamon and cardamom to the flour, then stir the flour into the egg mixture. Add the sour cream and oil, and stir just to mix.

3. Spray a waffle iron with nonstick spray and heat it. Pour $\frac{1}{2}$ cup waffle batter into the preheated iron and bake until the waffle is nicely browned. Continue until all of the batter is used.

Nutritional analysis per serving:

CALORIES	PROTEIN, GM.	CARBOHYDRATE, GM.	FAT, GM.	SATURATED FAT, GM.
177	7	18.2	8.3	3.4

SODIUM, MG.	CHOLESTEROL, MG.	FIBER, GM.	CALCIUM, MG.	CALORIES FROM FAT
67.4	78.6	0.6	38	42%

Swedish Pancakes

Swedish Pancakes make a great dessert—serve them with fresh fruit or sugar-free preserves in the middle! Of course, they are also delicious for breakfast.

SERVES 6

1 whole egg
4 egg whites
1 cup nonfat milk
1 cup flour
1 tablespoon sugar

1. In a medium-size bowl combine the whole egg and the egg whites. Stir to mix well. Stir in the milk.

2. Add the flour and sugar to the milk and egg mixture, beating by hand until well mixed. The batter will be thin like crêpe batter.

3. Spray a griddle or skillet with nonstick spray and heat it until a drop of water sizzles in the pan. For each pancake, carefully pour 2 tablespoons of batter into the pan. You can make 3 or 4 pancakes at a time.

4. When the pancakes are brown on the edges and bubbly in the center, turn and cook them briefly on the other side. Remove to a heated platter to keep warm.

Nutritional analysis per serving:

CALORIES	PROTEIN, GM.	CARBOHYDRATE, GM.	FAT, GM.	SATURATED FAT, GM.
101	5.3	17	1.1	0.3

SODIUM, MG.	CHOLESTEROL, MG.	FIBER, GM.	CALCIUM, MG.	CALORIES FROM FAT
46.8	35	0.5	8	10%

Swedish Pound Cake

Here's another version of the basic pound cake.

SERVES 12

4 tablespoons butter
1/2 cup sugar
4 egg whites
1 1/2 cups flour
1 teaspoon baking soda
3/4 teaspoon cinnamon
1 teaspoon cardamom
1/2 cup reduced-calorie sour cream
1 teaspoon vanilla

1. Preheat the oven to 350°F. Prepare a loaf pan by spraying it with a nonstick spray.

2. Cream the butter and sugar. Stir in the egg whites and mix well. Do not overmix.

3. Sift together the flour, baking soda, cinnamon, and cardamom. Stir 1/2 of the flour mixture into the butter mixture.

4. Stir in the sour cream, vanilla, and the rest of the flour. Mix just enough to combine the ingredients. Pour into the loaf pan.

5. Bake about 50 minutes, or until baked through. Be careful not to overbake. Cool thoroughly before slicing.

Nutritional analysis per serving:

CALORIES	PROTEIN, GM.	CARBOHYDRATE, GM.	FAT, GM.	SATURATED FAT, GM.
137	2.9	19.6	5.2	3.2

SODIUM, MG.	CHOLESTEROL, MG.	FIBER, GM.	CALCIUM, MG.	CALORIES FROM FAT
155.9	13	0.4	12	34%

Spanish Cuisine

Introduction

Spanish cooking brings to mind bullfights, flamenco dancing and, of course, the masterpieces of Goya. The Spaniards are great snackers; their main meal is eaten between 2:00 and 3:00 P.M. Spaniards often meet friends at midday at bars called tascas, where they enjoy wine, beer, or sherry accompanied by tapas, which are small portions of food. They have dinner between 9:00 and 10:00. Now you can understand the need for a siesta!

Mexican and Spanish cuisine are similar. The main difference is that Spanish cooking has a French influence and is more delicate in flavor than Mexican. Spanish cooks simmer their foods slowly in clay pots. They use simple spices—thyme, bay leaf, cayenne, paprika, parsley, and saffron—in moderation.

SPANISH DINNER PARTY

Entertain your dinner company with a Spanish flair. Have flamenco music playing in the background. Use brightly colored tablecloths and napkins and candles.

Serve dry Spanish sherry with the appetizers, a red Spanish wine with the entrée and Spanish champagne with dessert. Here's something to get you started.

Appetizers
  Tequila Marinated Shrimp
  Crudités

Salad
  Tossed Green Salad

Entrée
  Paella

Dessert
  Bowl of Fresh Fruit
  Strawberry Sorbet
  Cookies

Spanish Rice

You may use white rice for this as well.

SERVES 4

1 tablespoon olive oil
1 medium onion, chopped
2 cloves garlic, chopped
1 green bell pepper, chopped
1 medium tomato, peeled and chopped
1/2 teaspoon cayenne pepper
1 cup brown rice
2 1/2 cups chicken broth

1. Heat the olive oil in a Dutch oven. Sauté the onion, garlic, and bell pepper until soft.

2. Add the tomato, cayenne pepper, and rice, and stir. Add the chicken broth, and bring to a boil.

3. Reduce the heat to a simmer. Cover and cook 45 minutes, or bake it at 350°F for 45 minutes.

Nutritional analysis per serving:

CALORIES	PROTEIN, GM.	CARBOHYDRATE, GM.	FAT, GM.	SATURATED FAT, GM.
183	5	30.6	4.7	0.8

SODIUM, MG.	CHOLESTEROL, MG.	FIBER, GM.	CALCIUM, MG.	CALORIES FROM FAT
249	0.0	2.8	33	23%

Spanish Salad

This is a good summer salad or side dish.

SERVES 8

4 cups cooked brown rice
6 red, green, and/or yellow bell peppers,
   roasted, peeled, and cut in strips
2 red onions, halved, thinly sliced
6 tomatoes, peeled, cut into eighths
1 can (4 ounces) sliced green olives,
   drained
¾ cup Vinaigrette Dressing (page 22)
Freshly ground black pepper

1. Put the rice on the bottom of the serving dish. Arrange the peppers, onions, tomatoes, and olives on top.

2. Pour the dressing over the top and sprinkle with the black pepper.

Nutritional analysis per serving:

CALORIES	PROTEIN, GM.	CARBOHYDRATE, GM.	FAT, GM.	SATURATED FAT, GM.
175	4.3	37.4	2.2	1.8

SODIUM, MG.	CHOLESTEROL, MG.	FIBER, GM.	CALCIUM, MG.	CALORIES FROM FAT
288.3	0.0	4.2	32	3%

Baked Spanish Halibut

This dish is delicious and simple, and very low in fat.

SERVES 6

3 white onions, cut in half, very thinly sliced
2 pounds halibut
½ teaspoon freshly ground black pepper
1 garlic clove, minced
1 cup dry white wine
2 tomatoes, peeled and sliced
2 bay leaves
4 undercooked potatoes, sliced

1. Preheat the oven to 400°F.

2. In an ovenproof serving dish sprayed with a nonstick spray, layer ½ of the onions. Place the fish on top and cover with the pepper, garlic and wine.

3. Cover with the remaining onions, tomatoes and bay leaves. Place the potatoes around the fish.

4. Bake for 45 minutes, or until the fish is done. Baste occasionally with the cooking juices.

Nutritional analysis per serving:

CALORIES	PROTEIN, GM.	CARBOHYDRATE, GM.	FAT, GM.	SATURATED FAT, GM.
267	31	23.9	2.1	0.5

SODIUM, MG.	CHOLESTEROL, MG.	FIBER, GM.	CALCIUM, MG.	CALORIES FROM FAT
135.4	72.6	3.1	55	7%

Paella

Paella is a wonderful entrée to serve to company. It is a very pretty one-dish meal.

SERVES 6

8 ounce raw chicken breasts, boned and skinned
1 tablespoon oil
6 pieces Guiltless Chorizo (page 280), cooked
1 onion, chopped
1 clove garlic, minced
1 teaspoon paprika
2 tablespoons chopped fresh parsley
1/4 teaspoon pepper
1 cup tomato juice
1 cup light beer (or 1 cup chicken broth)
1 cup brown rice, uncooked
2 tablespoons pimento, sliced
1 package (9 ounces) frozen artichoke hearts, thawed
1/2 pound large shrimp, cooked, or 6 fresh clams, or 6 mussels in shells
1 cup fresh or frozen peas

1. Cut the chicken into chunks or strips, and brown in the oil.

2. Add the chorizo and heat. Remove the chicken and chorizo from the skillet, and sauté the onion and garlic until lightly browned.

3. Add the paprika, parsley, pepper, tomato juice, and beer. Bring to a boil.

4. Add the rice and pimento. Cover and simmer about 45 minutes, or until the rice is done and most of the liquid is absorbed.

5. Add the chicken pieces, chorizo, artichoke hearts, and shrimp. Sprinkle the peas over the top. Cover and simmer about 10 minutes, or until the artichokes are tender and the other ingredients are heated through.

Nutritional analysis per serving:

CALORIES	PROTEIN, GM.	CARBOHYDRATE, GM.	FAT, GM.	SATURATED FAT, GM.
269	27.8	26.7	5.5	1.1

SODIUM, MG.	CHOLESTEROL, MG.	FIBER, GM.	CALCIUM, MG.	CALORIES FROM FAT
245	112	4.3	76	18%

Spanish Chicken

Use the different colored peppers to add a variety of color.

SERVES 4

1 tablespoon olive oil
1 garlic clove, peeled
4 (4 ounce) chicken breasts, boned and skinned
1/2 teaspoon freshly ground black pepper
1 medium onion, chopped
2 red, green and/or yellow bell peppers, seeded and chopped
1 tablespoon paprika
1/4 teaspoon saffron
1 can (15 ounces) diced tomatoes
1/2 teaspoon cayenne pepper

1. Heat the olive oil in a large skillet. Sauté the garlic until golden brown, and discard.

2. Add the chicken breasts and brown on both sides. Sprinkle with pepper. Remove from the skillet and set aside.

3. Add the onions and peppers to the skillet and sauté them until soft.

4. Add the paprika, saffron, tomatoes, and cayenne, and mix.

5. Place the chicken back into the pan. Cover and cook on low until the chicken is done, about 20 minutes.

Nutritional analysis per serving:

CALORIES	PROTEIN, GM.	CARBOHYDRATE, GM.	FAT, GM.	SATURATED FAT, GM.
218	28.3	10.1	7	1.4

SODIUM, MG.	CHOLESTEROL, MG.	FIBER, GM.	CALCIUM, MG.	CALORIES FROM FAT
79.4	72.7	3.1	53	29%

Spanish Pork

Serve with a tossed green salad.

SERVES 6

1 pound lean pork shoulder, cut into
   1-inch cubes
2 garlic cloves, chopped
1 small onion, chopped
1 can (28 ounces) whole peeled tomatoes,
   drained (reserve liquid)
3 green bell peppers, seeded, cut in half,
   and thinly sliced
1/2 teaspoon saffron
2 tablespoons chopped fresh parsley
5 cups water
2 cups short-grain brown rice
2 low-sodium chicken bouillon cubes
Freshly ground black pepper

1. Heat a large Dutch oven, and spray it with a nonstick spray. Brown the pork cubes on all sides. Remove them from the pan and set aside.

2. Add the garlic, onion, tomatoes, and peppers to the Dutch oven. Sauté, stirring constantly.

3. Add the saffron, parsley, and pork to the Dutch oven. Add 1 cup water. Cover and simmer for 20 minutes.

4. Preheat the oven to 350°F.

5. Stir in the rice, and add 4 cups water along with the reserved juice from the tomatoes, chicken bouillon cubes, and black pepper. Cover and bake for 1 1/2 hours.

Nutritional analysis per serving:

CALORIES	PROTEIN, GM.	CARBOHYDRATE, GM.	FAT, GM.	SATURATED FAT, GM.
302	20.2	40.8	6.2	2.1

SODIUM, MG.	CHOLESTEROL, MG.	FIBER, GM.	CALCIUM, MG.	CALORIES FROM FAT
301	45.6	4.1	131	19%

Tequila Marinated Shrimp

Use a good tequila for this and serve the same tequila in margaritas with the appetizers. This marinated shrimp can be used as an appetizer on a toothpick, as a first course or salad, or as a cold main dish.

SERVES 6

1 pound medium-to-large shrimp, cooked
1 tablespoon olive oil
¼ cup tequila
¼ cup lime juice
¼ teaspoon paprika
¼ teaspoon chili powder
1 clove garlic, crushed

1. Place the cooked and shelled shrimp into a large glass bowl.

2. Combine the rest of the ingredients and pour over the shrimp.

3. Cover and chill for several hours or overnight.

Nutritional analysis per serving:

CALORIES	PROTEIN, GM.	CARBOHYDRATE, GM.	FAT, GM.	SATURATED FAT, GM.
153	20.3	1.8	4.1	0.6

SODIUM, MG.	CHOLESTEROL, MG.	FIBER, GM.	CALCIUM, MG.	CALORIES FROM FAT
128.1	151.3	0.1	54	24%

Orange Frappe

You may use orange juice with lots of pulp to make this. If you do, use 1½ cups of the juice.

SERVES 4

4 oranges, peeled
1 envelope unflavored gelatin
½ cup 1% milk
Mint leaves
4 orange slices

1. Section the oranges into a bowl, removing the membranes.

2. Drain the accumulated juice into a small saucepan. Sprinkle the gelatin over the top of the juice and let it sit for 1 minute.

3. Heat the juice-gelatin mixture and cook until the gelatin dissolves, about 4 to 5 minutes. Set aside to cool.

4. Place the orange sections into a blender and blend to liquefy. Gradually pour in the milk while blending, then blend in the cooled gelatin mixture in the same manner.

5. Pour into 4 half-cup dessert dishes. Chill. Garnish with mint leaves and a slice of orange.

Nutritional analysis per serving:

CALORIES	PROTEIN, GM.	CARBOHYDRATE, GM.	FAT, GM.	SATURATED FAT, GM.
87	3.1	19.3	0.5	0.2

SODIUM, MG.	CHOLESTEROL, MG.	FIBER, GM.	CALCIUM, MG.	CALORIES FROM FAT
45.2	1.2	3.5	98	5%

Strawberry Sorbet

You may use any frozen fruit or even mix your berries.

SERVES 6

1 bag (20 ounces) frozen strawberries,
  no sugar added
1/4 cup sugar

Put the strawberries and sugar into a food processor with a steel blade and blend until the mixture turns into strawberry ice. Serve immediately or store in the freezer until ready to serve.

Nutritional analysis per serving:

CALORIES	PROTEIN, GM.	CARBOHYDRATE, GM.	FAT, GM.	SATURATED FAT, GM.
64	0.4	16.6	0.1	0.01

SODIUM, MG.	CHOLESTEROL, MG.	FIBER, GM.	CALCIUM, MG.	CALORIES FROM FAT
2	0.0	1.9	15	1%

INDEX

side dishes, 166–176
soups, 161–162, 165
gingerbread, upside-down
apple, 86–87
grapefruit, baked, 288
Greek cuisine, 193,
195–196
appetizers, 198, 202, 206
desserts, 222–225
fish/seafood, 210–211
meat dishes, 213–214,
216–221
poultry, 212–215
salads, 197, 199, 204
side dishes, 208–209
soups, 203, 205, 207
green beans
basic, 48
in salad, 311
guacamole dip, 263
gumbo, 64

H
halibut
baked Spanish, 339
cacciatore, 251
on skewers, 210

herbs
choosing of, x
dried, 239
potatoes stuffed with, 35
honey cakes, 223
hummus, 202
Hungarian noodle bake, 169

I
Italian cuisine, 227,
229–230
desserts, 254
fish/seafood, 251, 253
meat dishes, 252
meatless dishes, 242–246
pasta, 235–241
poultry, 250
salads, 233–234
sauces, 247–249
soups, 231–232

J
jambalaya, xv
chicken gizzard, 63
pork, 72
jasmine rice, xv

jicama, xii–xiii
salad, 264

K
Kir Royale cocktail, xxi
kitchen
equipment for, xxiii–xxv
supplies for, xxv–xxviii
tips for, ix–x

L
lamb
buying of, xvii
loin of, 216
moussaka, 213–214
shish kebab, 219
stuffed peppers, 220–221
leeks
carrot and potato soup,
102
salad, 164
soup, 316
lemons
cheese pie, 78–79
storage of juice, x
yogurt cake, 80

lentils
in Mexican soup,
266–267
in spinach soup, 205
lettuce, drying of, ix
lima bean soup, 265
liver pâté, 127

M
macaroni and cheese, 107
marinade, 57
meat dishes
beef and beer, 105
beef Provencal, 146–147
beef roulade, 181–182
beef stroganoff, 148
cabbage rolls, 183–184
fajitas, 278
flank steak roulade, 71
fruited pork tenderloin,
185
lamb loin, 216
meatballs marinara, 252
Mexican pizza, 281
moussaka, 213–214
pancake pie, 301–302
pastitsio, 217–218

peppers
  eggplant, tomatoes, ziti and, 235
  pepper pots, 68
  roasting of, ix
  stuffed, 220–221
phyllo dough, 206
pies
  lemon cheese, 78–79
  pancake, 301–302
  potato, 39
  salmon dill, 108
  tamale, 284
pilaf, xvi
  brown rice, 33
  bulgur, 34
  orzo, 208
pizza, Mexican, 281
poppy seed dressing, 20
pork
  chops with potatoes, 186
  fruited tenderloin, 185
  jambalaya, 72
  Spanish, 342
potatoes
  cakes with mushroom sauce, 296–297
  carrot and leek soup, 102

dumplings, 170
French salad, 126
German salad, 163
herb stuffed, 35
leek soup and, 316
onion cake and, 111
oven chips, 36
oven-roasted, 37
pancakes, 171–172
parsley, 38
pie, 39
pork chops with, 186
roasted, 114
sour cream salad, 319
whitefish and, 177–178
poultry
  barbecued chicken, 57
  cabbage rolls, 183–184
  Cajun oven-fried chicken, 58
  chicken breast supreme, 59–60
  chicken cacciatore, 250
  chicken Creole, 61–62
  chicken cutlet, 299–300
  chicken enchiladas, 274–275
  chicken gizzard jambalaya, 63

chicken gumbo, 64
chicken paprikash, 179
chicken salad, 24
chicken sandwiches, 94
chicken stroganoff, 141
chicken with lemon and capers, 142
chorizo, 280
Coq au Vin, 143–144
Cornish game hens, 65–66
creamed chicken, 106
dirty rice, 67
fajitas, 278
German chicken, 180
lemon chicken, 212
moussaka, 213–214
mustard chicken, 145
paella, 340
Russian cutlets, 303
sauce, 248
Spanish chicken, 341
spicy apricot-Dijon chicken, 69
tacos, 283
turkey chili, 70
turkey marinated with lemon and herbs, 215

turkey salad, 24
prunes
  carrot muffins and, 10
  chocolate cake and, 75
pudding
  apricot, 73
  brown rice, 74
  cheese curd, 304
  Greek rice, 222
  peach, 225
  tapioca, 85

Q

quesadillas, 282
quiche, 128–129

R

raspberries
  corn muffins, 12
  sauce, 5
ratatouille, 242
red beans and rice, 54
red cabbage
  with apples, 173–174
  confetti, 42
  Russian, 298